PINK
LEMONADE

FRESHLY SQUEEZED INSIGHTS TO STIR YOUR FAITH

Thanks for the Awesome! show!

Gayle Zinda

with

JOHN WINCEK

To Chris Stir your faith,

Pink Lemonade™

PRESENTATIONS LLC

Stoughton, Wisconsin 53589
www.lemonmotivators.com

Library of Congress Control Number: 2005911240

Publisher: Dr. Michael W. Zinda
Marketing Manager: Adam Rizzo
Editor: Rhonda Wincek
Cover and Illustrations: John Wincek
Design and Composition: Aerocraft Charter Art Service

Published by The Lemonade Stand Publishing Co.
Pink Lemonade Presentations, LLC
dba The Lemonade Stand Publishing Company

ISBN 0-9770368-0-4

10 9 8 7 6 5 4 3 2 1

CONTENTS

1   Honey, I've Been Waiting for Your Call   *1*

2   Out of the Frying Pan . . .   *15*

3   Tune In, Turn On, Drop Out   *27*

4   Things Are Tough All Over   *41*

5   Flying Solo   *57*

6   The Weight of the World   *75*

7   Broom Closet Meetings with God   *85*

8   Beware the Ides of March   *107*

9   A Helping Hand   *133*

10   My All-Volunteer Army   *149*

11   Lemonade Stand, Live!   *165*

12   It's Better to Give Than to Receive   *183*

13   Lemon Blossoms   *203*

14   Making the Most   *223*

15   A Whole New World   *239*

16   Cha-Cha-Cha Changes   *267*

17   A Glass Half Full   *283*

18   When Life Gives You Lemons . . .   *307*

19   . . . Make Lemonade   *321*

EPILOGUE   Now That I Think About It . . .   *331*

Dedication

For my husband Dr. Michael Zinda,
and my sons, Adam and Nick.
Without their patience and love,
I would not have been able to complete this project.
It is my honor and joy to be part of your lives.
I love you.

For Rita Snider,
who changed my life
when she gave me a new purpose.
She was a tough act to follow.

ACKNOWLEDGMENTS

My love and gratitude go out to my parents, Albert and Bernice Litmer; my brother and sister-in-law, Jim and Cecilia Litmer; my best friend and inspiration, Saundra Strunk; and my spiritual advisor, Bill Huston. Your faith in me keeps me going.

There are so many people who helped me with this book. I just could not have done this without them. To John and Rhonda, my life is deeper because our paths have crossed. Thank you for listening and hearing the call to this project. To Edna and Rose, I cannot explain how grateful I am for covering this project with prayer and wisdom. I am forever indebted to you both.

Thank you to the many good people, and their families, who allowed me to tell a small part of their story: Jerry Snider, Giancarlo Bonutti, SM, Evelyn Wildeboer, Steve Smith, Eleanor Smith Robinson, Kim Marcum, Mary Lou Welch, John Wernke, Mary DeCioccio, Jerry Decker, Bill Sammons, Carol Perez, Marcia, Luanne Mattingly, Dr. John Sacco, Dr. Todd Cook, Dr. Mike Cross, Russell Dean, Dr. Peter McKenna, Dr. Phil Schworer, Lynn Smith, Eileen Stern, Taffy, and Charlene Wynn.

To my entire family, and to the friends and colleagues I failed to mention in the book, thank you for the memories and support of a lifetime. I so appreciate all the acts of kindness that helped the company grow.

1

Honey, I've Been Waiting for Your Call

This is nuts, I thought. *What am I doing here?* I pulled up to a Cincinnati address that I'd been given, not quite sure why I'd come. I never suspected that this was the first step in what would prove to be a life-changing journey.

It was a hot, sunny day in July 1989. I parked the car in front of an ordinary office complex. Nothing exciting, lots of concrete and glass, a few trimmed shrubs and dwarf trees. I was looking for a sign: "The Lemonade Stand". *Must be a restaurant or something,* I thought. No one had told me.

A medical supply sales rep had cornered me at the office and said, "you gotta meet this woman." She wrote down the name and number on a slip of paper and passed it to me. *Yeah, right,* I thought at the time. *I'll call her right away.* I dropped the note in my purse and forgot about it. Completely.

It was almost a year later, during a moment of quiet time between patients, when I remembered that old note. I dug it out of the bottom of my purse, where it was buried beneath a year's worth of accumulated debris, and thought, *well, why not?* So I called. A nice lady answered and I introduced myself. She replied with, "Honey, I've been waiting for your call." I didn't hear much after that. *What did she say? She'd been waiting for my call?*

You don't even know me! I thought. Then she said something about how I was the answer to her prayers. After that, there was some rambling about Jesus. Finally, she invited me down to her business, so that we might get to know each other. She went on about doing something good together, and I tried to take it all in; but my mind struggled to catch up. *Well, maybe she's a little bit crazy,* I guessed. I wasn't even half sure what she was talking about. Funny thing though: she did remind me of my Granny and I found myself wanting to meet her. Before I knew what I was doing, I replied, "Okay, when should I be there?"

Now I *was* there, and I spotted a carved wooden sign bearing a large cutout of a lemonade pitcher. *This must be the place,* I said to myself. The sign read: "The Lemonade Stand—a Place to Come and Be Refreshed." It didn't look like much of a restaurant, but at least I'd found it. As I approached the door, I made out the smaller type at the bottom of the sign: "Wigs, Breast Prostheses, and Makeup." *Okay, probably not a restaurant,* I thought. *Momma didn't raise no dummies.*

I started to put the pieces of the puzzle together. At the time, I was a nurse administrator for a group of doctors specializing in obstetrics and gynecology. We delivered babies. We worked with new and expectant mothers, doing happy things with happy people. It was a bright and sunny world. But I knew what wigs and prostheses really meant. Cancer: the dark side of medicine—a kind of scary, shadowy world best not spoken of. I took a deep breath, pulled open the door, and went in . . .

. . . And stepped through a "looking glass" of my own. Now I found myself in a plush, turn-of-the-century East-coast parlor. Stepping through that door felt like walking into the dawn. The room was sunny and welcoming, beautifully decorated with precious Victorian furniture. Right away, I felt completely at home. A velvet sofa crouched on walnut lion's feet against a wooden chair rail. Tiffany lamps cast their golden glow over richly upholstered armchairs. It was so warm and inviting that I expected to see a fire crackling in a fireplace. The only thing missing was the smell of fresh-baked bread—or maybe chocolate chip cookies. *Maybe they haven't gone into the oven yet,* I thought to myself. It was a nice room. I liked being there.

Through a wooden archway I saw two women. One was sitting in an antique salon chair, while the other hovered about working on her hair. The stylist-lady waved me towards the sofa and said she'd be with me in just a minute. Behind her stood a large cherry armoire, filled with wigs and supplies. Nearby was an old waterfall vanity, from which she plucked a pair of scissors. She returned to work, and I chose a place to sit down.

It was comfortable there, and I felt an almost irresistible urge to simply curl up with a good book. Instead, I settled in and watched the two of them, and pretended I wasn't eavesdropping. They were chatting and laughing together, as the customer in the chair tried on a variety of wigs and hats. I understood that this was some kind of salon; but there was more to it than that. There were no cheap fashion magazines or tabloids on the coffee table.

There was no tinny pop music to assault the ears. If I remember right, it was something soft and classical. Or it might have been some Sinatra; I don't know, it just felt nice.

Best of all, there were none of those catty stylists you sometimes run into, the kind that spend all day chatting away in endless gossip. These women seemed to genuinely care about each other in a way you don't often see. It looked like the grownup version of little girls playing dress up, with the loving way that little ones do. (This is before they grow into teens and the claws come out!) These two women were clearly enjoying each other's company. Even so, it was obviously a professional operation. The woman doing the dressing had a skilled, delicate touch, and a clear eye for color and style. I watched as the lady in the chair transformed from pale, bald, and self-conscious to smiling, radiant, and confident. It was all done with a little wig work, some makeup, and a few kind words.

When they finished, the customer said her goodbyes and left with a bright, happy smile on her face. She was literally glowing. It was almost as if her whole body was smiling. I could see that she felt wonderful inside—no, better than wonderful—she looked ready to take on the world!

The stylist was dressed sharp and done up nice, just like it was Saturday night—or Sunday morning if you prefer. She was on the lighter side of 40 and she looked beautiful; wearing a bright, white, fitted shirt over a denim skirt that sparkled with silver sequins. Her hair, nails, and makeup were impeccable. This lady obviously took pride in her appearance. She put down her scissors and comb and then, surprisingly, she picked up a silver-handled cane, and walked toward me very carefully, even gingerly. As she approached, I remember thinking, *Wow, if she looks that good, why is she walking with a cane? What's wrong with her?*

She sat down next to me and I introduced myself. Then, boldly, she took my hand in hers and looked me straight in the eye. "Honey, I'm Rita," she said. "I'm dying and I know it—but the Good Lord told me that if I hung on long enough, He'd send someone to carry on this business. As soon as you walked in the door, I knew that person was you."

Huh? I thought. Excuse me?

Umm, hello? Earth to Rita? Is there anybody in there? After all, we had only just met! *Like, ten seconds ago!* It took me a moment to get my head around what she'd said. This beautiful but frail lady was actually telling me that it was God's will that I take over her business for her! And she was serious! *Umm, yeah. Okay. Just let me hang up my coat!* I quipped silently. *What? Is she kidding? I mean, come on! God's will?*

I thought I was a pretty good person. I was brought up to be a good little Catholic girl. Oh, I wasn't perfect, by any stretch; but I always tried to do the right thing. Be nice and polite. *Be kind to crazy people!* However, I just wasn't accustomed to people saying "God said" *this* or "God said" *that*. And certainly not about what *I* was supposed to do! I smiled weakly at her in reply. I think I was starting to feel ill. *Is the room getting hot?* I wondered.

My discomfort must have been written all over my face. Rita gave me a long, slow grin and squeezed my hand. Then she patted my arm and put her hands in her lap to put me at ease, before she went on to tell her story. She had been diagnosed with breast cancer at the age of 36. Over the course of the treatments that followed—including chemotherapy and radiation—she had lost her hair nine times! And not only her hair, she'd lost her eyelashes and eyebrows as well. Nine times!

Chemotherapy is rough business. It is designed to make life impossible for cancer cells. Unfortunately, this makes it tough on other cells, too. Some patients get sick like they've never been sick before. They become exhausted—totally and completely wiped out. After that, their skin and lips dry up, and their hair falls out. To top it all off, people often look upon cancer patients with pity, or even fear. And if that's not enough, a patient will often be stunned to see that the face that looks back from the mirror is one that they barely recognize.

Rita was not about to take all of that lying down. She felt like she was losing her femininity. It seemed like they'd revoked her license, and she didn't get to be a girl anymore. Never one to whine and complain, Rita decided to adapt and evolve. So she set out to solve the problem. Beginning with the big department stores, Rita decided to do something she had never done before. She was going to buy a wig. While she was at it, she would find something to put into her bra to make her look like a woman again. Her clothes didn't fit right anymore, and she wanted to fix that. Rita wanted to feel good about herself again. Besides that, she wanted her family and friends to see her looking well, too. Not only would it ease her burden, it would ease theirs as well.

This certainly made sense to me. Nobody likes being an outsider all of the time. Humans are very contradictory creatures. Even as we pride ourselves on our individuality, we all want to fit in just a little bit. We want to be unique; but we don't want to feel like freaks. Rita confirmed this by saying that she'd grown tired of the pitying stares, and fearful looks, that her appearance inspired. It was nobody's fault; some people just can't help themselves. When confronted by something different, people look. Sometimes, they even stare. Rita wanted to look and feel normal again—at least, as much as possible.

With her plans for restoration firmly in mind, Rita headed out the door, and ran smack into the real world. Most of the department store salespeople didn't understand her situation. The few that did were pretty short on tact. Neither did they take into account just how humiliating it was for Rita to be missing her hair. And if they failed to make that simple leap of imagination, then they would never understand what it meant to have lost a breast. When she asked one sales clerk about a bra and a breast form, the dimwit yelled across the room, "Can anybody fit this kid for a prosthesis?!" Rita was mortified. It's not like the *whole world* had to know. She wanted to crawl under the counter, melt into the floor, dry up and blow away. Or maybe slap the clerk senseless.

But she did none of those things. Instead, she stood her ground. Rita needed help and so she stayed and endured the humiliation. It wasn't that the salespeople were heartless, or stupid—just ignorant. Uninformed. Okay, and maybe a little stupid. Rita explained that she didn't need to be handled with kid gloves. She simply wanted to be treated with a little respect. To be left a little dignity.

Rita Snider, the founder and guiding light of The Lemonade Stand. *She was both the beauty and brains behind the operation.*

When the clerk got no response to her insensitive shout, she sighed heavily, turned and trudged into the back room. After a moment, she returned with two different styles of bras. Carelessly, she flopped them onto the counter like they were a couple of old dead fish at the butcher shop. Rita picked one up. doubtfully. Just as she thought, they were totally and completely inappropriate. *They were big, old lady bras!* Rita weighed, like, 98 pounds. She could almost climb inside them! They looked like grocery sacks full of over-ripe melons—just big, round bags of water. "This, *this thing,* was to supposed replace *my breast!*" she said indignantly. "I felt more humiliated than ever."

As she left the store, outraged, Rita decided that other women should not have to face this kind of embarrassment. She was determined to find a way to make a difference.

The search for a wig began almost as badly. Wig shops don't exactly sprout up on every street corner. The nearest one Rita found was well across the tracks, on the seedy side of town. This was a shop that catered primarily to strippers—sorry, exotic dancers. It also served others engaged in entrepreneurship that

When life gives you lemons. . .

Try something you have always wanted to do!

If you're going to have "down time", why not make the most of it? A year from now you might look back and say, "I learned to cook, write, paint, play, travel, set priorities, and revolutionized the way I live."

These little pearls of wisdom accompanied gift baskets for Lemonade Stand patients. Universally effective, you'll see them sprinkled throughout the text.

was even less mainstream. This was not exactly her neighborhood, and Rita was more than a little nervous as she made her way there. As it turned out, the shop was run by a lovely, little Korean lady. Even smaller in stature than Rita, this little lady provided service that was far superior to that of the big, expensive department stores. In the days ahead, Rita and the shop owner grew together in a professional relationship that lasted for years. That little shop prospers to this day.

To Rita's great relief, the wig store was a lot of fun. Once she'd adapted to the customers in stilettos and skin-tight minis, the shop began to look like a real fashion playground. There was a wide selection of styles and colors to experiment with. Rita timidly selected a few of the more conservative, understated cuts to begin. But when you're sampling ice cream and you have 31 flavors to choose from, it's hard to stay satisfied with vanilla. She started to wonder what it would be like to be a blonde. While she was at it, how about a platinum blonde? After that, it was raven black. Then fire red. *Why not?* she thought. *When you're bald, you have nothing to lose.* It wasn't long before Rita began trying on some of the most adventurous cuts and colors. Long and straight, big and curly, short and spiky; blond, black, red, purple . . .

Rita's creative streak took over then and it was like she was compiling data, experimenting and cross-referencing, determining how she might put this palette of styles to work one day. In a way, it was liberating—this ability to change identities with each cut and color. That kind of freedom and fun could do a lot for a woman's morale. And so a plan began to take shape. What had started as a quest to fulfill a personal need was quickly evolving into an idea that might help hundreds, even thousands, of others.

The visit to that little wig shop opened up an exciting, ego-boosting new dimension to Rita's sense of style. In the years ahead, she would often come to work with a different hair color. With her creativity and fashion sense, Rita always managed to pull together new looks that were bold and innovative, yet still stylish and sophisticated. She was the Rembrandt and the Warhol of hair and makeup. One by one, each creation became another tool in her kit. Every new look became another way to rebuild a shattered spirit.

Inspired by the positive and negative experiences alike, Rita began to create the place that she had imagined. This was where breast cancer patients would come to be re-energized. Here they could find the wigs, breast prostheses, and makeup they needed to help them feel good about themselves again. Not only would she sell those products, Rita would offer caring, professional attention in choosing, fitting, and applying all of these items as well. A new, positive self-image would go a long way towards helping these patients to deal with their affliction. All they needed was a little help—and a nice place to go.

One night, Rita awoke with a start, suddenly knowing the name. She would call her new business "The Lemonade Stand." To her mind, a lemonade stand was a place where people stopped for refreshment. That was just how she wanted her clients to feel. After several months of hard work, and a lot of support—both physical and financial—from her husband Jerry, Rita's first shop was opened. As the new patients came in, she helped them to choose attractive wigs and appropriate breast prostheses. She taught them subtle makeup application, and demonstrated revitalizing skin care techniques. The idea was to put these women back together again, and teach them how to do their own maintenance. If they looked good, then they would feel much better about themselves. Rita gave her clients the care and understanding she hadn't found anywhere else. By the time those women left her store, Rita had restored their dignity and brightened their outlook on life.

I sat there quietly for a moment and took it all in—this beautiful little Victorian office and this oddly radiant woman. I thought about what she'd said—about divine inspiration and messages from God. To me, this was a new way of looking at life. It would take a little getting used to. Let's be honest, it would take a *lot* of getting used to. Even with my upbringing, it all seemed a little improbable. She talked like she actually *knew* God! Like they were on a first-name basis! To say the least, it was a new perspective. Then, Rita did something else that was outside of my experience. Way outside. Gently taking my hand again, she looked me in the eyes and said, "Have you ever asked Jesus to come into your heart?"

My stomach did a slow roll and I thought, *Uh oh, Bible thumper alert! Watch for holy rollers!* I bit the inside of my cheek and tried not to grin at her. I mean, sure, I'd gone to church. I tried to do the right thing; be good; blah, blah, blah. But what kind of question is that? *What is that supposed to mean?* I wondered. "Ask Jesus into your heart?" *Umm, okay. Sure. Is there,*

like, a line, or a window or something? Do I need to take a number?
But Rita wasn't kidding; she was completely serious. So I put my
wise-guy thoughts aside and tried on a puzzled expression.

While Rita waited patiently for me to answer, one corner of
her mouth turned up in a wry smile. To this day, I'm sure she saw
right through me. Sheepishly, I told her that I didn't really know
what she meant by her question. I said that I felt I was a good person, and I was raised Catholic; but I wasn't really sure that I
understood. What exactly did she mean by, "ask Jesus into my
heart?" She grinned and said, "Just that, honey! You need to stop
and just ask Jesus to come into your heart from this day forward."

Really? I thought, *That's it? Doesn't sound like much of a plan
to me.* But I told her I was willing to try.

With that, she said a prayer while I silently followed along.
At her prompting, I did ask Jesus into my heart. I felt a little like
a phony; but for Rita's sake, I tried my best to be sincere. Rita
smiled, patted me on the arm, and said to me, "There, Honey.
Now you don't have to worry any more." I raised an eyebrow,
thinking, *oh, really? So I'm covered now?* Rita continued, "all you
have to do is take care of the people God sends, and He'll send
you all the help you need." *Hmmm,* I thought to myself, *if she's
really right about that, this might work.* "Just be open to his guidance and direction," Rita finished, "and you'll be fine." *Okay,* I
thought. *I'll try to keep an open mind.*

Still, wisecracks aside, as Rita and I prayed together, I felt the
warmth of her hands and saw the intensity of her gaze. Some
might call it a light in her eyes. Anyway, *her faith* was palpable.
If it were any more intense, you'd be able to pick it up and hold
it in your hands. Without a doubt, this woman knew something
greater than I knew. Whatever it was, she was definitely tapped
into *something.* I wanted to know more. More about her, more
about her drive to help others, and maybe I would learn a little
more about her "journey with God." Just the fact that I was
thinking things like "journey with God" was remarkable in

itself. I didn't know if *she* was crazy, or was it *me?* Either way, I thought I would try to listen and learn.

W hen I was growing up, Granny Rose—my Mom's mom— was the most spiritual person I had ever known. Not that I'd known a lot by then, but I could tell that she was something special. Granny Rose lived nearby, and whenever we went to visit, we'd find her sitting on the porch out front, rocking in her chair and praying to Jesus. My mom laughingly called her "our resident holy roller", almost as if she thought Granny was a little nuts. But I'd never thought of Granny as crazy. She was a good grandma, and she was a hard worker. She was *real.* And she was always showing the presence of Jesus in her life.

As a young girl, Granny told me it was important to pray for your family, your future children, and your children's children. At the time, all of that seemed a little hard to imagine. It seemed so far away. I did try to pray . . . whenever I remembered—or when someone reminded

My Granny Rose, who had taught me the importance of praying for the people in your life.

me. You know how it is. Kids are busy, and not all that reflective; but I tried my best.

Granny Rose had taught me to pray as a kid, but growing up tends to wash away some of the innocence—and some good habits along with it. Now, all these years later, Rita was challenging and inviting me to actually *know* Jesus. As an educated, sophisticated—and jaded—adult, I simply wasn't sure what to make of it. Rita seemed so *certain!* So positive. I figured that it couldn't hurt to try.

By the end of that first meeting with Rita, my head was spinning. I left The Lemonade Stand and drove down William

Howard Taft Boulevard in Cincinnati, thinking about everything that she had said. To hear Rita tell it, I was the answer to her prayers and the solution to her problems. That seemed a little unlikely to me. I hadn't even figured out my own problems yet— and I had a stack of them!

Sure, Rita was a nice lady—but I wasn't job hunting! I wasn't even in the market. I was happy where I was. Bringing babies into the world, making people happy; it was positive, life-affirming work. My position paid a good salary and it had tremendous benefits. I had the respect, and friendship, of my colleagues. I was a success! Why would I give all that up?

Sometimes though . . . sometimes I didn't exactly feel like a rousing success. Every once in while, I felt like I was just running around in circles. For all of the salary my position paid, I wasn't taking very much home. A messy divorce a few years back had left me with a mountain of debt. I had two school-aged boys to raise on my own and things were tight as it was. My parents were a big help, and Adam and Nicholas were supportive, hard-working angels. But the long hours had me worried that I wasn't spending enough time with them. First, a broken family; then, a pair of latch-key kids and a mom who worked all of the time. Was I cleaning up the mess, or making it worse? In darker moments, I wondered if I were doing anything right at all.

Up until then, I had thought I was doing pretty well. I was working hard—*but why wasn't I getting anywhere?* Then I asked myself, "if I'm doing so well, then why was I even considering Rita's offer? It's not like there's a real, concrete proposal on the table." It was just a vague notion of an opportunity, an alternate future. "Why am I suddenly willing to leave it all behind me now and jump off this cliff?" And now, to top it all off, here I was *talking to myself in the car!*

"Oh, God," I said out loud, "if you are for real, and what this lady asked is real, then you sure have a lot of work to do before I can help anyone!"

I laughed at my sad, pathetic, crazy, mixed-up self and thought about things some more. I figured that, if Rita was right, then God was well aware of my challenges. If she was right, then He knew and *still* thought it was a good idea. Still, it was hardly an iron-clad guaranty. *Nothing set in stone here,* I thought. Even so, something called me to work with Rita, to join her in her mission. I couldn't believe I was seriously considering it. I was at the same time excited and terrified. My hands were shaking on the wheel. I was confused, on the brink of tears, and even—to my surprise—wildly elated! In short, I was *a basket case.*

And I was driving. D.W.C. Driving While Crazy. "I guess this is what they mean by 'take it on faith'," I told myself.

I knew I had just experienced something that would change my life—one way or another. Either I was becoming a wild-eyed zealot or I was following a crazy woman. The funny thing was, as I calmed down again, I found that I felt totally peaceful. The very idea sounded better and better. I just knew that somehow Rita was right. She said that God would take care of me if I took care of His people. I was starting to believe it. Sure, there was a nagging little voice of doubt—*okay, a nagging big voice of doubt;* but I knew that I had to follow my heart. Plain and simple, it felt like it was the right thing to do. I decided I would take the leap of faith.

Being with Rita that day had refreshed me in a way that I hadn't known was possible. While I'd enjoyed my work up until then, I also felt a bit like I was spinning my wheels and going nowhere. I was just a cog in the machine. Now I felt alive with possibilities. I wasn't sure what they were, but I sure was *alive* with them! I began to wonder if there was more to this than just wigs, prostheses, and makeup. *Did God have a hand in this?* I wondered. Had He refreshed my spirit? *Was I really even thinking these things?*

Maybe it was all just the idea of a change.

I gave my employers my two weeks' notice. Someone asked me what I was going to do next. I told him, "I'm going to work in a lemonade stand!" He looked at me like I'd lost my mind.

CHAPTER **2**

Out of the
Frying Pan . . .

Well, my hair's all gone—again!" Six little words that had practically become a mantra for Rita.

She was a beautiful, dynamic young lady—only 36 years old when she was diagnosed with breast cancer. I still couldn't believe that she'd lost her hair nine times in six years. Amazing. *How did she cope with it?* I wondered. One bad haircut could

throw me off stride for weeks! To *lose* it all . . . then lose it again
. . . and again . . . if that wasn't enough to break a person's spirit, then I didn't know what was. And then, to feel sick on top of
that—how did she keep such a positive outlook on life, when
life seemed so determined to beat her down? Yet, through it all,
Rita maintained her good humor and radiant personality. I don't
know how she did it.

While undergoing her radiation and chemotherapy, Rita visited several cancer centers and saw other women suffering
through their treatments, too. Everywhere, it was the same.
Along with their appearance, their self-esteem was crumbling.
These women—most with no hair or eyelashes, no makeup, and
missing breasts—looked all too much like tortured POWs. Even
worse, they began to act like them too. It broke Rita's heart to see
them feeling so helpless and alone. Ever the optimist, she knew
there had to be a better way.

Amazingly, Rita was no different than these women. Cut from
the same cloth, she *was* one of them; and she felt a kinship with
them. As with real prisoners of war, Rita felt a camaraderie with
them, a bond born of similar suffering. There was only one difference; Rita wasn't one to take things lying down. She ached to
help them, and it drove her to do things she'd never done before.
Rita was not a businesswoman. She had never owned a store, or
run a business. She had no "real world" experience. But Rita did
have two things going for her: she had a creative streak and she
was driven. Rita truly had a natural flare for color, makeup, and
style, and somehow she remained beautiful throughout her
ordeal. Although frequently exhausted by her own cancer treatments, Rita was determined to help other women. She knew she
could return them to their beauty, in the midst of their heartache
and challenge.

As I came to know Rita better, I stood in awe of the strength
of her personality. This little hundred-pound ball of fire burned
ever brighter under a deluge that would drown most stronger

souls. She simply refused to let her illness douse her spirit. Rita had a mission, and she would find whatever she needed to get the job done. And if it didn't exist, she would build it herself.

Having learned firsthand how painful it was to find her first breast prosthesis and wig, Rita decided this was her natural starting point. With a handful of wigs, and a mountain of determination, she traveled to local cancer centers and announced that she was now open for business. Just like that. It didn't matter that it hadn't been done before. Rita simply decided what had to happen, and then she *did* it. The Lemonade Stand was open, and Rita was ready and able to help other women in her situation. If they couldn't cross the tracks to the wig store, then she would bring the wig store to them.

Selling a wig, properly, is not as easy as it sounds. A wig doesn't just "fit." You don't just pop it on. It has to be styled, trimmed, and thinned before there's even a chance a woman will find it comfortable. Rita had no formal training. But with her natural sense of style and creativity, somehow she was able to work wonders with wigs and scissors, hats and accessories. She simply had "the eye" for such things.

The process began with a carefully fitted wig, trimmed and adjusted until it was right as rain. Then she would add the perfect hat, scarf, or bandanna. Maybe she would pull some of the hair up or back with a tasteful ribbon or barrette. Touches like that created the illusion that the client had pulled up their own, natural hair. Then Rita would apply a touch of makeup with loving care and respectful attention. In doing so, she would transform a woman physically, mentally, and spiritually. Her clients were literally created anew. One look in the mirror, and the resulting wide smiles and happy chatter renewed Rita and the customer alike. It was as good for her as it was for them.

Under Rita's care, even very ill women could learn to take charge of their appearance again. Long since resigned to feeling helpless, regaining this small bit of control was often enough to renew their spirit. The simple acts of putting hair on the head, adding a hat or scarf, and applying a little bit of makeup would completely revitalize them. The small boost in self-confidence snowballed, and made them stronger and more determined to fight their cancer. It wasn't long before dozens of women were being referred to Rita, and she developed a reputation as a miracle worker.

Even as the business took shape, Rita continued her own cancer treatments. There were times when it was a struggle for her to simply get through the day. Even so, Rita somehow found the energy to encourage others to feel good about themselves. She would focus completely on each client, and never rushed through an appointment, no matter how tired she was. Her capacity for giving was astonishing. Anyone who came to know Rita quickly discovered that her inner beauty far outshone her outward radiance.

In the beginning, her family thought the business was a kind of hobby for Rita; but it was so much more than that. It became her passion to help other people, and her efforts made her feel better about herself and her own troubles. Rita knew she was doing God's work, helping women who thought they could no longer help themselves. She knew firsthand of the overwhelming exhaustion these women experienced during their treatments. They simply did not have the energy to go to one store for a wig, another for a breast prosthesis, and still another for skin care and makeup. If The Lemonade Stand was to be that "place to come and be refreshed," then Rita knew that she had to offer all of these services, in privacy, under one roof. She created just such a place—warm and welcoming— and that was where I found her on that late summer day.

Rita had been running her business for about a year-and-a-half when we met, and was taking care of about 50 clients. Still suffering from her own treatments, she worked every hour that she could manage. When I joined her, it was through a simple

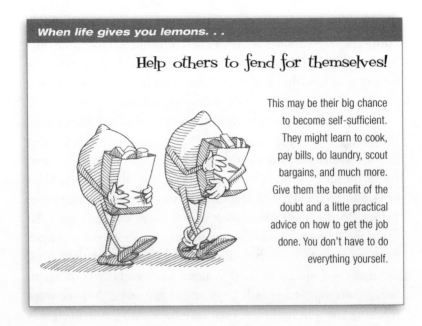

When life gives you lemons. . .

Help others to fend for themselves!

This may be their big chance to become self-sufficient. They might learn to cook, pay bills, do laundry, scout bargains, and much more. Give them the benefit of the doubt and a little practical advice on how to get the job done. You don't have to do everything yourself.

verbal agreement between the two of us. No contracts or hand-shakes were necessary; she asked and I said "yes". To get me started, she asked me to "be her legs." I would travel to the treatment centers for her and help those who were unable to make it into the shop. I was The Lemonade Stand on wheels.

There was no time for an instruction program or long, drawn-out apprenticeship. We hit the ground running. It was definitely on-the-job training. With the consent of her customers, Rita taught me how to help our clients look and feel better. While she worked her miracles on them, she was instructing me. These women were only too happy to oblige. It seemed as if, by volunteering to be my "guinea pig," they were doing their part to help others. As the weeks progressed, I learned first how to demonstrate wigs and how to select and apply makeup. Then, Rita taught me how to measure clients for a wig. There is more to it than you would think. Next, she taught me how to cut, thin, and trim a wig to create a soft, natural look. Once I'd

learned wigs, she taught me how to mix in hats, scarves, and tur-
bans creatively and to the client's best advantage. Over time, Rita
gave me all of her wonderful techniques for bringing out the
beauty in a face that had been ashen and fearful. In so doing, I
also learned how to revive their flagging spirits.

With each successful transformation, I began to understand
the charge that she got out of it. There was a rush of excitement
as we finished and each patient took that final look in the mirror. Without exception, their smiles reached all the way to their
eyes, and I felt a sense of accomplishment in my work like never
before. To my mind, the closest comparison was the rush I felt
upon the delivery of a healthy, squalling, newborn baby to first-
time parents. As I watched the light come back into their eyes,
the deadened spirits of these women were literally born again.
Sure, there might be dark days ahead for some, but we were
teaching them to find their own way back into the light. It was
very rewarding.

One day, just a few months after we'd begun working
together, Rita failed to arrive for work. I didn't have a set
of keys yet, so I couldn't open up the shop. Unable to do
anything else, I hit the road and began making my rounds.
However, as the day progressed, and I heard not a word from
Rita, I began to worry. With a few phone calls, I discovered that
she had been hospitalized. Even worse, she was in a coma—one
caused by her disease and its treatment. Now I began to worry.
I'm ashamed to say that it wasn't entirely about Rita. I was worried about *me!*

Without Rita's steady hand to guide me, my nerves began to
crumble. This was a precarious situation for me. *What am I going
to do?* I panicked. I know, "poor little me!" Here my mentor is
struggling for her very life and I'm worried about myself! Not
exactly my proudest moment, but I'm only human. Did I mention that I have my share of flaws?

When faced with a crisis, we don't always respond rationally. That is a learned skill, and I still had much to learn. At the time, none of that higher-level thinking occurred to me. All I could think about were my problems. My nursing position was gone. I was an unpaid volunteer. I was still learning the job. I couldn't get into the shop. All I had was a car full of wigs and makeup; how was I supposed to do business with that? At the time, I didn't even know Rita's family. How would I keep things going? Who would I talk to? *What should I do?* I thought, *how do you run a business when you can't even open the door?* I felt truly foolish.

With Rita unavailable as a source of support, I began to doubt myself. "What have I done?" I whined to myself. I had quit a good job to step onto this path—and I had no idea where it led! I'd given up everything to walk with this woman on her journey. Now that she was no longer there, I truly felt lost. Even worse, I felt like I had put my young sons, Adam and Nicholas, in jeopardy. *I've screwed up, big time,* I thought to myself.

It didn't take long before I realized that I was being selfish. My problems paled in comparison to Rita's. I realized then just how much I had been leaning on her for support. And she had held me up! Along with all of her clients, tiny, frail Rita had been keeping me going, too. So I asked myself, "What would Rita do?" The answer was, she would soldier on.

My first response to the bad news had been pure panic. I felt like I was out of the frying pan and into the fire! But as the waves of fear receded and I thought about what came next, my true position became clear. I imagined that I was like a baby bird that had been pushed out of the nest early. It was time to flap my wings and fly—before I splattered all over the sidewalk! So I faked it. I continued to travel to the hospitals with the hair and cosmetic samples that I had in the car. I continued to do my job and help our clients. I acted like everything was business as usual, and hoped that Rita would be back soon.

Basically, I tried to do what I thought she'd want me to. The truth was, *I didn't know what else to do.* I wasn't even sure that Rita would return!

I spent the next two months—two long months—in limbo. I moonlighted at odd jobs during my off hours, trying to keep my family solvent and The Lemonade Stand alive. Sometimes I wondered why I bothered to try—with no keys, no contacts, and limited supplies, it was a difficult prospect. At times, it seemed laughable. I was spending my nights doing anything I could to scrape up a buck, just so I could spend my days driving around and pretending to run a business out of my trunk! I couldn't afford to restock. My checking account was running on empty. *Should I go back to a "real" job?* I asked myself. *Is she coming back at all, or am I just wasting my time?*

It may seem foolish, but I was operating purely on faith. I made a few desperate prayers, but I didn't really have a solid relationship with the man upstairs. My faith was simply the forlorn hope that everything would be alright.

Rita had been my strength and inspiration, and now I was feeling very lost and alone. Still, I felt like I had to try. Something told me to just keep going. Working on the side to stay afloat, I took a night job as a limo driver, I freelanced insurance physicals, and took on brief stints of nursing in home-care cases. I did anything I could to keep it all afloat. It was a scatterbrained existence, and I felt like I was being pulled in a dozen different directions. So often, I wanted to chuck it all and go back to my "simple" old life. But then, one new smile from a patient, who hadn't had a lot to smile about, would give me enough inspiration to continue on to the next one.

Finally, after several months of chaos and confusion, I got a welcome phone call. A soft, tired little voice said, "Honey, it's Rita." I practically sobbed out my sigh of relief and I tried to stammer out a greeting. With a smile in her voice,

Rita went on, "You probably thought I was dead," I nodded mutely, "but my last treatment put me in a coma. I apologize, but I just couldn't talk to you." I had to smile at that—she was apologizing to *me* for not calling! I laughed to myself as I thought, *you know, I would have called but I couldn't get to the phone. I had this little coma thing going and all.* Unbelievable!

After so much time off her feet, Rita would have to stay home for a while to recover and rebuild her strength. She asked me to stop by her house and pick up the keys to the shop. She said, "You're going to need them so that you can keep on taking care of our people at The Lemonade Stand." *If I'm gonna what?* I thought. *She doesn't sound like she's coming back any time soon!* My doubts began to resurface and I started to slip back into my old role as apprentice. I protested, "I can't do it alone! I'm not ready!" But Rita would have none of it.

"You've been doing it already!" That tired, little voice on the phone projected strength and will. She was entirely confident that I could do it all—the fitting, the cutting, the thinning— everything! "You're a natural," she said. "You can make these women feel good again."

Despite her assurances, I still had my doubts. I had been winging it for months; but now that she was making it official, I was afraid it was all too much for me. I was still learning to be "comfortable" around cancer patients, and was still unsure of my abilities. It occurred to me, after we'd said our goodbyes, that Rita was more confident in me than I was in myself. I tried to shake off the self-doubt. With address in hand, I hopped into my car and headed for Rita's house.

Rita had warned me that she would still be in bed when I got there, so I was to walk right in and find my way around. As I passed through the sunny, cheerful spaces, I remember thinking about how a house reflects its owner. A white, baby grand piano shined from within a luxurious living room. It seemed like the ideal setting for Rita. The gleaming piano mirrored her strength and beauty. At the sound of footsteps, Rita called me into her bedroom. I found her laying in bed, with no hair or makeup on. I'd never seen her this way—she looked very weak and pale. I was struck dumb as the truth hit home. The reality of her situation was undeniable to me now. The woman before me was so unlike the woman I knew.

Rita was the foundation upon which my shaky self-confidence was built. At the sight of her, my will began to crumble again. My eyes welled up and I expressed my doubts about being able do everything that she seemed to have planned for me. Rita sat up straight and, with fire in her eyes and conviction in her voice, told me, "God will help you through. He will provide the people you need to continue His work." Then she laid back down again and relaxed. "All you have to do," Rita said, grinning at me, "is just remember to show up!"

Once again, poor, frail Rita had lifted me up, given me strength, and put me back on track. With her encouragement and inspiration, I would pick up just where we had left off. I told myself that, because Rita couldn't do it, *I had to.* I would continue to be her legs. But I found out that there was more to it than that. Being her legs, and learning about wigs and breast prostheses wouldn't be enough to get the job done. Rita knew there was something much more important that I needed to learn.

She asked me to sit down on the bed beside her, so I did—carefully. Softly, but firmly, Rita said to me, "Jesus is *my* source of strength; but I know that soon I'll be gone." I tried a few feeble protests, wanting to make her feel better—but even more wanting to believe it myself. She understood what I was lamely trying to do and gave me a warm smile; but her eyes told the truth. As she went on, I realized that her concern was not for herself—Rita was actually more worried about me! "My time is running low," she told me honestly. "That being so, there is something I want you to understand." Rita told me that I needed to learn more about Jesus, about how He would become my strength, just as He was for her. We prayed together, and she told me directly that the inspiration I would need in the days ahead must come from Jesus Himself.

Reluctantly, I got the message. When Rita was gone, I would need a greater source of strength if I were to continue our work. So I tried to understand, and because she asked, I would try hard to believe. As we all do when faced with impending tragedy, I questioned, *how can this be so?* How could Rita believe so strongly, when she suffered so much? Up until now, I had been doing it all for her. If she could face so much and still be so giving, then how could I do any less? Rita was, and still is, my inspiration—yet there she was telling me that it was just not enough. She said, "You have to look higher for your inspiration." While I understood her point, I wasn't quite sure how to go about it.

With my own eyes, I could see Rita's suffering. Just as clearly, I could see her giving nature. While I didn't really understand her strength, I could see it right in front of me. I could see it and be inspired. But, according to Rita, I had to look higher for my example. I thought I understood what that meant—I knew what Jesus had sacrificed. But knowing something in your head is one thing; knowing it in your heart is something else.

I wasn't entirely sure how my strength and inspiration were supposed to flow directly from Jesus. Entirely sure? I wasn't even remotely sure! Although I had prayed with Rita, and even asked Jesus into my heart, I didn't really feel plugged in yet. But, since Rita asked it of me, I would try to keep my mind open to the idea. *Still, it seems like a fuzzy way to get the job done,* I thought. *Not exactly a plan you can roll up and take with you. Directions would be nice, maybe an instruction manual or something.* Oh well, you take what you can get, you use what you have. Rita was still my role model in this, but I would try to open myself up to larger possibilities.

As I left Rita's house that day, I felt my confidence returning. While I had no idea where the road ahead would take me,

I did feel renewed and ready to step onto it once again. Then it occurred to me that, after another big talk with Rita, I felt renewed and confident again. *Beginning to see a pattern here?* I asked myself. Yes. I didn't know what the pattern meant, but I was beginning to see one.

Before I left, Rita had quoted a verse to me. She said it was from the Apostle Paul's letter to the Philippians. I didn't know what that meant, but Rita went on, "I can do all things through Christ who strengthens me." I thought I knew what *that* meant. Rita was now so weak that she needed me to be strong. She needed me to help her see the fruits of her hard labor. It was so important to Rita that The Lemonade Stand would be there to help others when she no longer could. I just couldn't let her down.

Okay, so maybe I missed the point by a little bit—at least my heart was in the right place. I knew I still had so much to learn. As I put the keys to The Lemonade Stand in my pocket, I realized that I was beginning the next part of this journey without Rita at my side. With her blessing, I was to continue on—with the Lord as my strength and my guide. I thought a map would have been nice. Since I wasn't going to get one, I'd try it her way.

3

Tune In, Turn On, Drop Out

had thought that *not* having keys to the shop was bad enough. But as I opened the door to The Lemonade Stand, for the first time in several months, I realized that actually *having* the keys might be worse! It occurred to me, as I went inside, that I was all alone here. It was up to me now. The store would sink or swim under my care.

I still felt like I was ill equipped to sell wigs and breast prostheses on my own. I did not yet have the expertise that I thought the job required. I knew that, to a certain extent, I was going to have to fake it. The idea made me nervous. The patients were depending on me to put them back together again. I simply could not let them down. "Anything is possible with God," Rita said, "if you'll just ask Jesus into your heart." For all of Rita's big talk, I still felt like I was way out on a limb, all by myself. Who was going to bring me a ladder? God?

To say that I had not yet developed a deep relationship with Jesus would be putting it kindly. A relationship? Ha! We weren't even nodding acquaintances. Up until a few weeks ago He had been less a divine presence in my life than a historical figure I had learned about. Rita tried to introduce us, but I felt like we hadn't even shaken hands yet. It was like He was a buddy of hers who had thrown me a little nod and said, "hey," and then went on His way. There was no "relationship" there—and I certainly didn't know what His purpose was for my life. You could say that I wasn't exactly tuned in.

What have I gotten myself into? I would often wonder. *It's not like this makes a lot of sense!* I continued to work nights and weekends at any odd job that I could get my hands on. That way, I could keep on working for free at something for which I had *no* business skills. None, nothing, *nada,* zip. There was *the business,* and there were *my skills*—but never the twain shall meet! One night I'm doing home health care; the next night I'm driving a limo. The night after that it is off to do insurance physicals. I was living a life of multiple personalities at night, all so I could pretend to know what I was doing the next day at The Lemonade Stand—where I lived still *another* personality. That may be a slight exaggeration. After all, I was still me—and not completely crazy, yet. But with so much going on at once, it could be difficult to stay focused. At that point, if someone had said that all of this was "God's plan" for my life,

I would have laughed. *This is a plan? Yeah! If this is a plan, we need a new architect!*

Taking on so much at once, there was a lot to be nervous about. At The Lemonade Stand, there were three big ones that really stood out. In the beginning, just the idea of working closely with cancer patients made me nervous. At the time, there was a stigma to the disease, almost as if the patients wore a scarlet letter. The very word triggered an almost primal, instinctive fear—even in a trained nurse. I knew it wasn't contagious. That didn't make me any less nervous.

Since then, education, prevention, and treatments have all done their part to change our more foolish notions. My change in attitude began not long after my first meeting with Rita. By the time she had me assisting with a client, I had pretty much come around. It didn't take long to see that these were people just like me—people in need of help. After that, training and normal human empathy kicked in and I was a nurse again.

I would simply ask myself, *how would I feel if it were me?* If I took a moment to imagine walking in their shoes, that was usually all it took to know how to handle the clients. *How do they want to be treated?* I asked myself. *The same way I do.* No one was looking for pity. If they were having a rough day, then a little compassion would be good. If they were exhausted, I would offer a helping hand. Otherwise, our clients wanted to be treated as the regular people that they were. And if they weren't feeling like regular people anymore, then it was my job to help them feel that way again.

I'd quickly gotten over my anxiety about cancer patients, but now I faced an even bigger dilemma. I wondered, *how am I gonna do this?* How was I *really* going to make my clients feel better about themselves? I mean, kind words and helping hands are nice and all; but cancer is about as serious as things get. We're talking life and death here. If a customer were dealing with issues as weighty as those, how were my puny efforts going to make a difference? Even worse, these people had to look in the mirror every day at a reflection that was not their own.

That is where it all starts, I realized. If they can see their own face in the mirror again, then I can connect them to their old selves once more. If the clients can feel like themselves again, then they will be better equipped to deal with their cancer. So, my job was to make them look and feel less like cancer patients and more like people. But only a short while before, I had been delivering babies! Newborns don't typically need a haircut, and they're certainly not looking for wigs. They don't need makeup because their skin is already perfect. You simply wipe them off and they're beautiful. Delivering babies hadn't really prepared me for this.

Other than the maintenance I quickly performed on myself each day, I wasn't exactly an expert at putting people back together again. But oddly enough, I did actually have a little training in my background that would come in handy.

A few years before all of this, my mother was at her beauty salon, waiting to have her hair done. She was flipping through a stack of old gossip magazines, when the stylist called her in to a chair. As she began her work, my mom chatted with her casually. It was just the usual small talk, but eventually it turned to a subject that made my mom's ears perk up.

To make money on the side, the stylist had taken up a distributorship in a cosmetics company along the lines of Mary Kay. According to the stylist, they supplied training not just in sales, but in makeup application, too. And they were always looking for new distributors! *Oh, boy.*

Of course, as soon as she heard about it, my mom thought of one person. Me. Her daughter, Gayle—the nurse. So in a backhanded attempt at career advancement, my mother gave the stylist/distributor my name and number.

A few days later, the stylist called. "Hi, Gayle. Would you like to find a way to make some extra money?"

Oh, boy! I thought, *Who wouldn't?* "Tell me about it," I said; and she did. The extra income sounded great. "Sign me up!" I told her. While all of this was going on, *my* stylist was into her own bag of tricks. A display had been set up in her shop. It was a contest. A drawing—the grand prize for which was a scholarship to beauty school. According to the rules, salon employees were ineligible; but she filled out a card anyway. She filled it out for me.

Of course, I won.

So, never having won *anything* in my life, *this* was the prize that fate decided to bestow upon me. *Beauty school. That's just great.*

Some might say it was God's will. I know Rita would have said so. But I'm glad nobody said so at the time! It would have badly shaken what little faith I had. After all, there I was, a practicing nurse. If it was God's will that I go to beauty school, then what did it say about His opinion of my skills as a nurse?! *Hey Gayle, nice job with the nursing. Why don't you try beauty school instead? Or maybe sell makeup . . .*

On the other hand . . . I never was one to pass up an opportunity. And the price was right. I asked myself, *so what have you got to lose?* Other than a little dignity, the answer was nothing. Besides, I had two boys to take care of; dignity could wait. I took the classes. And I took the training for the distributorship.

It went about as well as you might expect. Oh, don't get me wrong; it wasn't all bad. I spent my evenings in classes, studying and practicing. We learned some truly valuable techniques. But after about six months of classes, I just couldn't take it anymore.

The problem wasn't the workload. It was the student body. Pretty much every student in our group was fresh off her senior prom. No twenty-somethings, no thirty-somethings. Where were all of the "continuing education" adults, returning to school to pick up this valuable new skill? Well, they certainly weren't here. My classmates were all Tiffanys and Brittneys. Flocks of them.

When life gives you lemons. . .

Get good information!

This is a tricky thing. There's information and information overload, facts and rumors, knowledge that makes you happy or sad, new ideas, and the issue of what's going to happen to you personally. Recognize that much of it is a crapshoot, and combine what you hear with a respect for your inner voice and your belief in a Higher Power.

There I was—the single mother of two school-aged boys, and a practicing nurse—in the middle of a room full of young girls with big hair. My colleagues were doctors and nurses; their colleagues were Heather and Jessica. My concerns were about how to keep two growing boys fed, clothed, and educated. Their concerns were the new line of Guess? jeans and whether or not to get streaks and tips for Friday nights' hookup with Brad and Justin. Needless to say, I found it difficult to fit in.

I tried to tell myself that it was all for a good cause. The skills I was learning might have application in corrective cosmetics—helping burn patients or accident victims with heavy scarring. I tried to be positive and patient. I tried to find the value in the lessons; but as the classes progressed, the material became more and more faddish. I was a nurse, my job was to help people. I thought, *if I wanted to know about big hair, teased out bangs, blue eye shadow, and too much eyeliner, I could go to work at José Eber—or just hang out at the mall!*

My patients weren't going to be looking for blue streaks or purple lowlights. They were looking for serious help, not flights of fancy. I'd had enough. It was time for me to get back to work. Humming a little tune, I went down to the registrar's office and resigned. Running through my head were the words to a song from *Grease*, *"Beauty School Dropout."*

The makeup distributorship didn't last much longer. It must have been the nurse in me, but I just couldn't get excited about making pretty people prettier. They would be fine. But there were people in trouble who really needed me—accident victims and burn victims. People had been disfigured and I could help them fit in again. *That* was where I needed to be.

The constant pressure to sell didn't make it any better. It was always, "Sell, sell, sell!" But I didn't care, care, care. All the pink Cadillacs in the world—or whatever they gave away—weren't going to motivate me. Money was not what motivated me; but helping people did get me going. So I put an end to the distributorship.

I didn't regret the experiments—not at all. Both my mom and my stylist had my best interest at heart. They were only trying to help me make ends meet. Besides, I did learn a thing or few; and over the years ahead, I would put those skills to work.

While I may have gotten a little off track with the beauty school classes, I did actually pick up a few things that I could use. So what seemed like a diversion at that point, would prove very useful just a few years later. At the very least, I was more comfortable hovering around another person's head—and I knew better than to hold the pointy end of the scissors.

So as I thought about The Lemonade Stand, what else did I have to be afraid of? I'd overcome my irrational fear of cancer patients. The cosmetic skills I figured I could handle—with a little time and practice. What was it that had me so nervous as I entered the shop? After all, Rita had "given me strength" just the night before. Now I was woefully unsure of myself again.

At first, I thought it was my pathetic lack of business skills that had me so terrified about running the shop. But as bad as those skills were, I knew they would improve. I could learn, I could hire people, or I could farm things out. Running a business wouldn't be easy—especially for someone with no head for numbers—but it could be done.

The thing that terrified me the most, I realized, was the unknown. The lack of structure, the absence of any guidelines or instructions, was more than a little unnerving As a nurse administrator, the expectations had been clear. The roles were well defined. The tasks were carefully outlined and assigned. Even as a limo driver, I knew just what to do, and where to go. Finding the directions was a minor detail. But there was no road map for The Lemonade Stand.

Not only would I be taking care of the hands-on work with the patients, I would be wearing a number of hats that I'd never worn before. I didn't even know if these hats would fit my head! Business management, hiring, training, marketing and public relations, bookkeeping, inventory control. Those, and at least a dozen other things I'd never done, I would now have to do. *How am I going to manage all of this?* I wondered. *I must be crazy.*

I shared my fears with Rita, and she promised that we would have a little time of discussion and prayer early each morning. "The best way to begin your day is with prayer," Rita said. She reminded me of Jesus' promise: "For where two or three are gathered together in My name, I am there in the midst of them" (*Matthew 18:20*). I looked at her blankly, and shook my head— *huh?* "When we pray," she explained with a grin, "He will be there with us."

Oh, I nodded, and pursed my lips, *hmmmm.* "Okay," I said uncertainly.

That's it? I thought. *That's the plan?* I was supposed to manage all of these new roles and all I had for backup was the
religious equivalent of "trust me"? It didn't seem like much of a
hook to hang all of my hats on, and I said as much. Rita chuckled and replied, "Trust me. Honey, it's all you're ever going to
need." *Trust me?* I thought to myself. *She actually said, "trust
me?" They say that in the movies right before everything goes to
pieces.* But I swallowed my doubts, took a deep breath, and nodded an okay.

Hoping that a little one-on-one time might result in something of a road map, I gave it a try. Every day, when I got to the
office, I would call Rita and she'd read a Bible verse to me. There
was no lesson plan, no orderly progression. Rita would simply
pick a verse that she felt compelled to share with me that day.
The funny thing was; it did exert a calming influence over my
life. I began to look forward to my telephone time with Rita
every day. Up until then, it had never crossed my mind to begin
the day with prayer. I was 32 years old and I had never even
given it a try. Sure, I attended church every Sunday; but the truth
was, I had only been going through the motions. I'd never seriously read the Bible—not cover to cover. Let's be honest: other
than in church, I had barely even cracked one open!

Over time, Rita's words began to make a little bit of sense to
me. They kind of grew on me in a way that such things never
had before. Church, and the Bible, had always seemed somehow
separate from life. My life was one thing; the church was something else. I had never noticed a real connection. My life often
conflicted with church, but it never seemed to meet up with it.
Now my life had run headlong into it—in the form of this
strangely magnetic little woman.

Rita taught me that God's Word was so important—more so
than the business itself. That was a little hard to swallow at first.
It seemed to go against my better judgment. My instinct had
always been to put my work first. After all, I had a family to feed.

Rita explained that God and family should be my priorities, along with service to others. After that, the business would take care of itself. I was dubious. It is a difficult idea to get your head around when there are bills to be paid. But Rita was the expert, so I tried to take it all in.

The Lemonade Stand was not about marketing and accounting; although those things might have their place. The business was about service—service to God, through service to man. Our job was to do right by others, one day at a time, as best we could. One of Rita's favorite verses was "But the very hairs of your head are all numbered" (*Matthew 10:30*). That verse had a very special meaning to Rita. For every time she'd lost her hair during her illness, Rita knew that God cared. Just as He understood *her* struggles, He understood *all* struggles. Our job, for Him, was to ease the struggles and suffering of others.

Every day brought a new verse and a different lesson. Sometimes, the application was obvious, and the lesson was clear. On other days, it would take a while to sink in. Whenever I expressed a little confusion at her choice, I would hear the smile in her voice, as she told me, "Honey, just give it a little time."

On some mornings, her verses were like little, mental bolts of lightning. Others were like a slow summer dawn. I gotta admit, there were a few that were like spring after a long winter—they took that long to understand. Hours—or even days—later, I would finally get the picture, and her meaning would become clear. *I got it!* I would think to myself happily. Then I'd have to smile, or even laugh aloud, at her insight. These little outbursts of joy could raise a few eyebrows when they seemed to erupt out of nowhere.

Rita taught me one that I had to think twice about. "All Scripture is given by inspiration of God, and is profitable for doctrine, for reproof, for correction, for instruction in righteousness, that the man of God may be complete, thoroughly equipped for every good work" (*2 Timothy 3:16-17*). After thinking about it for a moment, or three, it sounded sensible enough. On the other hand, seeing it in action could be quite inspiring, even amazing! Most of us think of a Bible verse as something that applies to *other people*. We might shake our heads, and cluck our tongues, and say, "Oh, if only they knew about John: *this,* or Paul: *that*—then they wouldn't be in so much trouble." Usually, when we think of a Bible verse, it is in regard to someone else. Applying the verses to yourself—and truly seeing the application—is often remarkable, and occasionally stunning.

Don't get me wrong; they weren't all gold. Every day was not a Top 40 hit. Some verses were just little trinkets to make you smile and nod. But some were gems with fire enough to warm your very soul. The interesting thing is that, for each person they will be different. But whether they worked a little or a lot, at the end of each phone call I felt more than ready to face the day ahead. *Today's going to be a good day,* I'd think to myself. *Bring it on!*

Bring it, He did.

There were bad days, too; days when Rita and I couldn't talk. I sorely felt her absence then. But a bad day like that for me meant real trouble for Rita. She had several bouts of serious illness; some were bad enough that she needed to be hospitalized. During those tough times, I would go to visit, hoping to cheer her up a little bit. But there were days when the treatments and medication would leave Rita too weak to talk. Even then, she was determined not to "let me down." I was amazed. Struggling for her life, Rita was still concerned that my spiritual education should continue uninterrupted.

Her son, Stephen, planned to study to be a minister one day. When she was too weak to do so herself, she would ask him to read Bible verses with me. "Take my Bible, Stephen," she would whisper, "and read to her. Teach her the Bible, Stephen. It will be good for both of you." Sometimes we'd stay in the room to read and talk together, so that she might listen in.

You could see that it did her some good—if you paid close attention. A ghost of a smile, or a barely perceptible nod, told me that Rita was following along. I like to think that our discussions helped to lift her up and take her away, at least temporarily, from her dark world of suffering. If nothing else, the talks gave her something new to focus on—something that was important to her.

While some might label it a simple "distraction", others would say that she was in touch with God. At that point, I really couldn't have said. All I knew was that it made her feel better in a way that nothing else could. It left me feeling different somehow, too.

Finally, when Rita dropped off to sleep, Stephen and I would retreat into the hall to continue our studies. For such a young man, he had so much strength, and so much love to give. I was truly inspired by him. It hardly seemed possible, but this 18-year-old man seemed to know so much more about God, and life, than I did. How could I not follow his example?

It was around that time that Rita gave me her personal Bible. It was so precious to me. Not only did it serve as a way to get to know God, it was also a window into Rita's soul. She had all of her own personal notations jotted down throughout it. I saw her highlighting marks over the phrase, "the very hairs on your head are numbered." It was filled with dozens, even hundreds of little notes and comments that were just as personal to her. These markings and notations documented her struggle with cancer, and her journey through life. At first, when I began to read her Bible, I felt as though I were invading her privacy. It was like digging through someone's mental underwear drawer—this stuff was personal and private. Although, as I thought about it, I realized that Rita knew, better than anyone, just what was in there. It was her intent that I know her innermost thoughts. If Rita

Rita's family: her husband Jerry, the lady herself, her son Stephen, and her daughter Holly. Rita loved them all—along with her other children, Donna and Jerry—without end. I know, because she told me so.

couldn't tell me about them, she would have me read them for myself. It wasn't long before I began to gain a greater understanding of Rita and her source of strength. She was most definitely "turned on" to something important. It might take a long time, but if I had to read that book line by line, I was going to do it. I wanted to *know* what she knew.

If there was one thing I did know, it was that I really had my work cut out for me. I had so much to learn, about so many things. The notion of actually studying the Bible, and learning the Word of God, had really gotten under my skin. But at the same time, I had so much to learn about the business itself. I had to figure out how to run it, how to market it, how to pay the bills, how to buy the products, and how to fit those products to the clients. If I thought about everything at once, I quickly felt overwhelmed. Panic would begin to bubble to the surface. *Settle down,* I'd think to myself then. *One thing at a time.*

On days like those, I'd remind myself of the words of the Apostle Paul, "I can do all things through Christ who strengthens me" *(Philippians 4:13)*. That verse would become my tag line, my mantra, my guiding light. Over and over, I would repeat that phrase in the days ahead. It became my mental broken record.

Rita's Bible remained one of my most treasured possessions, until several years later when I returned it to her youngest daughter. Holly was having a rough time of her own, and I hoped it would give her some comfort and guidance. By then, I was firmly on course and thought it might help to steady up her rudder. Even so, it was difficult to let it go, and I really missed having it around. Rita's Bible had been my touchstone, my contact with her in her absence. But it wasn't the book that counted, so much as the lessons that had come from it. The lessons that Rita taught me will last forever.

4

Things Are Tough All Over

I was "all in". There wasa no going back now. It was all or nothing. I'd quit my nice, safe position at the doctor's office, but I still had the responsibility of raising my two young sons. Nicholas and Adam were 11 and 12 years old at the time, and they still needed plenty of care and attention. I hoped and prayed that I was doing the right thing by them. Looking at it objectively, the whole thing seemed foolish enough. I was a single parent walking away from a steady paycheck with good, consistent benefits to a life of unsteady pay and no benefits at all. So I tried not to look at it objectively. *The whole thing just feels right,* I tried to tell myself. *Everything will be okay.*

With all of the turmoil in my professional life, what I needed was a little peace and tranquility at home. *Yeah, right.*

With impeccable timing, fate decided to throw me a curve ball. Not to mention a couple of fast balls and a slider—all while I was hoping for slow and easy, straight up the middle. I had only just begun trying to do God's work, and already it felt like the devil was playing havoc with my life.

Two years earlier, the seeds were sown—in a big way. My little boy, Nicholas, started to have headaches. These weren't the usual little allergy or eyestrain headaches. They were real head-splitters. When one came on, it would have Nicholas staggering in from outside, drunk with pain. Playing with his friends was all but forgotten as he stumbled in, looking for help. We tried aspirin and cold compresses, but relief was always fleeting. After a day or two, things got so bad that he would wake up in the middle of the night, screaming with pain. On the third night, he begged me to make it go away. I spent the rest of the night trying to comfort him, but I was growing more and more alarmed. I had finally realized that something was wrong, really wrong. We went to see the doctor early the next morning.

Dr. Todd Cook was a really good guy—warm, open, and sympathetic. He knew how to talk to kids and was very good with Nicholas. At the same time, he was informative and honest with me. After a brief exam, he suggested that a CT scan might be appropriate.

I was friends with most of the nurses in the building, and there were several of us in the room with Nicholas to keep him company. We were kidding around with him, telling him that

the big tube he was sliding into would let us see how many mar-
bles were still upstairs. Nicholas seemed to treat it like a big
science adventure—all wide-eyed with curiosity. He was all
smiles, enjoying the company of the nurses; but I know he must
have been even happier to be getting some help.

The big machine did its work, and just a few minutes later,
Dr. Cook motioned me over to his side. As I leaned in close to see
the results, he sighed and bowed his head. Dr. Cook looked at me
with a long face, and mouthed silently, "We found a tumor."

The room went completely silent then; all sound faded away
and I went numb. The other nurses could read lips as well as I
could. Tears began to run down their faces, as they struggled to
put up a brave front. I began to feel a little lightheaded then, and
the room took on an alarming angle. I looked for a chair, to sit
down for a moment. Something was really wrong with my son,
and it was literally scaring the sense out of me. My training
helped me to maintain a calm facade—at least I think it did. I
don't know. Inside, my head was reeling and the seconds seemed
to stretch out endlessly before me. But as quick as you can think
it, the nurses swung into action. Dr. Cook told me that they
would take care of it immediately.

Of course, Nicholas knew something was up right away.
There's no fooling a kid. He adopted the calm demeanor of the
other nurses and took the news stoically. I don't know if he really understood how serious it was, but now that he knew what it
was, he was prepared to face it bravely.

The next morning, Nicholas was admitted to Children's
Hospital in Cincinnati, for brain surgery. It was a twelve-hour
procedure. I sat in the chapel and prayed and waited, and waited and prayed, for that whole, long day. It was agonizing and
endless. My family and friends shared the wait until the surgeon
came out to see me. He sat down with us and explained the procedure, then he said, "I'm confident that we have removed all of
the tumor. However, we'll have to send away for lab work to be

certain that the margins are all clear." We wouldn't get the final results until after the coming weekend. From Thursday to Monday I prayed for the best, and feared the worst. It was the longest weekend of my life.

Adam and I would go in to visit Nicholas every day, to try to keep him feeling positive and happy. He responded well and showed little of the worry that must have been eating him up inside. He had a steady stream of company as his teachers and classmates came in groups to visit. They filled Nicholas' room to overflowing with new hats for his little shaved head. Along with all of the cards and balloons, there were plenty of books and comics to help him pass the time until he could return to school. His room was filled with positive inspiration. It was easy to see how much love people felt for Nicholas and his family. It had to be good for his spirits. I know it was good for ours.

On Monday night, the surgeon returned at about nine o'clock. Nicholas was lying in the bed, looking tired, frail, and pale as a ghost. He seemed so fragile, and looked top-heavy with a big, white dressing wrapped around his head. Carefully, the doctor helped Nicholas up and began to unwrap the bandages. As he did so, he told us that everything appeared to be "A-okay" with Nicholas' test results. He would need no further treatment. I practically melted with relief at his words. I was nothing but a big, sobbing puddle of happiness.

Nicholas recovered from surgery quickly, and it wasn't long before he was back in school again. His shaved head had grown back into a short brush cut. With a few careful nips, the barber's clippers transformed the surgery scar into the letters of his initials. His classmates were greatly entertained when he doffed his cap to reveal a hairstyle that was far ahead of its time. It was just a few years later that fashion caught up with him. With the addition of baggy pants and oversize shirts, all of the boys were emulating Nicholas' old grade school style. When I saw what had developed, I laughed to myself as I thought, *been there, done that.*

Back up to full-speed again, Nicholas resumed his sports program with enthusiasm. He was back on the diamond almost before I got my "okays" out. One afternoon, he was up to bat, with his cutting-edge hairstyle safely secured beneath a plastic batter's helmet. The pitcher was burning them in, right over the plate, and Nicholas had his eye on the ball. He got a little piece of one, and fouled it away.

That near-hit must have thrown the pitcher off his stride. On the next pitch, he put a little too much knuckle on the ball. He knuckled it right into Nicholas' head, and knuckled Nicholas right off his feet! That little playground Nolan Ryan went white as a sheet and dropped his mitt. Then he dashed off the mound and was instantly down in the dirt, helping Nicholas climb back to his feet. Those safety helmets really do the job. Nicholas shrugged the whole thing off with a laugh, waved to the stands, and took his walk to first base. The poor, shaken pitcher returned to the mound. There, he proceeded to send Nicholas, and the next three batters, all across home plate. One by one.

The worst was over, but we weren't out of the woods yet. Nicholas would still need follow up CT scans every year, for the next five years. At the time, that was just fine with me. I was working happily away at the doctor's office, and I had plenty of insurance to cover the follow-ups. But several years later, everything had changed. By then, I was at The Lemonade Stand without a "real" job or paycheck. My insurance was ancient history, and Nicholas was in need of another expensive CT scan. I didn't know how I would come up with so much extra money. After all, we were talking about a thousand bucks!

I hoped and prayed—and tried to have faith—that somehow the Good Lord would provide. In His own good way, I suppose He did. I continued to work several side jobs at a time, trying to make ends meet. All the while, I spent my days with Rita trying to learn everything I could about The Lemonade Stand, and all that went with it. Underlying everything were my continued efforts to learn the Bible. Rita felt that my studies were as important as anything else I was learning. She told me it was crucial to the spirit of the business, and said "it's just not possible to have the one without the other."

Somehow, we kept the hounds at bay and the bills paid—but only just barely. The boys did their part, by helping around the house, and never asking for *anything*. I continued to find jobs as a home healthcare provider—with one case here, another there. I also ran around, all over town, to give insurance physicals. I visited peoples' homes, one after another, to draw blood, run tests, and take samples for the lab. My job there was to check people over to see whether or not they could qualify for their life insurance. While those two jobs might seem vaguely related, my other job wasn't even a distant cousin. Besides the other two, I spent many a long, late night at work driving limos.

All over town and all night long, I chauffeured celebrities big and small. They were mostly of the smaller sort—there aren't a lot of real celebrities in Cincinnati. My customers were more of the business sort, with more than a few weddings and proms mixed in.

One night, I did have the thrill of driving a real celebrity—but only if I could find her. While I knew my way around town, I knew nothing about the airport. Bette Midler's plane was landing in minutes and I was lost among the twists and turns of the airport corridors. At my wit's end, I spotted an airport police car and screeched to a halt alongside it. I frantically explained my predicament. "Can you help me?" I pleaded.

"Bette!?" the officer exclaimed. "She's coming here?" He practically squealed. Adopting a serious demeanor, he ordered tersely, "Follow me!" And with lights and sirens blazing, he peeled out. Racing along the access roads and down the tarmac, it must have looked like we had the president on board. We pulled to a stop alongside the plane with not a moment to spare.

When life gives you lemons. . .

Write things down!

Memories go haywire in a crisis. Use tape recorders, planners, and journals to keep track of what people are saying, what you have to do, and the thoughts and feelings that run through your head. This helps to maintain a sense of confidence and order now, and is invaluable learning for the rest of your life.

As the air-stairs unfolded, I hopped out and opened the passenger door. Together, that officer and I played it totally cool. We were professionals, after all.

"Ms. M.," I nodded, as I held the door for her. Once I'd closed the door behind her, I looked up at the policeman again. His eyes were as big as mine.

It seemed like I drove to the ends of the earth in that limo. Every once in a while, the jobs might overlap. Then I would find myself making a quick drop-off at the lab, while on my way to pick up another limousine client. Never have urine samples ridden in such high style.

Somehow, I nickle-and-dimed my way through paying for the scan that year. Even so, things were just too tight. I had to face reality. I was the owner of a house with no equity, and I couldn't afford the mortgage anymore. It was a struggle just to make the utility payments. It was time to cut back. I called a friend, who had just earned her real estate license, and told her that I needed to sell my house. It was the middle of winter—the worst time of the year to try to sell a house in Kentucky. But it had to go.

My misfortune was her big opportunity. She was so excited, because it would be her very first listing. *Nothing like going with experience,* I thought to myself, *but beggars can't be choosers.* Rita had put her trust in me—another novice—so I would do the same for my friend. She recommended that we get it all cleaned up while we waited to put it on the market the next spring. I shook my head and told her, "I can't wait. It has to be done right away. By spring, the house will probably be in foreclosure." In order to continue working with Rita, I had to reduce my bills. That included selling my house, right away—before I lost it!

We did some sprucing up, put it on the market, and crossed our fingers. It sold within a week. From that moment on, I had a feeling that God really was working in my life—or at least, influencing events. It seemed as if He were eliminating the hurdles in transitioning from my previous life into my new one. Some people may think it sounds a lot like I'm crediting divine intervention for things that real estate

My older son, Adam. Even as a young man, he was always bold and resourceful, almost fearless. He was an enormous help to me.

agents do every day; but that's truly how it seemed to me. I know it was not exactly the parting of the Red Sea, but it was a small miracle to me. It may not seem like a big deal; but anyone who ever sweated out late mortgage payments, or tried to sell a house quickly, knows what a blessing it was. I felt like God was helping to clear away the obstacles for me, so that I might begin walking this new road and doing His work.

Of course, with the house gone, the boys and I needed a new place to live. There was a beautiful apartment complex nearby with lush landscaping and cozy little buildings. Every time I drove past I wondered why I never saw a "for rent" sign outside. The complex was nice enough that I could certainly understand why. It had a very "homey" feel to it. *Who would ever want to leave?* I asked myself. I knew I wouldn't, even as I wished someone would.

A few days after we put our house on the market, I was in a plastic surgeon's office, where I was telling the staff about The Lemonade Stand. I hoped that we could take care of any patients who might need help with their makeup. The office manager and I were getting along pretty well. As we talked, I learned that the doctor she worked for was also the owner of the apartment complex that I'd admired for so long. She and her husband actually managed it for him. I expressed my interest in the complex and lamented the fact that there were never any units available. Okay, so I whined.

A few days later, the office manager called. There was an opening in her building, and the boys and I could move in right away. I was so happy, because it was such an inviting place. Better yet, I'd been spared that

My younger son, Nicholas. To this day, he is a quiet, thoughtful, and gentle soul. I could not have succeeded without him.

"lost in limbo" feeling that comes from being between homes. Not only that, I'd been saved the headache of trooping around the city on an extended apartment hunt. With my hyperactive schedule at the time, that was a big relief.

Another prayer answered? It sure seemed that way to me. To someone else, these might seem like small things, disconnected events. To me, coming one right after another as they did, they began to add up to something. I had the feeling that, once again, the Lord had provided. The road ahead was smoothing out, as each pothole was filled in.

I told the boys that I'd found us an apartment. I was fairly nervous about it—afraid that they might interpret it as a step backward. After all, giving up your house is usually seen as a bad thing. So I emphasized the positive. It was a wonderful complex, and it was closer to school. They'd be able to make the trip more quickly, simply by walking. We would save on expenses, and be able to dig our way out of the financial hole I'd gotten us into. I thought it was a good thing, and I hoped they would respond well.

I shouldn't have worried. They were both very excited and said, "Okay, Mom. When do we go?" I felt like yet another weight had been lifted from my shoulders. I honestly don't know if they really *were* excited about the change. Maybe they were putting up a good show to keep up my morale. I wouldn't be surprised if that were the case. Adam and Nicholas always supported what I was trying to do. There they were, doing it again.

I always kept my sons involved, and let them know what was happening with everything. It was probably more than they wanted to know, but they were always in the loop. From business developments to Bible studies, I kept them up to date on everything that I learned. They seemed to understand that business and the Bible should be intertwined. Then, as Rita said, "Each one acts in service to the other." The idea that I was trying to do good work, for people in need, must have been what put it in perspective for Adam and Nicholas. They never complained about the hardships we endured.

The boys and I went without a lot of things, and they never asked me for anything twice. If I had to say "no", they understood why. Times were tough, and we scrimped and saved to get by. We did more than our share of hand-me-downs and do-it-yourself, bargain shopping and buying generic. If there was a cheaper way to get things done, we did it.

I know it was tough on the two of them, especially during their high school years. Later on, as their friends were getting cars, my boys were getting sneakers. There was no money for nice clothes, only necessities. "Sales" were good, "clearance" was better; and if we had to swallow some pride for a little "second-hand," we did that, too. With that being so, there was certainly no money for yearbooks or class pictures. Class rings might as well have been diamond rings. They just weren't happening. I couldn't afford any of it and still my sons never complained. When he was barely 14, Adam took an after-school job at a gas station, so he could help me with buying clothes. Nicholas made up for his absence by doing more than his share of housework. I don't know if they realized just how much I depended on them. I tried to let them know how proud I was, and how much their help meant to me. They would simply shrug it off, "No problem, Mom."

We were not unique in our situation. As with many families, it always seemed like life was a continuous struggle—one highlighted by emergencies designed solely to test your strength. No sooner did one drama end than another one began. Almost as if on schedule, we were faced with another crisis. Adam was diagnosed with asthma, a serious case requiring a lot of expensive treatments.

Once again, God showed His face to me by leading me to the right place at the right time. Dr. Phil Schworer was a physician in private practice who was very helpful to me. He knew I was a nurse, and that I ran a small business where I tried to help cancer patients. I guess Dr. Schworer thought my "one good turn" deserved another, because he told me to just bring Adam in. "We'll take good care of him," he said to me. After that, Dr. Schworer always saw Adam quickly, took great care of him, and never charged us for a single thing. Lab tests, medicines, office visits . . . nothing. There were always plenty of "samples" to cover Adam's prescription needs. When we finished with a visit, the doctor simply gave me a pat on the shoulder as he left, and whispered, "Keep up the good work." When I got to the front desk and pulled out my pocketbook, the lady there would shake her head and say, "We won't

Dr. Phil Schworer cared for Adam's asthma, and never charged a dime, as I struggled to care for cancer patients. He thought it was a fair trade.

need that today. It's all taken care of. Now, when can you come in again?" If that's not God's hand at work, I don't know what is. Does that count as a miracle? Even a small one? It sure felt that way to me.

I t used to break my heart that I couldn't buy the boys the extra things they wanted—or even everything they *needed*. We worked hard and struggled along, doing our best to get by. Somehow, whenever a desperate need arose, there was always an angel at our doorstep, ready to provide. At least that's what it looked like from my point of view. No matter what it was that we needed, by God's grace, people would show up with it. Whether it was clothing, food, or toys, whatever was most needed at that very moment seemed to arrive just in time. After a while, a pattern began to emerge and I found myself doing less doubting and more accepting. I was beginning to make connections between what Rita was teaching and what I was seeing in my life. More than just seeing the connections, I was feeling them.

The happy moments weren't all "big miracles". There were lots of little ones. And it's not like I was on a regular delivery schedule or anything; but it did seem as if my uncertain prayers were being answered with surprising frequency. It felt like I had a direct line. I could almost imagine God rolling his eyes and sighing, "Oh, Me. Again? Don't tell me, it's Gayle. She needs another one."

I came home one evening after a long, exhausting day. Between The Lemonade Stand and the freelance gigs I had wedged in, I was wiped out. The boys and I were preparing dinner and discussing what tomorrow would bring. They were going on excitedly about a field trip that was scheduled for the next day, when I realized that I was in trouble again.

My purse was empty. I didn't have the money to pay for their lunch, much less the field trip. The banks were closed by then— and my account was probably empty anyway. It was getting too late to call anyone, and I didn't want to go begging to my folks or my friends—again. They were probably getting tired of it. It's funny how a few dollars can become a big problem. I was really struggling with my little dilemma. It wasn't so small to me! *What kind of a provider am I?* I worried. At a loss for a solution, I tried a desperate prayer. "Lord, I don't know what I'm going to do, but I really need your help here."

Earlier that day, as I was closing up the shop, the phone rang. It was my mom's best friend, Evelyn. She was caring for her mother, Rosa; and all day long, Rosa had been asking if I would come by. I said yes, even though I would rather have waited another day. Just a few days before, I had set Rosa up with a breast prosthesis and bras, so I knew she didn't need anything important. I wished it could wait, but I'd already agreed to visit her at home. So . . . I would.

It wasn't until after dinner that night that I remembered my promise. It had been such a long day, and now I was busy stressing over how to pay for field trips and lunches. *Why do I have to go all the way out there?* I whined to myself. *Why couldn't she just tell me what she wanted?* I was tired. And grumpy. I really didn't want to go back out, but it seemed important to Rosa. I quit my little pity party, made sure the boys were positively occupied, and I got back into the car.

I arrived at Rosa's house a short while later, where I found that she was confined to bed. Right away, I felt stupid for fussing like I had. We talked for a little while, mostly about inconsequential things. Her spirits seemed to lift as we chatted. It looked like all she needed was a little company. She asked about my sons and I said good things. I wasn't confined to bed, so I certainly had nothing to complain about.

Rosa patted my hand after a bit, and said, "I'd better send you back to your boys." She took up my hand then and asked me if I'd pray with her. When we were finished, she said, "Thank you for coming. I'm grateful for your time and I appreciate your praying with me." Then she took my hand into both of hers, pressed a note or something into it, and gave it a firm closing squeeze to go with her "goodnight." I stuffed the note into a pocket and gathered up my purse and coat. Quietly, I let myself out the door, as I fished around for my keys.

As I left Rosa's house, I was glad I'd gone to see her, and felt much better for it. You might even say I felt a little at peace. But as I climbed into my car, the reality of my own life struck me again. By then, it was very late, and I still had no idea how I would meet my sons' needs the next morning. That warm, fuzzy feeling began to fade away as I got caught up in my own concerns.

I remembered Rosa's note then, and dug it out of my pocket. I was hoping for a few kind words to lift my spirits before I returned to my life. I unfolded the page. There were a few kind words in there all right. *A hundred of them, with Ben Franklin's face on the front.* What a wonderful surprise. A hundred bucks would take care of that field trip. It would also take care of gas and groceries for the week!

Rosa had no way of knowing that I was all out of cash—flat broke and busted. During her visit to the shop, the business would have appeared to be flowing smoothly. She couldn't know that there were no paychecks to be had. I certainly hadn't burdened her with my problems during our visit. Lucky for me, Rosa had been inspired to place that money in my hand. Once again, when I was down and out, scared and upset, God showed His face to me—this time through Rosa. At the sight of that hundred dollar bill, my eyes teared up and I nearly wept with relief. I would be able to take care of my boys' needs after all. As silly as that might seem, it was so important to them. That made it important to me, as their mother.

Not long after my visit, Rosa died. She probably never knew how important she'd been to me, and to my family. I'm so thankful to God, for sending Rosa to me when she needed help. Little did I realize that the visit was for my sake as well as hers. In answering *her* prayers, He answered *mine*. Or was it vice-versa? Rita said that if I took care of the people God sent, He would send the people I'd need. I found this to be true so many times. And I would again.

One of the verses that Rita shared with me, during our morning chats, was John 15:7. "If you abide in Me, and My words abide in you, you will ask what you desire, and it shall be done for you."

Hmmm. Almost unbelievable isn't it?

Flying Solo

R ita did her best to instill in me every ounce of Christian spirit that she could. With her as my role model, I had been a willing student—even if I was a little slow to catch on at times. Rita was so concerned that I understand that there is a purpose for our lives. As I worked alongside her, putting our customers back together again, I began to think that I had found mine.

Having a hand in a patient's transformation was an almost magical experience. Watching a drawn, worn-out face lift up into a light, happy smile, I couldn't help but feel that we were doing good work—especially when the smile stayed in place. It was almost like we were helping them to rediscover their sense of self. When a client looked in the mirror and saw her own face again—the one that she thought was gone—it was like a lost and weary soul had come home again.

After working with Rita for only ten short months, she lost her long battle with cancer. She was gone. Knowing it was coming hadn't made it any easier. Our time together passed so quickly. Even as Rita said her time would be soon, I didn't want to believe it was true. As anyone would, I hoped and prayed that she would pull through. Other people had, why not Rita, too? But she would have shaken her head at me, smiled sadly and said, "It wasn't meant to be."

But why? I wanted to know. It's enough to make you ask some serious questions of God. *If our work was so important, why couldn't Rita continue to do it? And, what about Rita's dreams? Doesn't she get to have hers? How about those she loved?* The questions quickly became too painful to contemplate. But whenever I found myself going over them again, I would see Rita's face. In my mind, I could see her smile and say, "Honey, you're just wasting your time. You have a job to do—so do it!" I thought she'd rather have me *doing something,* instead of sitting around mourning. So I tried my best to do just that.

As near as I can tell, some lessons have to hurt to be learned. Some examples must be harsh to be remembered. Doesn't the story of Jesus Himself seem to say as much? If He were just another teacher, just another rabbi, would we remember Him so well? His lessons are what we try to live up to, but it is the crucifixion that makes the lessons stick. It is the way He lived His last moments that shame us, or inspire us, to do better. It is sad that it should be so, but doesn't it seem to be true? At least for some of us? The painful lessons are the ones most clearly remembered.

Think about it. We all know about The Good Word, The Ten Commandments, and The Golden Rule. We all understand, "Do unto others . . ." But how many of us really *do* it? Of course, we try. But then we slip. Or procrastinate. Or cut corners. It's in our nature to look for the easy way out—we actually have to work at it to rise above ourselves. Even when we do, all too often it's so easy to go on a little vacation. So some of us turn to the church to help us keep ourselves in line—to keep us in touch with "the better angels of our nature." But even in church, how many of us simply nod in agreement at what we hear—and forget all about it when we head for home?

The good lessons are all there. Your church, and the Bible, are just sloppin' over with them. The positive examples are just waiting to be read, or heard. But still we procrastinate. Some of us are a little slow to catch on, or a little too lazy to do the work. I count myself among them. We know what we *should* be doing, we simply figure that we'll get to it later.

So I have to wonder if God doesn't place reminders all around us. Some are small, some are large—reminding us that He is there, and reminding us that we can aspire to something greater than we are. Sometimes we pick up on the little ones and get back on the proper path. Sometimes we miss the big ones completely. We're all different, so the reminders are always out there, in all different forms—small and large, beautiful and tragic. You just never know what is going to click with a person.

Rita was my inspiration.

Her work, to ease the suffering of others, set an example for all of us to live up to. But would I have given up my job on account of her work? Would I have walked away from my safe, comfortable life just to follow the example that she set? I like to *think* I would have. But would I *really*? I don't know. I might simply have expressed some admiration and returned to my life. If Rita were just another normal, healthy person doing good work, I probably would have said, "Isn't she something? God bless her." Then I would have gone about my business.

The fact that Rita did as she did, even as she suffered from the same malady as her clients, made it so much more remarkable. *That* would be hard to walk away from. How could I *not* help? But if Rita had recovered, would I have stuck it out as long as I did? If everything had turned out okay, would I have stayed the course, and fought my way through the rough seas ahead? Would I have continued to struggle so hard just to keep the business afloat? Or would I have jumped ship and moved on to something calm and safe?

Don't misunderstand me. I'm not saying that Rita's suffering was solely for my benefit. It was for no one's benefit. But the way that Rita faced it would inspire many others to do the right thing in their lives. I was just one of the many whose hearts she touched. Others may have taken different meanings, or inspirations, away from her life. But inspire others she did.

Rita bore her burden stoically, and fought the good fight right up until the end. She was a lifesaver to dozens of women in dire need. Amazingly she did it all on her own, even as her illness worked to bring her down. But Rita was only one. She could do only so much. But because of her example, my colleagues and I would go on to help many thousands more. Some of those thousands would go on to help many more in turn. Some of them would even come full circle to help us at the shop when we needed it most. Like a pebble dropped into a pond, Rita's impact continued to ripple outward through the lives of others.

On that first day that we met, Rita had said, "I'm dying and I know it. But the Good Lord told me that if I hung on long enough, He would send someone to take over." In that moment, my fate was sealed. Oh, I may have thought that I was "thinking it over." But no, the decision was already made.

To me, Rita was almost a saintly figure. It is an exaggeration, I know—she was all too human—and I don't presume to canonize her myself. But it seemed to me that Rita's suffering—and her rise to the challenge—were meant as symbols for the rest of us.

I don't mean that God pointed to her and commanded that she become a sacrificial lamb. He did not "visit upon her an affliction" so that she might serve as an example to others. No. It may be that these things happen on their own. Whether it is by accident or by choice, by free will or fate, by genetics or by chance, things simply happen—both good and bad. But even if you believe that God determines the outcome of every event, the truth is in how we face up to them when they come. Whether an event is good or bad, some people respond well and others react poorly. Some don't respond at all. But there are those who look to God for guidance—in times of triumph *and* in times of tragedy. When they do, He delivers to them the strength, or wisdom, to handle things in a God-like way. God helps people look past their own selfish interests to see the bigger picture. Rita did exactly that. She looked past her own interests to see the bigger picture. And she inspired others to do the same.

For all of my struggles to understand, I know what Rita would have said. With a little tilt of the head, and one raised eyebrow, she'd say, "I know what my purpose is. And I'm content with it." Then a little grin would slide across her face and she'd say, "You need to quit worryin' about my purpose and attend to your own!" Then, with a little pat on the back or a squeeze of the hand, she'd finish with, "Now, get going. There's work to be done."

Right up until her final moments, Rita constantly assured me that, even without her, I could take care of the business. If I continued to stay focused on God first, and kept asking for His guidance and direction, then together we would accomplish more than I ever dreamed was possible. I promised Rita that I would do everything I could to keep the business going for at least another ten years. I'm not sure why that number popped out; but now that I was all alone, it sounded like a lifetime. I'd always known that, one day, I would be running the business on my own. Now that the time had come it truly seemed impossible.

Rita had two daughters, but to my knowledge they weren't going to continue with the business after Rita was gone. My contact with them had been limited. The family hadn't really taken an interest in The Lemonade Stand, at least not from what I had seen. Perhaps they saw it as a charitable hobby, or maybe just a simple distraction for her. I hope they didn't feel like the business was taking her away from them. I know that was not so. She loved her family without end.

But The Lemonade Stand did give Rita purpose, and it gave her suffering meaning. To Rita, it was better to stand up and fight, to spend her days helping others, rather than to curl up at home and wait for the end. She had never been one to stand and wait. But sadly, Rita didn't feel that it mattered to anyone else what happened to the business after she was gone. The Lemonade Stand was her passion, and she wanted to know that it would continue. So I made my promise to make a good go of it, for at least ten years.

The trouble was, there were no contracts between Rita and me. She simply wasn't a by-the-numbers, paperwork kind of person. Her word was her bond—and that was all right by me. But as you might imagine, a lawyer would make a hash of that arrangement in a New York second. I had to make things legitimate.

It looked like I'd have to go it alone. Rita's family was finished with the business. That was understandable. After all, they had just suffered a grievous loss. The last thing they were looking for was a daily reminder of that loss. Besides, The Lemonade Stand just wasn't *their* passion.

Since I didn't know what the long-term intentions of Rita's family were, I thought I had better start from scratch. Rather than continue to do business as The Lemonade Stand, I changed the name to Image Insights. A few years earlier, I'd run a little business on the side, helping people who had been bruised, scarred, or burned in accidents. With paramedical makeup and a little instruction, I would help them to restore their appearance. I originally picked the name because I felt like I was helping people return their outer appearance to a match with their inner self image. It was just a small, freelance business, but its goal had been to help people look and feel like themselves again. Since The Lemonade Stand had a similar mission, it seemed like a natural transition to me.

Even with my Image Insights experience, I had no real business background. I'd never had a retail space before. I'd never had to keep a store stocked, or worry about the sell-through. I didn't have any family or friends who had ever owned a business, or even had any business education. My credit was still terrible and I had almost no money in the bank. A single parent, with no child support, I thought I was a most unlikely candidate to own a business. But I knew I had to keep this one going. I'd made a promise to Rita, and I knew that there were people out there who needed my help.

The Lemonade Stand was located right in the heart of Cincinnati, close to all of the major hospitals. This had been perfect for Rita—it was near her home and her treatment centers. Best of all, her husband had been willing to help her pay the rent. I didn't think he'd be willing to help pay mine. I couldn't afford to stay there, so the first thing I had to do was find a new location. I'd worked for many years in hospitals in northern Kentucky and was more familiar with that territory. Since I still lived in Kentucky, I began looking for a place that would keep me close to home. That would allow me a little more time with my sons. My parents, who were always so supportive, also lived nearby. Staying near home would allow me to better take advantage of their willingness to help.

I started searching for places to set up shop, and one day I found myself in Covington, Kentucky. It was only ten minutes

When life gives you lemons. . .

Look your best!

Forget outdated notions of glamour and hype and begin finding and enhancing your own uniqueness. Above all, do take the time to look your personal best. Doing this will reinforce energy and confidence.

from where I grew up, but I couldn't remember ever having been there before. It seemed like a nice, little town, so I decided to look around.

I drove circles around Covington, trying to figure out what to do next. Business planning was not my forté, and I was a little light on advisory boards; so it seemed like I was always driving around in circles, trying to figure out what to do! I'm fairly sure that this is not how they teach it in Business 101.

I turned a corner, and drove right past a little white building that was for rent. *Worth a shot,* I thought; so I pulled a quick U-turn and went back for a look. As soon as I walked inside, I saw that the border along the ceiling was purple—my favorite color. *That's it,* I thought. *This is the place.* I know, it's silly sometimes, the things that we base our decisions on. Even so, purple was the color I'd used for my first Image Insights business. When I saw the purple there, I felt like it was the right place at the right time. Upon investigation, the rent seemed afford-

able—provided I could make the business go. If I were to continue the work that Rita had begun with The Lemonade Stand,
it would be right there.

Now that I had a location, there were a few minor details to
attend to. Before I opened the doors, I had to find out how and
where to buy the products, how to stock the shelves, how to find
clients, and how to set up a functioning office.
Like any good kid (read: clueless), I called

*My dad, Bert; an awesome carpenter, and
all-around talented guy . . . oh, and a full partner
in the Bert and Bernie Savings and Loan.*

on my parents for help. In the beginning,
they thought I ought to be measured for a strait-
jacket—my dad thought I'd completely lost my mind. "Why on
earth would you give up a nice, secure job to do something like
this? The whole thing sounds so risky?" There would be days
ahead when I wondered the same thing.

However, once my folks understood my goal, and saw my
determination, they climbed aboard. My parents helped me out
financially when the banks wouldn't touch me. I had tried to
explain the business to the bankers, but they just wouldn't
believe in me. The loan officer must have thought I was a fig-
ment of his fevered imagination. Believe in me? Ha! It's a wonder
they could even see me through their tears of laughter. No, there
would be no bank loans for me. I had to do my borrowing at the
Bert and Bernie Litmer Savings and Loan.

My folks didn't exactly have a lot of extra money just lying
around. Still, they lent me what they could to get things started.
It meant a lot to me. That they would risk their savings in order
to help, it was a big show of faith in me. I couldn't let them down.

Not only did they help financially, my folks were willing to
get their hands dirty, too. My dad was a carpenter by trade and

did excellent framing and finishing work. He helped me with the necessary repairs and a complete re-painting. He built cabinets for the products and shelves to display the wigs. With a lot of hard work, and a little help from me, my dad turned a beat-up old office into a smart, professional storefront. My mother had spent more than a few years as a secretary, so she knew what it took to get me up on my feet. She helped me set up my client records and got some of the paperwork problems solved. She answered phones and helped me attend to an endless array of other details. I couldn't have opened up without them. Because of their faith in me, and their hard work, I was finally beginning to look like a real business. Only one minor detail remained. None of us knew anything about finding the products.

I had to learn everything I could about wigs, but had no idea where to start. This was all before the Internet was available in everyone's home, making its wealth of information easily accessible to everyone. You couldn't just flip on the modem and type a few words into the search engine. I don't think search engines were around yet. It wouldn't have mattered if they were, because I had no idea what a modem was.

I certainly couldn't walk into a local wig shop and ask them to tell me everything they knew. They would rather sell and fit the wigs themselves. I wasn't sure how I would find out what I had to know. While sorting through my incoming mail one morning, the answer fell into my lap. It was a newsletter from Ava Gabor Wigs. A front page article highlighted a lady in Chicago who'd been in the wig business for seventeen years. *I should just call her,* I thought naively.

Then I imagined calling Ava Gabor Wigs with my little Kentucky/*Green Acres* accent:

Ring, ring. "Hello, *dahhhling,* Ava Gabor Wigs. How may I direct your call?"

"Well, hi y'all. I was lookin' for . . ."

Click. Bzzzzzzzzzz.

Still, I supposed that was the worst that could happen. *Not calling certainly wouldn't work.* So I called the lady in the newsletter—her name was Bonnie. I explained to her what Image Insights was, and how I had come to own it. I probably talked a little too fast, but there was so much to say. I told her that I had only a casual background in wigs, and very little knowledge about how to help someone to choose one for themselves. Then I asked if she knew anyone that could help me. *Why should she?* I fretted to myself. *Why should an Ava Gabor pro, from the bustling metropolis of Chicago, want to waste any time on a know-nothing nobody in Kentucky?*

Of course, Bonnie was wonderfully helpful, and a literal gold mine of information. She even invited me to Chicago to spend a little time with her, in order to show me a few tricks of the trade. I was excited, but also a

My mom, Bernie; good-natured, organized and efficient, and endlessly patient— even with me pushing her buttons.

little nervous about the trip, so my mother went along for moral support. When we arrived, we found Bonnie's mother in the store helping her out, too. Right away, we had something in common. Like peas in a pod, the four of us spent several days together.

Bonnie was a real professional. Smart and successful, but still down-to-earth, she was totally willing to share. If anyone could be titled a "true wig expert," Bonnie would be that person. She showed me everything I'd need to know about wigs. She taught me how to order them—not as easy as it sounds. She explained which companies were best, and why. And she showed me what quantities, colors, and styles of wigs were best to keep on hand. She even gave me a copy of her list of business contacts. Bonnie was like the Encyclopedia Britannica of wig knowledge, full of every technical detail and creative option imaginable. Best of all she was a delightful person to spend time with.

That little newsletter in my mail—was it a lucky bit of chance? Or a gift from God? I know what I think. Oh, I know all about direct mail, and mailing lists, and all that. But talk about the right person at the right time—Bonnie was an open book to me. She was so willing to help me along on my journey that I couldn't thank her enough. I don't know how I'd have started if not for her. I might have found another resource; but not one with the quality of information, and generosity of spirit, of Bonnie.

My next order of business was to learn about the breast prostheses. That was a subject I truly knew nothing about. At the time, one of the leading manufacturers was Colaplast, in Atlanta, Georgia. Encouraged by my experience in Chicago, I called and made an appointment to visit the factory. I wanted to see how a breast prosthesis was created, how it was meant to fit into the pockets of the bras, and how the bras themselves were made.

I drove all the way down to Georgia in my worn out, old Chevy. With no heat or air-conditioning, and no radio, it was a long and lonely drive. There was nothing but the hum of the engine and the roar of the wind to keep me company. I had to stop more than once for a little wake-up call and a smooth, delicious cup of truck-stop battery acid, er, coffee.

Once I arrived, I made myself as presentable as I could, under the circumstances. I was more than a little nervous again. After all, I was there simply to make demands on their time. Hoping I wouldn't be an imposition, I squared my shoulders and stepped through the front door. What I found, once I stepped inside, was the definition of Southern hospitality. Those folks just could not have been any nicer.

There I was, arriving to interrupt their day, and they treated me like a visiting dignitary. The Colaplast people took me on a tour through their factory and showed me everything that there was to know about a breast prosthesis. Who knew there were *so many* different kinds?

It's one of those things you don't give much thought to—but they certainly had. I'd come in with a notion that I'd see a small, medium, and large line of breast forms. There were dozens upon dozens, if not hundreds of breast forms in every size and shape. It was really quite startling to see them all. But it makes sense when you stop to think about it. After all, women come in all shapes and sizes. I had to know how to properly fit each and every one that came through my door. The Colaplast people were more than happy to teach me everything.

The generosity of the people I encountered was astounding. I had a wonderful time in Atlanta, learning about something that was entirely new to me. My lack of knowledge seemed to make them all the more conscientious. I was sobered by the realization that there was a need for an outfit as large as Colaplast. Up until then, my perspective had been one of helping just a few clients at a time. Here was a company that thought in terms of millions. Once I realized the implications of all those breast forms, it became a staggering thing to behold.

After my time in Chicago and Atlanta, I felt well-equipped to help those who would come to see me. I was beginning to feel pretty confident. At the very least, I thought I could put on a professional face and *appear* knowledgeable. The rest I would have to make up as I went along.

Professional appearances aside, my courage and self-esteem were still fragile things. Deep down inside, I was scared. I'd been leaning on Rita for so long that sometimes I found it difficult to move ahead without her. I was still grieving her, and I missed her tremendously. Every day, I reminded myself of Rita's encouraging words. "You can do this, honey," she would say to me, "with God's help, you can do it."

Rita encouraged me to pray constantly. She told me I should always be open to God's presence in my life. Through the words and deeds of others, He would speak to me. Through friends or strangers, through clients and their families, and through others I had yet to meet, God would speak to me. But only if I would listen. "How can you hear, if you're not listening?" Rita asked me. There would be many opportunities, many different ways, in which God would guide me. If I were open to the idea, He would show me how to make my way through the hurdles that lay ahead. At that point, I was definitely open to new ideas.

It's almost like you have to get out of your own way. I think if people stopped looking so hard for God, they might find that He's already all around us. We simply have to do our part and do what's right. If people quit getting so caught up in the clutter and chaos of life, then they might find that things are simpler than they'd imagined. It's like that old saying about not being able to see the forest for the trees.

For me, reading the Bible a little every day helped me to find my center. Oh, I'm not saying I was perfect. There were weeks when I read it only in fits and starts; but I'd resolved never to quit. There would be many a day when I'd be caught up in life's little dramas—not to mention life's big ones. There would be days when I'd be up to my eyeballs in drama, and sinking fast. But, if I could remember to do it, I would always be amazed at how a few minutes with the Bible could bring me back to earth. Reading just a few passages—even a few lines—was often all it took to calm frazzled nerves. A few more, and a moment of quiet, would help to put things back into perspective. And if that wasn't enough, there was always prayer.

I finally had a dream and a purpose in life. It had been passed on to me by a woman who believed and knew the Lord with all her heart. Her dream was mine now, and I planned to keep that dream alive. I didn't have all the answers yet. I wasn't sure how I'd get through the next day, much less the next ten years; but I knew that

I had God's blessing. I drew a little closer to Him each day by studying the Bible and praying, and asking for His guidance. God was answering my prayers, it seemed to me; leading me to people who would teach me everything I had to know. With God's help, and everything I'd learned from my wig expert, Bonnie, and the folks at Colaplast, I was ready to help any woman who came into my store. I would help each lady pull herself back together again. Then, I'd send her on her way, with a spring in her step and a smile on her face—just like Rita used to do. I finally opened the doors at Image Insights, eager to help anyone the Lord sent my way.

He sent a man.

To my great surprise, the first client I had was not a woman at all. With all of my newfound knowledge, I simply had not learned how to fit a wig for a man. I'm embarrassed to say that it hadn't even crossed my mind. My first male customer came in and he said "hi", and I said "hi", and he said, "I need a wig." And I . . . just . . . stared . . . with a big, goofy grin on my face.

And then I remembered to close my mouth.

Forgot a little somethin', did ya Gayle? I thought to myself. That poor man just stood there watching me, with a slightly puzzled smile on his face. I stood there and tried to process this new information—or rather, my complete lack of it.

He gave me a long, slow wave, just like in the movies. I blinked and fell out of my little trance in a burst of laughter. Then I stumbled over my words, for a minute or two, while I tried to cobble together an explanation. I told him that I was a little new at this and I didn't have all of the answers right at that particular moment. He just smiled and said, "That's okay. I have all day."

It's a good thing he did. Lucky for me, my first customer was a man who was so patient, and so kind. He was an executive for a large corporation, who would be starting cancer treatments soon. He felt it would be better for company stability and morale if it didn't look like the boss' hair had just fallen out overnight. While a bald head had become cool by then—

thanks to Captain Picard on *Star Trek*—it was still not a widespread fashion choice. My client wanted things to develop gradually, as his treatments progressed, and the word got out. Once the company was comfortable with the knowledge, he could begin sporting his chrome dome.

We looked through several catalogs together and compared hair-color samples. Then I called my sales rep, Laurie, at the wig company. She walked me through all of the steps we had to puzzle out. Over the phone, the three of us worked together, taking measurements and selecting colors. When we were finished, I quoted him the price. I promised that he could return the wig if he was less than happy with it. Since we weren't able to see the actual wig yet, I didn't want him to feel railroaded. He smiled and said, "I'm sure we'll be just fine." Then he paid me in full and left.

When the wig arrived, I called him and he came back in for his fitting. It was simply amazing—the wig fit perfectly. Thanks to my little beauty school detour, I was able to cut and thin it properly. By the grace of God, we got it looking just right for him. Once we'd finished, and he turned to face the mirror, he was surprised and impressed with the final result. He stood up and gave me a big bear hug. Then he said, "You've been a great help to me—not just on the outside, but on the inside as well." Between my work and our conversations, he told me that he felt much more confident about the trials he had to face. He thanked me warmly then, and expressed the hope that I would continue to help others, just as I had him.

I felt like a million bucks.

This had been my first solo flight. I'd made it around the course, and the parting words of my first customer were my perfect three-point landing. I said a prayer of thanks to God for walking me so calmly through the experience, every step of the way. Then I said another one, for sending me a man who was so kind and patient. He was willing to be my guinea pig, to allow me to learn as we went along. It was such a blessing that he let me be honest and open with him, as I found my way.

For my first learning experience without Rita, it had gone pretty darned well. Through it all, I was reminded of a verse that she had read to me, a time or three: "God is our refuge and strength, a very present help in trouble" *(Psalm 46:1)*.

My first customer had given me such a boost of confidence, that I thought Image Insights could set the world on fire. Although I knew, at the rate of one person at a time, it would never be much more than a flickering candle. Not that that's so bad. Helping one person at a time is a noble goal for anyone. It should be a goal for everyone. But I wanted to do better. That array of breast forms, at the factory in Atlanta, made a big impression on me. There were a lot of women—and men—out there in need of help. If I were to take care of more than one at a time, I would need some backup.

CHAPTER 6

The Weight of the World

With the tireless help of my family, Image Insights became a functioning reality. The Lemonade Stand was born again. While it had a new face and a new name; I still had the same mission, and the same sense of purpose. Image Insights was The Lemonade Stand in a new wrapper. The driving force was still "service to God through service to man."

My first two volunteers were my sons, Adam and Nicholas. The boys came into the shop to back me up by answering the phones and tracking down the clients' wigs. The older ladies loved them. Their positive attitude and sense of humor never failed to make people smile or laugh. I think my boys really helped to put the women at ease. It has to be good for a girl, no matter what her age, to have a couple of nice young men close at hand. They were always joking and kidding around. I'm sure the teasing must have helped my clients to feel like girls again, rather than just cancer patients.

I was always amazed at how comfortable Adam and Nicholas were around these women, and how enthusiastically they helped out. They made me proud. After all, there was nothing in it for them. I couldn't afford to pay the boys anything, so they weren't in it for the money. We weren't exactly a hot, fashion store at the mall, swarming with teenage girls. This was a business dealing primarily in older women in trouble. They were upset, worn-out, and looking less than their best. Adam and Nicholas never seemed to see them that way. Of course, they did see them after we'd put them back together again. That had to be as good for their spirit as it was for mine.

The boys continually surprised me with their selflessness and willingness to give—I don't think I could choose one moment that impressed me the most. I lost count of the number of times when a client would put a hand on my shoulder and lean in to voice a quiet compliment. "Your boys are such *angels*," they would say. "So well mannered and polite. Young gentlemen, they are."

My boys? I would always blink in surprise. But then I'd think about it, and I'd have to smile and nod. Then, I would thank my client for the compliment, because . . . well . . . the customer is always right.

Oh, Adam and Nicholas weren't exactly saints, but they certainly were blessings. Heaven sent.

nce the company was up and running, I began my mornings by making the rounds of the hospitals. I didn't have any money for advertising, but I did know that most of the hospital staff came in at seven. So, bright and early every day, I was out talking to doctors about how Image Insights could help their patients. Doctors weren't my only objective; I tried to spend at least two hours every morning talking to as many nurses as possible.

Nurses get things done. The good ones have more influence over their doctors than those doctors may be willing to admit. They are a lot like sergeants in the military. The generals may give the orders, but the sergeants make things happen. Just as a good officer listens to his sergeants, a good doctor listens to his nurses. So I talked with any nurse that would listen. After two hours of that, I would hurry back to the shop to open the doors by nine.

Throughout the day, whenever I had a quiet moment, I'd pick up the phone and call hospitals and doctors' offices. With no budget for publicity, I had to get the word out to everyone I could. Eventually, all of that leg and phone work paid off. It wasn't long before doctors and nurses in the area hospitals began telling people to "go down to that little place in Covington". As business picked up, the word began to spread. Soon, the local social workers, and the friends and families of patients, began to say good things about us. People began to drop in, without appointments, all day long. I had to be there every minute of the day, so that I wouldn't miss anybody. Any networking had to be done before or after business hours.

Before I knew it, I had clients coming in from all over. My little shop was drawing people in from Kentucky, Indiana, and Ohio. It broke my heart to see them struggle into the shop, so exhausted by their treatments that they could barely stay upright. Some of them began their chemotherapy at eight o'clock in the morning; then they would go home and rest for awhile. At the end of the day, they would return to their treatment center for another session. More than a few of my clients were terribly sick. But as bad as they felt, they still didn't want to be seen without hair. It was so important to them to maintain their normal appearance.

Some clients would leave the doctor's office and come straight into mine for help, before heading home to rest. I usually spent about an hour and a half with each person. As we worked things out together, I could see each one fighting off the fatigue, struggling to remain focused and alert. Every waking moment was a battle for some people. If they weren't hurting, they were tired from hurting. Relief, when it came, was fleeting.

It was terribly sad to see how sick and worn out some of the patients were. As if that weren't bad enough, it was easy to see how draining it was on some of their families. Getting a patient to an office visit twice a day was really hard on some of them. It was a time-consuming responsibility that must have weighed heavily on them when added to all of the other demands on their time. Of course, the patient would know what a hardship it was for their family. Just getting to all of those hospital visits adds up to a lot of time and money. This would add to the stress of many of the patients. Nobody wants to feel like a burden. Even when family members took up the slack with a smile, and not a word of complaint, it was plain to see how it wore on the conscience of some of our clients.

After a few months, the continuous sadness and sickness took its toll on me too. There were too many days when I would hear that a client I'd taken care of had lost her battle with cancer. Too many times, I would read in the paper that someone else had died. I quit reading the paper. We've all lost someone we know. We've all had to deal with the shock and despair that results from a loss. If we're lucky, that kind of thing is very rare.

I wasn't that lucky.

When life gives you lemons. . .

Come to terms with the question "why me?"

The story of gain and loss, of sorrow and joy, of life and death, is inside each of us. If we don't come to terms with life's unfairness, the question may forever rise to choke us.

It's not like we lost everyone. But even one is too many—and we lost a good many more than that. Between the losses, and the almost endless suffering of the rest, it was almost more than I could bear. *Am I really helping anyone?* I would wonder. *Does it even make a difference?* Sometimes it seemed like there was just no point to it all. *What good does it do to help,* I asked myself, *if they're not going to make it?* Then I would go home at night, and cry myself to sleep, totally overwhelmed by everything I'd been through that day.

Alone in my room one night, I cracked. I literally cried aloud to God and asked, "Why? Why am I doing this?" Feeling particularly pitiable, I complained to Him, "This is so sad. It is just not any fun. Rita's not here to help me, and nobody understands. It's just too much."

Yes, it was self-pity; but I thought I was entitled to a little. The continuous tragedy and almost ever-present sense of loss really wore me down. Yes, my troubles were blissfully small compared to theirs. They should *be* so lucky to have troubles like mine. It's not like I hadn't known the facts going in. I was a professional, I should have been prepared. It should not have been a surprise.

But it was.

I was feeling bad for these dear people, and the trauma they were going through. On top of that, I was failing to handle my own problems. I was spending so much time worrying about them, that I wasn't giving the business the attention it needed simply to survive. I was always short of money. I never knew if there was enough in the account to order a wig before a client paid for her fitting. It was like walking a tightrope, balancing happy cancer patients against financial disaster. I was probably lavishing too much attention on individual clients and not charging enough for my time—but I couldn't imagine any other way of treating people. They were so sick. If I could help, I would. Then I'd worry about money later.

Back in the early 90's, I had to buy the wig first, and then the client paid once the wig was cut, fit, and ready to wear out the door. Much like in a salon, I was paid upon completion of service. If an insurance company was involved, I might have to wait a month or two for a payment. Once the red tape and restrictions were sorted out, I would often see just a percentage of the claim—if I saw anything at all.

When I first opened Image Insights, I contracted with several insurance companies to cover services. Many of my clients were stretched as thin, financially, as I was, if not worse. If insurance didn't cover my services, then they never could have come in. They simply would have done without.

We welcomed everyone into the shop—insurance or not. If enough of them were able to pay with cash, then I knew that the rent was paid. If the patients used insurance, then I knew it might help with the next month—or the one after that. Sometimes a patient had no cash, *or insurance.* How can you say "no" to someone who is suffering and asking for help? We didn't. We just helped anyway. So if I kept my customers happy, then I courted disaster for my business. But if I ran the business by the book, then I would have a lot of suffering people going without. And if I had to turn people away, then what was the point of being there?

Wigs, prostheses, and other related items don't come cheap. Not by a long shot. So even as I knew that I couldn't say "no" to someone in need, I understood the damage it was doing to the business when we didn't get paid. Even *with* insurance, things were still incredibly difficult. The claim forms that I had to file had to be filled out meticulously, down to the last detail. Miss one tiny, seemingly insignificant little thing and the claim is rejected. There were no polite phone calls. No one was going to ask, "Did you miss this little check box? Here, let me mark it for you." That kind of thing only happened in my dreams. In the real world, if I made a mistake, then I might wait another month for a rejection notice. Then I had to begin the whole process again. Even if I dotted every *i* and crossed every *t*, I wasn't home free. In the end, the insurance company decided how much they would pay—if they paid at all.

I'd never had a head for numbers, and now I was drowning in a sea of them. Even as I struggled every day to stay afloat, I had to keep up a positive, happy face for my clients. Their troubles were so much worse than mine. It seemed small and petty to call my miseries "troubles" at all. But no matter what you call them, they were dragging me down. I was miserable.

By then, I began to doubt the wisdom of my decision to go into this business. Was I really helping anyone? *Let's be honest,* I asked myself. *Do they really need me here? Does it really matter?* Between the constant financial chaos and all of the human suffering and loss, I began to wonder what I'd gotten myself into. *Is this really worth it?*

The next morning, I would put on a happy face again, and return to work. After all, I had appointments. People needed my

help. I couldn't very well disappoint them—but how was I going
to carry on like this for another ten years?

O ne fine, bright shiny morning, a nurse came by the office
to look us over. She wanted to see for herself what kind
of services we were offering her patients. I answered her
questions and we talked for a while. As we did, I found myself
sharing some of my worries and frustrations with her. I'm not
sure why I started dumping my problems into her lap. She was
just so easy to talk to, so understanding. I had been missing an
outlet like that since Rita died. I had no sounding board, no
punching bag, no shoulder to cry on. For months, I'd been winging this business essentially on my own. There was no one else
to lighten the load. I was making things up as I went along and
trying my best not to let Rita, or my clients down. On top of that,
I was trying to share the grief and lighten the burden of every
person who walked through my door. "It's no wonder I'm crack-
ing up," I told her.

After a while, I realized that I was unloading on her, and I
tried to make myself stop. "You must think I'm a basket case," I
said to that nurse. "You come in here with a few questions and I
dump my life's story on you!" She smiled and shook her head,
as if to say it was okay—and I went on talking! I just couldn't
seem to help myself. "I miss having someone I can talk to," I told
her, "someone who knows what I'm going through." There was
no one who understood the hurdles I faced every day, both business and emotional. It was wearing me down. Things had been
so hard, and I wasn't sure how I was going to make it.

This kind woman quietly listened to me feeling sorry for
myself. She just waited for me to wind down. When I was done,
she said softly, "Gayle, don't you realize that you're helping these
people live—and sometimes die—with dignity? If you weren't
here, where else do you think they'd go?"

I blinked at the statement. *Where else would they go? . . .* I thought for a second . . . *There aren't a lot of places like mine around.* Actually, there were almost none. I looked up at her and nodded. "Yeah," I agreed, "where *would* they go?" Now that she'd said it, the light finally came on in my head. I had been so overwhelmed by the struggles I faced each day, that I'd lost sight of why I was doing it in the first place. It wasn't about me at all. My struggles were not what was most important.

I wasn't the one fighting for my life.

I sighed heavily. Then I smiled at her and rolled my eyes— *What was I thinking?* clearly written all over my face. She leaned over, gave me a hug, and whispered "You'll do all right." And I realized I would. I had a whole new outlook on the business, and my purpose in it. All from two little sentences.

It was like she'd given me permission to put down the burdens I'd shouldered, allowing me to concentrate on the work at hand. I understood that I didn't have to carry the weight of the world on my shoulders anymore. I didn't have to solve all of the problems of everyone who walked through my door. I only had to solve one—the one that brought them to me for my help. Whether a client's time on earth would be long or short, my job was not to save them all. My job was to make them feel good about themselves again.

There aren't many people who get to experience God first-hand in their lives. I felt like I had, again. I wondered if that wasn't at least part of why that nurse had come to visit. Was it really *just* to look the place over? Maybe that's all the visit was to her; but to me, she was the right person at the right time. A perfect point of contact. Like Rosa, she was exactly what I needed at that precise moment.

If I took care of His people, God would send the people I'd need. Rita had said it was so. Once again, it looked to me like it was true.

I nstead of feeling only sadness and despair, I began to see strength and encouragement in many of my customers. Some of them would quietly come and go. I'd give them a lift and they would give me one. Others would have a tremendous impact on my life. I met some of the most amazing people in that shop. In ways large and small, many would demonstrate the same strength of character that Rita had shown. Now my days were filled with moments of inspiration.

I had lost perspective, and then I'd lost my way. All it took was a gentle nudge to get me back on track.

Late one day, a businessman came in for a wig fitting. Everything went well, smooth and simple. When he left, that man took my hand in his and said, "Thank you for being here. Please, don't ever quit." He passed away only two days later. Two short days.

I knew then that I wouldn't quit until God said it was time to do so.

CHAPTER 7

Broom Closet Meetings with God

Image Insights began to grow as it became more and more popular with the patients and their doctors. The appointment book filled up quickly, and walk-ins occupied every spare moment, and then some. It was getting busy!

While that might sound like a good thing, in reality I found that I was being stretched way too thin. With a full appointment book and so many walk-ins, every minute of my day was occupied. I was left with little or no time to take care of the business itself. Numbers remained uncrunched and paperwork stacked up by the ream. To top it all off, everything was tied up in enough red tape to choke an army.

When a client arrived for her session, I would spend at least an hour with her. If I could, I'd block out an hour and a half. I wanted each person to know that they had my complete and undivided attention. For that hour or more, I was *theirs*. No matter what a client needed, all would be taken care of. It was important to me that no one feel like they were getting the bum's rush. Image Insights was not an assembly line. It was a personal service. I was there for *them*.

The trouble with personal service though, is that it's time consuming. At this rate, I would never be able to see more than 6 or 8 people a day. While that might make for some nice sessions on the part of my clients, it was not nearly enough to cover my overhead. It didn't matter how personal the attention was, if I couldn't meet my expenses there wouldn't be any attention at all.

In order to stay in business, I had to get more cash coming in through the door. The trouble was, I didn't want to start raising prices on everyone. The patients had it bad enough as it was. Besides, the insurance companies weren't going to be interested in paying any more. So, as far as I could tell, there were only two ways for me to generate more income. I could get more help, so we could handle more customers, or I could move more merchandise. At that point, "more help" sounded like an option that I couldn't afford.

I was working late one evening, when a nice looking man came in. I called out a greeting. He nodded politely in response, and turned away. *Not ready for help*, I thought. *I'll let him look around.* He was wearing an expensive suit and he carried himself well. He had the look of an executive—top drawer, highflying.

This guy looked like he was comfortable with money. He casually circled the shop, inspecting the wigs, examining the prosthetics, and just generally checking the place out.

I stayed busy with my work and just watched him out of the corner of my eye. After a few minutes, I approached him and asked if he needed any help. This power executive actually flushed a little as he replied. He stammered as he explained that his wife was preparing to begin treatments of her own. He had noticed the shop on his way home from the office and mentioned it to her. She asked him to stop in and look around. "My wife is a little shy," he finished.

What a wonderfully supportive husband, I thought. After all, how many men are willing to stop by even a lingerie store to pick up something personal for their wives? Not too many. And my store was nowhere near as fun. I offered a hand and told him my name. He shook it politely and introduced himself as David. "So, what would you like to see?" I asked. "It would help if you told me a little about her."

"Well, she's a brunette," David explained. "Dark haired, and only a few inches shorter than I am." He paused a moment, thinking. "She doesn't tell me what she weighs. Let's say about 150—I don't know." He flushed again, and then continued. "She's a big girl—bigger than you are. When she wears heels, she's as tall as I am."

David stopped talking then, and his eyes flicked over to the breast forms. He opened his mouth to continue, then clamped it shut. "Yes?" I prodded gently.

"I don't know how to explain it," he resumed. "She's not just bigger than you are . . . she's . . ." He fumbled around with his hands, then he shrugged helplessly and stuffed them into his pockets. He looked away and mumbled, "she's *bigger* than you are." He was embarrassed.

"I get that all the time," I kidded him. "Come on, we'll get it figured out somehow." I led David over to the prosthesis area.

There followed several minutes of awkward silence, as we examined the breast forms. He seemed a bit taken aback by them. I pulled a few samples and encouraged him to pick them up. Once he'd hefted and compared several, we began to narrow down the choices. The nervousness melted away as he experimented and David finally began to smile. "We're getting close." He actually winked at me as his composure returned.

"I want to understand absolutely *everything* that my wife will go through," David explained. Then he asked if I would show him how the forms worked with the bras. I took down the appropriate size and showed him how things fit together. "Well that makes sense," he nodded thoughtfully.

Frown lines wrinkled his forehead. "Will this be uncomfortable?" he asked. "Will it bother her to wear it?" He paused thoughtfully. "I wonder how it's going to feel for her to have it on." I opened my mouth to reply, when David held out his hands for the bra. "Do you have a dressing room, where I can see for myself?" My eyebrows went up as I handed it over.

Wow, this is about as supportive as it gets, I thought. *Truly above and beyond the call of duty.* Yes, it was an unorthodox request—but I didn't want to discourage his noble intents. I showed him to the dressing room, and busied myself with tidying up as I waited for him to finish.

A few minutes later, the dressing room door swung open and I looked up with a smile. David stood there, arms flung wide, with the bra strapped on over his button down shirt. "Now, how about a wig!?" he exclaimed triumphantly.

My mouth fell open. *You're kidding me!* I thought. *Here in Covington!?*

At my look of stunned surprise, David hurriedly stripped off the bra and rushed over to me, apologizing all the way. Yes, it was true; they actually *were* for him. He went on to explain that he'd been searching for a discreet source of "accessories" for a long time. It turned out that David had many friends and acquaintances, all with similar requirements. With my permission, they would be more than willing to visit quietly, after hours. Best of all, it would be a cash business.

I was still a little bewildered at the sudden turn of events. I had no idea how to reply. He smiled at me, "I can see I've given you plenty to think about." I nodded dumbly.

David gathered up his suit coat and briefcase. As he buttoned up his jacket, he pulled a business card from the inside pocket. "I hope you'll consider it carefully," he said as he handed it to me. "This could become a nice extra revenue stream." I promised to give it some thought and bid him a polite goodnight as I closed up the shop. Yes, I had some serious thinking to do.

A cash business. *Wouldn't that be something?* I thought. There would be no red tape, no forms to fill out, no long waits or rejected claims. If David was telling the truth, I could have a whole new client base. They were people who would be willing to buy expensive merchandise outright. Even better, they would need only a fraction of the "hands-on" time that my clients did. These customers weren't looking for counsel or comfort. They probably wouldn't need help with selection or fitting either. Most of them probably knew just what they wanted.

This could solve a *lot* of problems. These guys could keep my bills paid, and I could go on helping my clients without a care in the world. I wouldn't have to worry about how many clients I saw in a day. I wouldn't have to raise my prices, or hire more help, and I could keep the doors open. It seemed like the perfect solution. I wouldn't have to change *anything*—and I could keep providing the same level of personal service that everyone was used to. It would be so easy.

I thought about it all night. I prayed on it. Then I thought some more.

The next day, another "businessman" stopped by—discreetly, at the end of the day. It seemed that he had similar requirements. *Coincidence?* I wondered. *Or has David already put the word out?*

Over the next few days, other male clients quietly dropped in just before closing time. It looked to me like David was encouraging a positive decision with a little demonstration of buying power. One evening, a well-dressed older woman showed up. It wasn't until we were halfway through our transaction, that I realized this was one of my "new breed" of clients. I would never have known if he hadn't let me in on it by dropping David's name.

That guy, er person, had been impressive—but his appearance raised a little warning flag in my head. People are different. Some have sophisticated tastes. Others are attracted to the bold and gaudy. I knew that some of those men had more taste and fashion sense in their little finger, than I would ever have—or even know about—in my life. On the other hand, there were some who were so flamboyant they could make Joan Rivers' hair stand on end. This wasn't West Hollywood. It was small town Kentucky. I was worried. Could David's colleagues remain as discreet as he suggested?

It looked like I was worried for no reason. These men remained polite and low key. On Saturday afternoon, I had a surge in business as a handful came into the store all at once. It really was shaping up like David said it would—a large cash business with little or no fuss. The next week went the same way—a few good evenings and a busy weekend. The following Saturday, one group begged me to set up a booth at their next convention! I realized that there could be serious money in this.

It wasn't until about a month in that the trouble began. In the middle of the day, a woman came into the shop. She was dressed garishly, and *way too young* for her age. Her miniskirt and spiked heels reminded me of the wig shop that Rita had described—the one where she'd found her first wigs. I remembered how, in the story, the shop had been on the wrong side of the tracks, and catered to girls in exotic and entrepreneurial professions. It looked like one of those girls had just found Image Insights. Even so, I was doing my best to help her, when she looked me right in the eye and smiled broadly. "Gayle, you don't even know who I am, do you?"

"I'm sorry?" I blinked at her, "*Do* I know you?"

"Bobbi Johnson," she said brightly. "We met last weekend at the benefit dinner?"

I thought for a moment. The past weekend, I'd gone to a benefit dinner. It was at the opening of a new cancer center at a local hospital. There I'd met a number of donors. I hadn't met any Bobbi's, and I said so. "I did meet a *Robert* Johnson, but," I paused, "*He* was a . . . loan officer . . . at . . . a bank." I trailed off. He was married to a nurse I knew at the hospital.

Bobbi just grinned at me and batted her false eyelashes.

So much for discretion, I thought. If a *banker* was going to come sashaying into the shop in the middle of the day, all tarted up . . . how was I going to maintain control? I wasn't. That's how.

Sure enough, the next day another of my new clientele dropped in while I was out of the shop. Christie, one of my hairdressers, and Saundra, a client and volunteer, were there to help. This fellow must have been new to the game, because he wasn't very good at it. In fact, he was terrible. This poor man made Robin Williams look feminine. The girls did their best to help, and bit down on their tongues to be polite. But eventually, they had to take turns retreating to the back room to quietly regain their composure.

The next morning, I called the number on David's card. I thanked him for his offer and for all of the new business he'd sent my way. Then I told him that I could no longer continue to see his colleagues. There were several "fashion" wig shops in the area that would be thrilled by his offer, and I was able to direct him to several. After that, I put a sign up in the window—one explaining that our services were "for medical purposes only". David and his friends politely respected my wishes.

Some people might think that they know why I made my choice. *Oh, she's got religion now. She's holier than thou.* But no, others can think what they want to. I know why I did it.

As to any social or political issues, I'll leave the complex questions to God. My job was to help people *in need.* Simple as that. As that visiting nurse had said, just a short time before, "You're helping people to live—and die—with dignity." Nothing else could measure up to that.

David's offer had been sorely tempting and I had struggled with it. I'd prayed on it and thought about it a great deal. In the end, I came to the conclusion that it was a distraction from my mission. It was important that I stay focused on the people who truly needed my help. "God will send the people you need . . ." Rita had said. So I trusted in Him. There were two real problems with David's offer. One was that it would give my business a split personality. My job was to improve the well-being of people who were struggling to *stay alive.* This was serious business. We weren't selling toys. There were other places in town that could do that.

The other problem was that his offer represented an easy out. I wouldn't have to change anything. Each day, I could handle a half-dozen clients and everything would be fine. That may not *sound* like a problem, but it was. It was a prime example of thinking too small.

In her short time, Rita had helped dozens of women in need. Now, with just a few employees and volunteers, we were capable of handling hundreds. But the breast forms at Colaplast told me that I should be taking care of *thousands.* There were too many people in need for me to play it safe and keep things small. No easy outs, I had to do this thing right.

To do this right, I had to grow. For the longest time, I had run the shop as a one-woman show. After a while, I picked up a few volunteers. Most of them were clients, or former clients, who appreciated what we'd done for them. They

When life gives you lemons. . .

Get creative with potatoes!

When you feel too sick to eat, but need to keep your body going, potatoes are a lifesaver. They're easy on the stomach, and take little energy to digest, but they provide lots of the nutrients that your body really needs.

came in for a half day here, or a whole day there, just to help out at whatever they could.

These generous souls offered their services *for free*. My volunteers were such a big help. There is no way I could have made it as far as I did without them. More times than I could count, volunteers would be instrumental in the life of Image Insights. They literally kept it going—all because we had been there when *they* needed a little help to keep going. I hope they thought it was a fair trade.

As important as my volunteers were, it wasn't fair to rely on their help. As time went on, I added one employee, and then another, and another. They were part-timers at first, but eventually that changed. But even with the help I had, Image Insights seemed to reach a plateau beyond which it would not grow. My experiment with David and his friends turned out to be a failure—or more precisely, a detour. Moving more product to other communities was not the solution to my problems. It simply was not what I was supposed to be doing. If moving more product was not the solution, then helping more people was. But to handle more clients, Image Insights would need even more help.

Up until then, the few employees that I had were hired as extra hands for me. If I could bring in a stylist to handle trimming and thinning, then I could handle more clients. If I could hire someone else to answer phones and schedule appointments, then I could handle even more. But Image Insights needed more than that to grow. We needed more stylists, more office help, and even specialists to handle other aspects of a clients' recovery.

As I took up the challenge of finding new employees, I found that it was even tougher than I'd expected. I needed employees who were special. My people had to have the skills that I needed, along with an understanding of what Image Insights was really about. To tell the truth, it hadn't been that long since I'd figured it out for myself—what Image Insights was *really* about, at its core. But now that I had, I didn't want to dilute its meaning, or have it wander off course under someone with different ideas.

Service to God through service to man. That was still our guiding light. Our customers were the center of our attention, the focus of our concern—and I understood that more clearly with each passing week. Nothing mattered more than our clients. All else was secondary. *A good employee,* I thought, *will understand that.*

But I soon discovered that good people are terribly hard to find.

People who are both resourceful *and* compassionate are a rare commodity. I would find people who were one or the other, but not both. I needed both. It was crucial to me that they could take charge and solve some of the problems that cropped up on a normal day. They were there to leverage my time, so that I could take on more clients. *I had to.* Otherwise, how would I make their payroll?

Unfortunately, it soon became apparent that some of my hires wanted to be taken care of just like our clients. In my work, I provided comfort and counsel as I helped patients put themselves together again. When we were done, the clients left happy. I sometimes wonder if those employees saw that and wanted a little for themselves. Whether it was a little insecurity or serious marriage trouble, they let their personal troubles affect their work. Either that, or they looked to me to solve their problems for them.

Some of my employees looked at me as if I had all the answers. *All of the answers? Me? Ha!* What they didn't know is that I was pretty short on decent answers myself. But I was always willing to *do* something. Oh, I might stall, or complain, or even wail about a problem—but eventually I would do something. If *that* didn't work, I'd try something *else*. Most of the solution to a problem lies in *doing something* about it. Whether at work or at home, that was all they had to do, too.

Too many employees could be tripped up by the tiniest thing. One little surprise and they would be paralyzed by inaction. What I needed were people who would *do something*. At times, it could be very frustrating.

When a new client came in, I had to do an interview to learn their likes and dislikes, style preferences, and something about their personality. That way we didn't choose something crazy for them, when they were looking for conservative—or vice versa. The whole point of the process was to make them *feel* better. To do that, you had to know a little bit about them. If I could get someone to handle the interview for me, and fill me in, we could serve more people.

I hired someone to handle initial consultations with the clients. That person would take down the clients' preferences and narrow things down before I came in. Then I would help the customers make their final selections. Like nurses assisting doctors—it was that simple. Or it should have been. Often, the employee would start the interview, but then she would stop and second-guess the answers. With no clear information to work from, I'd have to do the interview again, which would put me behind.

Another employee's responsibility was the filing of insurance claims. This was important work, and it had to be done just right. Otherwise, we wouldn't be reimbursed. As a primary source of income, there was little room for error. Well, that employee might fill out the forms, but she would neglect to make sure that *everything* was filled out. Simple stuff, like entering a name and address, but not bothering to look up a claim code. No code—no reimbursement. Claim rejected, time wasted, and do it all again.

I was *paying* for *this?*

Don't get me wrong. They weren't all bad. Even the bad employees weren't bad people. They simply weren't bringing to the table what I'd expected them to. If Image Insights was a pot luck dinner, we were getting too many jello salads and not enough meat.

It seemed as if I attracted everyone in town with low self-esteem. It could be maddening. There was so much to do, but so few hours in a day. *The last thing I need to do is babysit someone I hired to help me out,* I growled to myself. My patience was wearing thin. *I shouldn't have to hand-hold them through their work.*

To me, the clients came first. I thought it was important that I be "up" for them. They were terribly ill, and really did need someone to hold their hand. My clients needed a hug and someone to tell them it was going to be all right, at least for that day. I *had* to be in good spirits for them, to ease some of their burden. These were people who needed it. *My employees should be fine,* I thought. *They're not sick!* Being a cheerleader for my staff was a burden that I didn't feel strong enough to bear. I felt like a few of my employees were absorbing all of my energy. At times, I'd find myself getting angry and impatient with some of them. Whenever I did, I felt ashamed. *Look at how negative I'm getting!*

In an effort to do better, I tried to help them solve their problems. *If they could just get past their roadblock,* I thought, *then they'd be free to do their jobs.* Sometimes it worked, and I ended up with another valuable employee. Other times, clearing up one obstacle only revealed another, and another.

One night over dinner, I confessed my cares and woes to a friend. Or, more accurately, I whined and complained. I needed to vent. When I finished, my friend suggested that I might be missing the point. "Your unmotivated employees are broken people."

"I *know*," I nodded glumly.

"It's not that they don't have initiative," she went on, "they don't think things are even *possible* for them. They can't *imagine* success, big *or* small."

"I *know*," I repeated, sitting up straight.

"They're so afraid of failure, they won't *do anything* if there is risk. Any risk at all, no matter how small." She leaned back in her chair and shook her head mournfully. "They're looking for someone to hold their hand."

"I *know*," I agreed vehemently.

She chuckled and said, "They're looking for the *strength* they don't have.

"Yep," I nodded, "I *know*."

She nodded at me. "They see that strength in you."

"Huh?" I replied, brilliantly.

She went on to explain that most people had a lot of lemons in their lives. My employees were attracted to the "lemonade mentality" of what we were trying to do. "They don't know how to get things done," she shrugged. "They think that you do. You're like a magnet to them. They're looking for strength from you."

"Well how am I supposed to give them that?" I sighed.

All she said, with a shrug, was, "I don't know."

I n the days ahead, the pressures of dealing with suffering clients and difficult employees left me feeling helpless. There were just too many problems for one person to solve. At my wit's end, I gave these matters the careful consideration that they deserved.

There was a small broom closet in my office. I went inside and hid.

I would close myself in that little room and say, "Okay God, it's just me and You now. I know You mean for this business to be successful, but I'm feeling overwhelmed right now and I need a little help." But I didn't stop there. "I'm having trouble helping my clients to the best of my abilities, because I don't know how to help my employees to help me. I really need Your help with this." I was looking for more than just guidance in general. I was after specifics.

Whatever the problem was, I would get down to brass tacks and come right out with it. (No, I didn't ask to win the lottery.) Keeping in mind my purpose in His good work, I would present a specific question, like, "I can't get so-and-so to focus on the details; so I end up re-doing her work. How can I teach her how important this is?" Or, "I can't get such-and-such to trust her own judgment. She's constantly second-guessing herself and asking me to confirm everything!"

Somehow, after a few quiet moments in that closet, God would always inspire me. I felt relaxed and at peace again. I could think calmly and clearly, rather than react from raw emotion. Once my frustrations were no longer getting the better of me, I could see my way clearly to a solution. Calm and self-possessed, I could leave my little sanctuary and re-enter the real world.

After my little break, I was often able to say just the right thing to a difficult employee. Usually a few kind words and a gentle nudge would help motivate them to take charge of their situations. Suddenly, they would stop leaning on me for every answer and actually make decisions on their own. I was stunned at the difference a little, verbal shot-in-the-arm could make.

Looking back, I feel like I let more than a few of them down—especially my first troublesome hires. I should have figured it out sooner. I should have been able to help them, too. All that time, I'd had words of encouragement for my clients, but never enough for my employees. Those people were reaching out for help too, each in her own awkward way. But I had been too blind to see it. Once again, I'd been so caught up in the drama of life that I failed to see the bigger picture. Rita told me that if I helped the people God sent my way, He'd send me the people I needed.

Nobody said they all had to be patients. They could be employees too.

Once I discovered my little broom closet sanctuary, I was able to do a better job. There were far fewer troublesome employees after that. It looked like the trouble wasn't just with them. Was I really getting in a better crop of people? Or had my quiet time with God taught me a little patience and made me a better boss? I only wish I had cleaned out that closet a little sooner.

There were a few, really choice employees that did bring the proper skills to the table. And if they lacked skills at first, they more than made up for it with positive attitude. Christie and Bill were among my best. Taking a chance on people who might not fit really paid off with those two.

Christie was a young, little thing, fresh out of beauty school. Her aunt was my best friend, and it was at her suggestion that I met with Christie. I was a little nervous about the idea; hiring a friend of a friend is often a recipe for disaster. Christie turned out to be the exception to the rule.

With absolutely no medical experience, and no real-world cosmetology experience, Christie was not the ideal candidate. She was, however, the ideal employee. Based on her schooling, Christie knew that she wanted little to do with mainstream salons. She had no interest in gossip and had little more interest in the faddish nature of "pop" salons. Here today and gone tomorrow was not her style. Christie wanted her work to have some meaning. She wanted to make a difference with people.

As a refugee from beauty school myself, I knew just what she meant. I hired her. She turned out to be one of the best hires I ever made. Christie was caring and kind—even devoted—to her clients. They loved her in return. Christie was like a little angel with scissors.

Terribly nervous, at first, about her lack of medical experience, Christie was unsteady and uncertain around the customers. Playing to her strengths, she stuck to hair and wigs at first—and became quite the master of her art. Like a little sponge, she soaked up everything that was going on around her. It wasn't long before she was fitting breast prosthetics and handling all manner of products. Clearly, Christie "got" Image Insights. She understood The Lemonade Stand spirit and her sole purpose was to improve the lives of her clients. Improve them she did, and her customers loved her for it. Christie's work had meaning and was important to a lot of people. She was happy, I was happy.

As employess go, Bill was another priceless gem. A young family man, he was an experienced hairdresser with a sparkling personality. Just being around him would cheer up a good patient on a bad day.

Bill was a warm and wonderful man—a real charmer, but he was also supremely talented with the tools of the hairdressing trade.

At first, the idea of bringing a man into the shop generated a good deal of anxiety. That concern was shared by employees and customers alike. Most of our clients were women trying to recover from a painful, personal trauma. There were many of us who weren't sure that a man would fit in—I was one.

But to know Bill was to love him. With his warm and friendly ways, he quickly won over even the most doubtful. To avoid any personal discomfort, Bill worked only in hairdressing and wig fitting. But there, he worked magic with his scissors and combs. With his skilled, professional touch, and the attention he lavished on his customers, Bill was a real ego-booster for the women who sat in his chair.

He was another one who truly understood what we were trying to do at Image Insights. Bill seemed to *need* to make a difference as much as his clients needed him to. Sometimes it happened in the strangest of ways. We picked up a client once, from the world of plastic surgery—a refugee, of sorts. Her name was Marcia, and she was having a bit of a midlife crisis.

Marcia was feeling her years and had grown tired of looking and feeling run down. Rather than do the hard work of diet and exercise, Marcia opted for the easy way out. As she will readily admit, Marcia decided that a nip here, a tuck there, and a little liposuction were just what she needed to get back into fighting shape.

While scheduling her "minor facelift," it occurred to Marcia that she ought to have her eyelids done, too. Then she decided that it wouldn't hurt to have her neck touched up. While she was at it, she thought it would be a good idea to have her tummy worked on. *And of course, those hips . . .* Marcia thought, *if anything needs done, it's my hips.* "Well, if I'm gonna do it," she convinced herself, "then I might as well do it all." In the interest of efficiency, Marcia decided to do it all at once.

Not a good idea.

It was a seven-hour procedure, and it was about as traumatic as a night in the ring with George Foreman. It was truly awful. Marcia looked like she'd gone ten rounds in Madison Square Garden and come out on the bottom. Everything was battered, bruised, and beat up. And as she hid out, resting and recovering, she realized that the damage wasn't going away. *This is going to take a long time,* Marcia realized, miserably. To make matters worse, there was some nerve damage and one side of her face drooped badly. She cried herself to sleep more than once, ashamed at the vanity that led to such a foolish decision.

When Marcia came to us for help, we set to work with paramedical makeup and used every trick in the book. Bill gave her a beautiful new hairstyle, one that really complimented the shape of her face. Then he added color that perfectly suited her normal skin tone and wardrobe. By the time we were finished, Marcia had the look that she'd hoped to receive from her surgeon.

On her next follow-up exam, Marcia's doctor was stunned to see how good she looked. He knew how long the recovery would take. To him, the transformation was miraculous. (To us, it was all in a good day's work.) Over time, Marcia did heal completely, and the nerve damage even repaired itself. She looks good now, but there have been no return trips to the surgeon. Now, Marcia maintains her good looks with those two foul words—diet and exercise. She works hard at it now, and she looks great to this day.

While Marcia's transformation may have seemed like a miracle to her and her doctor, I knew that it was entirely due to the hard work of Bill and the rest of my staff. The real miracle came a few weeks later.

Marcia's doctor was so impressed by our work, that he sent us a very special client. Carol Perez was a patient of his, and had been for a long time. Her heavy burden was a severe case of skin cancer. It was cancer of the face.

Carol's battle with cancer had been a long and brutal one. She'd had so many operations for skin transplants that she lost count. While the doctors had finally beaten the cancer, the victory had come at a high cost. Her face looked like a patchwork quilt. Carol had won her battle; but when she looked in the mirror, it wasn't her face that she saw anymore. It was the face of a battered stranger—but with her eyes looking back, plaintively, wondering where her old self had gone. As a result, Carol hid away from the world.

She hid for seventeen years.

Rather than face the looks of fright she would have received in public, this warm, intelligent, and completely capable woman lived the life of a recluse for nearly two decades. She hadn't wanted to stay stuck at home. Carol wanted to be as productive, and as social, as anyone. She wanted it so badly. But Carol knew what kind of reaction her appearance would inspire.

Her old, happy face—the one Carol had grown up with—was gone. In its place she had a look that would inspire horror and fear in others. For a few brave souls, it would be pity. It was more than she could take. The first few scars had taught her that. Carol had been hidden away ever since. That is, until Marcia's doctor sent her to us.

The first time Carol came into Image Insights, I have to admit, I was a bit taken aback. I'd been in the medical business for a long time. Even so, I was surprised. I hope I didn't let it show; but if I did, I know that Carol had a soul generous enough to let it slide. Bill came over and introduced himself, and together the three of us sat

Carol's battle with cancer left her with a seriously scarred face. She hid from the world for 17 years. A little help from Image Insights set her free again.

down to coordinate our plan of attack. I knew we had our work cut out for us.

Much as we did with Marcia, we made serious use of paramedical makeup. Every step of the way, we taught Carol what we were doing. She had to learn to manage it on her own. She was a willing and attentive student. Bill worked his magic with scissors and color, and created a beautifully stylish look for her—Carol's first in nearly two decades. He mapped out a wardrobe plan for her, so she would always look well put together. Her clothes, her hair, and her wardrobe were all color coordinated in a way that suited her completely.

When we were finished, it was impossible to tell what Carol had been through. Although it happened before her eyes—and she'd learned to do it herself—Carol still could not believe the change. After so many years, it was too much to take in. It was some minutes before she was able to respond; and when she did, there were tears—which she carefully dabbed away—along with the smiles. There was laughter, too. Lots of joyous laughter.

Carol returned to work almost right away. She took on *three* jobs at once. "What do I need to go home for?" she told me. "I've done that already!" She was so happy to be back around other people again. Eventually, Carol pared it down to two jobs, and then one—her favorite, which she has kept to this very day. I don't think she'll ever stop.

Bill's work was crucial in freeing Carol from her bondage. His work changed her life; and Carol is but one example of the good he did. He made such a difference to so many of our clients. More, I'm sure, than he'll ever know.

My employees were wonderful, each and every one. Whether they were terrific or troublesome, they all had their hearts in the right place. Over the years, I learned that if any of them did seem difficult, it was due at least as much to my real failings as to any I perceived in them. I had just as much growing to do as they did, if not more. Besides, it wasn't only employees who could seem difficult. At times, the patients could be just as frustrating. Of course, they had a darn good reason to feel out of sorts. But if I was having a rough day, then all the reason in the world wouldn't make it any less aggravating.

Enter the broom closet.

I might have been dealing with a client who was anxious and picky about a wig. *Try this one. Now that one. How about the other one? No, the other other one. Oh, I don't know. Let me see the first one again. No, the other first one.* The more anxious and picky they became, the less focused I would get. After too much mixing and matching, and fooling around, I couldn't see the solution anymore. When I got to that point, I'd excuse myself briefly and head back to my broom closet.

I did a lot of growing in there. Sometimes I had to hide in my closet for a little while, other times I was like Clark Kent ducking into a phone booth. By the time I came back out, I would know just the right piece for the job. We'd pop it onto the client's head and, before you could say, "Look! Up in the sky!" the client would exclaim, "That's it, that's the one! I love it!" I'd laugh to myself then, *Score another one for the broom closet!* It was amazing to me the difference that a little prayer and quiet time could make. Rita promised me that God would always help, as long as I stayed close to Him. It looked like He was delivering on her promise.

Some might say that I didn't really need God *for that*. It was simply the "time out" that helped me to solve my problems. After all, common sense and clear thinking can solve almost anything.

That's all true. But that doesn't mean that God wasn't there. I couldn't have done it all on my own. So much drama, so many dilemmas. There were just too many times when I ducked into the broom closet facing problems I had *never seen* before. Totally flummoxed, I would go in there with a puzzle that was completely outside of my experience. By the time I walked back out again, the solution had been laid bare. Common sense and clear thinking may do the job, but sometimes you need God to point the way.

"Do not be anxious about anything, but in everything, by prayer and petition, with thanksgiving, present your requests to God. And the peace of God, which transcends all understanding, will guard your hearts and your minds in Christ Jesus" *(Philippians 4:6–7)*.

I found peace and guidance in that old broom closet. My little "Chapel o' the Mops."

CHAPTER **8**

Beware the
Ides of March

mage Insights was growing again. My support staff was beginning to gel and take care of business on their own. Their efforts were finally paying off. They freed up more time for me each day, and I was able to take on more clients.

That was all well and good, but it wasn't long before I'd hit my limit again. There are only so many hours in the day; and one woman can do only so much, no matter how efficiently it is done. Yes, we were helping more people; and yes, that did generate more income—but my employees generated more expense. We were still treading water, just barely getting by.

So, I found myself at a crossroads again. Actually, it was the same crossroads, but I'd moved out of the slow lane. Image Insights had only gone around in a circle to meet up with the same dilemma again. Our growth flattened out. In what seemed like a very short time, we'd reached a plateau again. While it would have been nice to stay right there and operate at a comfortable level, it wasn't going to happen. Besides the fact that it didn't *feel* right, the ever-increasing flow of customers would not allow it. What was I going to do, start turning people away?

What I needed was a clone. Since that wasn't going to happen, I had to find someone just like me. I needed another professional; but they don't come cheap. It was Catch-22 all over again. I couldn't handle more clients without more professional help—but I couldn't pay for that help without more clients. There didn't seem to be a way out. In the end, my only option was to somehow get *even more* done each day. If I could manage to handle still more clients, then maybe I could get ahead enough to hire someone else one day.

I still couldn't afford any advertising, but our word of mouth was good. My brother, Jim, pitched in to help with his photo equipment, and we created a series of slide presentations and photographic portfolios of

My brother Jim helped to get the word out by creating a series of before-and-after images that communicated our abilites better than I ever could.

my clients. These before-and-after images told our story in a way that my words never could. Jim would shrug it off as no big deal, but it was terribly important to me. As soon as any doctor saw our portfolio, or a presentation, he immediately understood our abilities. Better yet, he understood what they could mean for the patients. The response was *always* good—more clients for us and more help for people in need.

Those portfolios really did the trick. The only thing wrong was that I could only hand them out one at a time. Still, the photos, and our good work, were having the desired effect. People were saying wonderful things about Image Insights and we were developing an excellent reputation. Patients and their families, doctors and nurses, secretaries and receptionists, and even our suppliers were passing the word about the store.

The medical secretaries and receptionists were probably some of my most important contacts. Doctors and nurses are busy people, usually overscheduled, so their time is short. But the ladies at the front desks had more time to talk with patients, and they

Lisa Yates is a medical secretary at St. Elizabeth's Hospital, with a bright and sunny disposition. Her referrals probably helped keep me in business.

often had more information available about the outside world. They knew where the best pharmacies were, they knew about the support groups, and they knew about Image Insights—and boy, did they spread the word.

The receptionist and secretary at St. Elizabeth's Hospital, Lisa Yates, was probably responsible for keeping me in business. Bright and cheerful, Lisa started work there right out of high school. Over the next two decades, she grew in experience and position, but she never stopped telling patients about us. She promoted Image Insights to patients in need as if the business were her own.

Then one afternoon, I got a call from someone who could really put the word out—a journalist at the *Kentucky Post,*

Richard Pridemore. He asked, "Are you the wig lady who takes care of cancer patients?"

I laughed and said, "That's me!" Rick replied that he had heard very good things about Image Insights. Then he asked when he could come by for an interview.

I was so excited. *The newspaper!* I was thrilled to have even a little bit of free publicity. It would probably be just a small blurb lost in the back pages of the paper—but it was free! Even if they put it in between the pork belly futures and last weeks Lotto numbers, it was publicity. And as the saying goes: any publicity is good publicity. This was a chance to spread the word about my business. Its reach would extend far beyond what I was able to do with my one-on-one chats.

One of my clients, a woman named Sue Welch, agreed to allow the reporter to interview her and her husband, John. I warned her that Rick would probably ask them deeply personal questions. It might be about their experiences with cancer and the treatments, or it could be about the services that we had provided—there was no telling. But they were game Sue was one of my very first clients, and she had become a very dear friend. Always willing to help, Sue was an amazing woman, and she had a warm and wonderful spirit. She taught me many things about grace under pressure, strength of character, and wisdom. With her giving spirit, she reminded me of Rita in so many ways.

John would faithfully accompany her to every appointment. Whether it was to Image Insights for help with her wigs and makeup, or to the cancer center for her treatments, he was constantly at her side. John's presence alone offered Sue comfort and support; but it went far beyond that. She was his sunshine and he was her moon, glowing in her warmth and reflecting it back upon her. It seemed like there was never a moment when he wasn't in her orbit. The two revolved around each other. *This is the definition of a supportive husband.* I thought. *I wonder where I can find one of those?*

In spite of her cancer, Sue was one of the luckiest women I had ever met. They were such an inspiring young couple; the love they felt for each other was plainly visible. I could see it, and I could feel it. Yes, I was jealous—but only in a good way. Whenever I saw them, I would pray that God might someday send me a husband just like him. I wished for a wonderful man, one who would be there

Sue Welch was a fearless clients. She literally bared it all, revealing her chrome dome to the newspaper when such things just weren't done.

through the good times and the bad—something I'd never had before.

I was so fortunate to have Sue and John at the shop the day the reporter came in. That they had volunteered was such a blessing for the store. There could not have been a better pair of role models to introduce to the reporter, and to the world at large. Such a warm, attractive, happy couple, Rick took to them right away.

Looking around the shop, practically drinking it in with his eyes, Rick explained that he'd never been in a place like this before. I showed him around and described our business. He was truly impressed when he learned what we did for our patients. After the tour, Rick sat down with Sue and John to get their side of the story.

It was plain to see that Rick was quite taken with Sue. She had that effect on people. While the rest of us got the polite-and-friendly reporter persona, Sue got to the man himself. To watch the two of them together, one would think they'd been friends for years. He wasn't just investigating, he was *attracted*. There was nothing inappropriate about it. Sue was an attractive person—she defined the term—so of course the reporter was attracted. Completely untroubled, John took it all in stride. No doubt, he'd seen it a thousand times before, but he knew to whom her heart belonged.

The reporter asked Sue a *lot* of questions, and his interview with her went on for quite some time. When they finally finished, Rick stood up to take some pictures. As he fiddled around with his camera, Sue removed her wig. Rick raised his camera to his eyes and, at the sight of her, he jumped back in surprise. He stumbled then, and crashed into the counter behind him, breaking several of the lights around the big make-up mirrors. We all got a laugh at his expense, and he took our ribbing with good humor. A little red-faced, Rick apologized for his gasp of surprise and explained that he was stunned when he saw her without her wig. Until that moment, he had no idea she had no hair.

Sue very graciously allowed Rick to photograph her, bald head and all. Then he took pictures of the two of us as I applied Sue's makeup, still without her wig in place. She smiled pleasantly as he worked around us, and told him more about her battle with stomach cancer. Sue literally bared all and shared everything with the reporter. I know it must have been terribly uncomfortable for her, and I was touched by her selflessness. There were other women out there who needed what we had to offer, but they didn't know where to turn. This was Sue's way of extending a helping hand. I think that cold, objective journalists' heart was melted a little that day by the story he heard from Sue and John. As he wrapped up, Rick told us when he thought the story might run, and he promised to let us know the night it went to press.

We waited anxiously to see our article in the *Kentucky Post*. When Rick called to tell us that it would run the next day, I could barely contain my excitement. I had trouble sleeping that night. I knew I was overreacting. After all, it was just a silly little article, stuck in the back, maybe with a cheesy black-and-white photo. But to us it was a big deal. It made Image Insights more legitimate somehow. *And who knows? Maybe it will bring us some more business!* So I hoped, anyway.

I drove in to work the next day on pins and needles, I was so nervous. When the paper arrived, I snatched it up, anxious to dig

Sue Welch and I made the front page! The article was our first serious exposure, and it changed the future of Image Insights.

Story by Richard Pridemore. Used by permission of The Cincinnati Enquirer.

through it for our article. To my complete and utter astonishment, it was on the front page! More than just *on* the front page, it *was* the front page! It was huge! A glorious color photo of Sue's bald head took up most of the space, and the article was quite long and detailed. The headline read: "Covering Cancer's Scars.

Image consultant rebuilds confidence, one stroke at a time." I went to the nearest newspaper machine and bought every copy.

I was so thrilled with it all—but then I felt a momentary stab of panic. Sue's atypical chrome dome was nearly life size—on papers throughout the tri-state area! I hoped she would be okay with the display. When Sue and John came into the shop, they were laughing with delight. Sue had made the front page—with no hair! How many women could say that? She was as proud as I was.

After the photo and story ran in the *Post*, the phone began to ring off the hook. It was non-

Fiery, but ferociously organized, my sister-in-law Cil was a master at making order from chaos. We gave her plenty to do in that regard.

stop chaos and clamor. The phones were so busy we couldn't cover all of the calls. I was pleased at the response, but desperate for help. My sister-in-law, Cil, volunteered to help, and not a moment to soon. Jim, my brother, had often said that Cil was the "Queen of Organization." I'm sure truer words were never spoken. Nothing fazed Cil, she could calmly handle anything. Cil could organize a riot and keep everyone orderly and happy, which she proceeded to do for us. Answering phones, scheduling appointments, and taking count-less messages from well-wishers, she was as busy as I was. It seemed as if everyone in three states wanted to congratulate us on what we were doing. As a result of that one article, we were getting busier and busier every day.

With all of the new clients we were attracting, it looked as though I might finally be able to get my head above water financially. If we could keep up the pace, we might be able to build enough of a reserve that I could hire another pro-fessional. Once we did that, we'd probably see a snowball effect.

As Image Insights helped more clients, it would lead to more hiring, and then to helping still more people, and on and on! I knew I was getting ahead of myself; but the possibilities were thrilling, so it was hard to resist.

After a few weeks at our new heightened pace, I was a little less than thrilled. Oh, intellectually I was still excited—in a distant, objective kind of way. Physically and emotionally, I was just plain worn out. Keeping up with of the tidal wave of new business was taking its toll. I was tired all the time.

One day, a woman came into the shop, holding that old issue of the *Post* in her hand. As so many others had done, I thought she was there just to wish us well. As it turned out, her reason for visiting was even better than that.

My visitor introduced herself as Kate, and I found out that she was the best friend of my next-door neighbor, Karen. "I saw you in the *Post*." Kate said, "What a wonderful story." She told me that she'd cried as she read Sue's story. Her husband was also deeply touched by the story—so much so, that he had a brilliant idea. Kate's husband thought that Image Insights was a noble cause and he urged her to come and help as a volunteer.

Kate admitted that she was fortunate enough not to have to work. She wanted to help simply because it was the right thing to do. While she'd never had any training in fitting prostheses or wigs, Kate actually *was* a nurse and even had a cosmetology background! Her career path sounded surprisingly familiar. *What had I been saying about needing a clone?* I happily accepted her offer.

A more perfect solution, I could never have imagined. I was overwhelmed with gratitude. Briefly, I ducked into my broom closet, closed my eyes, and said aloud, "Thank you, God." This one woman was the answer to so many of my prayers. Even though we were becoming busier each day, I still didn't have the money to pay for a professional employee. Kate's offer to volunteer was a godsend. Now, we could stay caught up with the new patients and, over time, get far enough ahead to make it a per-

When life gives you lemons. . .

Have a good cry!

Everybody says it helps to have a good cry, but sometimes people find this is difficult. Maybe they're trying to be strong, or they're in shock, or they don't want to mess up their make-up or tie. If all else fails, get the ball rolling with an onion.

manent and paying position. By the time Kate was fully trained and up to speed, it could be a real job with a real paycheck. I could almost see it now. The snowball that was the business was rolling downhill and gaining momentum.

With open arms, we welcomed Kate into the Image Insights family. Over the weeks ahead, I trained Kate the same way that Rita had trained me. I had her certified in breast prosthesis fitting, and taught her what she needed to know about skin care and makeup. Then, I taught her everything I knew about helping clients to choose wigs, and how to fit them properly. At last, I had someone to help me with the most important, and time-consuming, aspects of the business. Best of all, she was someone who was up to the challenge. In truth, I secretly envied her ability to work without worrying about money. Kate was my saving grace and—to my everlasting wonder—she didn't even *want* to be paid.

Kate worked hard, learned everything I taught her, and smoothly handled both patients and suppliers. *So this is what it's like to be a twin,* I smiled to myself. Eventually, we were able to help almost twice as many patients as before. More money was coming in to cover our expenses, and things were looking up! Soon, I would finally be on top of things. Once we'd put the financial worries to rest, I could focus on the business of helping others like never before.

As we trained together, I told Kate again and again how important she was to me. Her help was making it possible for us to grow. Soon, I hoped to ask her to stay on as a *real* employee. Then we would see if we could *really* make this thing fly. "Don't worry about a thing," Kate would smile and tell me. "I only want to help."

What a wonderful woman. You don't run into someone *like that* every day. There weren't words enough to express what I felt for Kate. She'd become so good at her job that I'd begun to think of her as an equal, someone in whose care I could safely leave the shop while I made my rounds. I'd even started to entertain fantasies about an actual vacation. Since I had a real backup now, it was possible for the first time in years.

Things were going so well at the shop. I could hardly believe my good fortune. It was time to make Kate an offer. Then, about three months after she started, Kate was gone. She just disappeared.

After one morning of making my rounds of the hospitals, I returned to my office. I was exhausted after several hours on the go. As I came through the front door, I was surprised to see a full waiting room. *That never happens!* I fretted to myself, *How can we be so far behind?* Cil was in the office, doing her best; but Kate was nowhere to be seen. When I asked about her, Cil whispered anxiously, "She called in this morning and said she had to quit. Her husband doesn't want her working here anymore."

I was stunned. "Just like that?" I blinked.

"Yeah," Cil nodded, "just like that."

I apologized to our waiting clients and promised I'd be with them shortly. I asked Cil to give me a few minutes, and then send the first one back.

Kate was gone. I felt like the rug had been pulled out from under me. This bit of bad news was not only unexpected, it was also contradictory to everything I thought I knew. I scratched my head and frowned, *I thought her husband loved this place!*

Shaking off my confusion, I focused on the job at hand. When I went into the fitting room, to prep for the next customer, I noticed that Kate's certification was gone from the wall. *It was there yesterday, wasn't it?* I'd thought it was. *She must have taken it down last night, knowing she wouldn't be back. But why didn't she tell someone then?* I wondered. The little voice in my head told me that something else was going on. Kate *chose* to disappear, rather than say goodbye to anyone. Curious. There was more to this than her husband not wanting her to work. I had no idea what was going on, and to be honest, I was a little afraid to find out. Kate had never said a word about leaving. I'd thought she was really happy with us.

Kate's sudden departure left me confused and saddened by the loss. I was also more than a little disappointed that the peace that had entered my life was already at an end. Things had just started to go smoothly, and now it was over already. Volunteers come and go—that much I knew. I had hoped that Kate and I might do some good things together; but I had to accept the fact that people have lives, and plans, of their own. After a few days with no word, I sent Kate a bouquet of flowers and a farewell note. In it, I wished her well and thanked her for the help she had given us. I also expressed my hope that she would come back to see us again soon.

Things quickly returned to normal at the shop, and I once again found myself overworked and overtired. There were days when I found myself alone in the broom closet, praying for someone else like Kate to come along. She was one in a million. By then, it had been several months since the newspaper article ran. While the clients continued to come in, the well-wishers and volunteers no longer did. We had our hands full again—and then some.

few days later, the UPS man came by with a delivery. Ted was our driver for years, and he was always cheerful and energetic. As a young man, he was tickled at first to find out that the packages he delivered were full of wigs and fake breasts. But when he realized what they were for, Ted turned very protective toward us. He put us first on his delivery list, kept us stocked with shipping supplies, and never missed a pickup. And he was very friendly toward my clients. It's funny how a conscientious worker can take something as simple as a package delivery and make it a bright spot in someone else's day.

So it was with his heart in the right place, that Ted turned to me and asked brightly, "So Gayle, how are things going at your other store?"

I frowned, "My *other* store?"

Ted, our loyal and faithful UPS driver, with another "first in line" delivery for the Covington store. He took care of us just as if our business was his. The appearance of Ted's sunny face was always a bright spot in our day.

"Yeah," he responded, "the one in Fort Thomas." At my puzzled frown, he went on to explain. Someone had opened a store just like mine—and it was right in my home town! He'd thought it was mine.

"That's funny," I said, puzzled. "It's not mine." At that, Ted shrugged and rolled the rest of our delivery into the back.

Another store . . . in my neighborhood. It was an interesting bit of news, to say the least. So I started to ask around about it. Many of the people I talked to thought that I had opened a second location. *Another location!? Ha!* I thought grimly. The very idea was laughable. I could barely afford the first store. A second one was out of the question.

Someone else had started up a competing business. The thing that really surprised me about it was how close they had located their store to mine. *You'd think they'd want a little distance between us,* I thought. It was beginning to make me nervous, so I decided to see what this new store was all about.

After calling information for an address, I gathered my courage and drove into Fort Thomas to look around. I found the new store, and as I walked through the front door, I was surprised to see a familiar face. It was Kate! Standing behind the counter alongside her, was my next-door neighbor, Karen! I just stood there, dumbstruck, and looked slowly around their beautiful store. Neither of them said a word.

Even though my mouth refused to function, my brain was working overtime. I may not be the sharpest pencil in the cup, but I could see what had happened here. Together, the two of them had taken everything I'd taught Kate and opened a competing business. The biggest shock of all was the number of familiar faces in the waiting room. So many of them were *my* current customers. Several of them smiled at me and said hello, like they expected me to be there.

Later on, I found out more from the clients in my shop. Kate had been telling people that she opened her location because she wanted to do something for her mother. Her mother had breast cancer, you see. It may be none of my business, but that smelled a little fishy to me. In all the time we'd spent together, she had never once spoken of her mother to me. For the best part of three months, we'd spent several days a week together helping women with breast cancer to find their old selves again. One might think that her mother would have come up in conversation, oh, maybe once or twice.

I felt utterly betrayed by this woman, and was doubly shocked by the fact that my neighbor was in on it, too. The woman next door was now competing directly against me. *Et tu, Karen?* Every day, when I pulled out of the driveway to take my boys to school, she would wave to me with a big smile on her face. Often, Karen asked me how things were going with the shop. Then, she would smile and tell me to keep up the good work. *Ouch . . . just a minute. . . . Let me pull . . . this knife . . . out of my back.*

I had no idea that they were planning this together. In fact, I had no idea *anyone* had been planning *anything.* Suddenly I understood that all of our good work together had been nothing more than an opportunity to Kate. It was a chance to steal my business, my meager little livelihood. I'd trained her up, had her certified, and taught her everything I knew. And in return for a short time with my clients, she'd walked away with a complete education—not to mention some of those clients.

I could hardly believe my eyes. Kate had only been gone for a few days! How does anyone remodel a store, stock the shelves with specialized products, and fill the waiting room with customers in only a few days? You don't, that's how! It's impossible. They must have used the supplier sheets and medical referral lists that Kate had access to at Image Insights. I could certainly tell that they were accessing our client base! But to have put together such a beautiful shop so quickly—they must have been working on it for months. In other words, it was in the works the whole time that Kate was at Image Insights. If I weren't so outraged, I would have thought it was pathetic.

I was devastated by their betrayal. On top of that, the smug, condescending smiles on their faces were almost too much to bear. They actually looked proud of themselves. *They really did this?* I wondered silently. It was like a train wreck, only I was the train. I couldn't believe what I was seeing, so I just stood there, unable to move, with my mouth hanging open. *Turn and walk away,* I kept telling myself, but my feet wouldn't budge. I couldn't imagine that someone would actually do such a thing. I hadn't been in business all that long, and I was barely making ends meet. Now I could see it all falling apart around me.

Later on, I found out that these two women were letting people think that their store was my second location. Even worse, they were capitalizing on the *Kentucky Post* article by allowing new customers to think that Kate was the nurse in the story. I don't know that they made the claim outright, but they never bothered to correct anyone. *What incredible, amazing, mind-numbing nerve!* To clean me out, take my customers, and then pretend that it was all my idea—or worse, that they *were* me—it simply boggled the mind.

The icing on the cake, for me, was that they both had husbands who were well off. They had money to burn. Kate and Karen could afford everything that I could not. They could furnish a fancier store, they could hire more help, and they could afford a better location. One of them also had a physician father-in-law who helped to promote everything they did.

Most of these things I learned in the days ahead. Standing there in the doorway, too stunned to speak, I had to struggle to tear myself way. I knew it would be terribly inappropriate to say any of the things I was really thinking. A few, choice, single-syllable words popped to mind—not to mention a few more than appropriate multi-syllable ones. I managed not to blurt them out. It wouldn't have helped matters, or changed a thing. It probably would have delighted them.

I don't know how long I stood there. Whether it was seconds or minutes, it seemed like forever. Eventually, I snapped out of it. I turned around and walked out as quickly as I could without actually running. I hoped I wouldn't trip on my way out and add further to my abject humiliation. It sounded like there was laughter as I walked out the door; it was hard to be sure. I couldn't hear anything over the blood roaring in my head.

Somehow, I made it home. Depressed beyond words, I just cried and cried. I had gambled my future, and that of my children, on Image Insights. I'd put everything into the company—everything into one roll of the dice. Now, in the blink of an eye, I thought it was all gone. The woman that I thought God had sent to save me, had instead taken everything away. And, as if to rub salt into the wound, the whole thing was sorely testing my faith. Struggling to hold on to my source of strength, I tried to pray for guidance. But even in prayer, my will crumbled. In a few short moments, I would slip into bitterness and recrimination. "How is *this* the answer to my prayers?" I cried angrily. "This is a nightmare! What in the . . ." I stopped, and sighed heavily. "What in the *world* am I supposed to do now?"

I thought about going in to work the next morning, and realized that I would still have to see my neighbor every day as I left home. "That's just great." I griped. "That way I can be humiliated first thing every morning—just before I go in to watch my business fall apart around me." *Thank you, God,* I thought sourly. *I don't know what I did to deserve this.* I was hurt. I was terrified. And I was angry that I had been so easily deceived.

Resigning myself to failure, I bowed my head in shame. I had let Rita down. Sad as I've ever been, I finally stopped all of my whining and mental complaining. I just sat there in silence and contemplated the enormity of the disaster.

"I let Rita down." The pain of it was almost like losing her all over again.

Then, like a bolt out of the blue, something that occurred a long time ago flashed into my mind. I remembered the day that I'd met a man named Bill.

Back when I first began training with Rita, I was working several side jobs to keep food on the table. One of them was giving insurance physicals. One late, fall evening, I called on a man in Newport, Kentucky. As I approached his house, I admit, I was a little afraid. Bill's house wasn't in a very nice neighborhood. Nobody sat out on their porch to enjoy the last of the sunset and the cool breeze. The streets were empty, and the houses were dark and quiet. *Not a nice place to live,* I thought. The grass was dry and the trees were bare, it was a colorless, lifeless neighborhood. I thought briefly about turning around and going home. Maybe someone else could take this one.

My father often warned me that, as a female, I shouldn't be going into the homes of strangers by myself. But there I was, in a bad neighborhood, ready to do just that. Plain and simple, I needed the money. So I continued to look for the house on the call sheet. Once I found the proper address, I breathed a sigh of relief. This house had a green, well-tended lawn and neatly trimmed bushes. Flowers lined the walkway up to the door. Feeling a little more confident, I got out of the car. Bill's porch lights were on, and a warm light glowed through the front windows. When I knocked on the door that evening, I had no idea that a wonderful experience was in store for me.

At my knock, an older black gentleman welcomed me into his home like it was Thanksgiving Day and I had nowhere else to go. He introduced himself, and he was a charmer. Bill Huston was a gentleman to the last. The insurance physical proceeded quickly and smoothly, and we chatted politely as we worked our way down the checklist. We were finished in short order. *Looks like I may get home early*, I thought to myself.

All in all, it was nothing out of the ordinary. We wrapped it up and I stood up at the table to collect my things. I was exhausted from a long day and ready to go home. Suddenly, Bill said, "Honey, if I gave you a spoon and told you to move this house, you'd figure out how to do it, wouldn't you?"

House? Spoon? What? I was so puzzled by the man's comment that I didn't know how to respond. I stared at him blankly for a moment, and he smiled and nodded at me. "Yeah," he drawled out to himself, "I do believe you would." I sat down in the chair across from him and raised my eyebrows expectantly. He just leaned back in his chair, closed his eyes, and nodded to himself, "Mmm, hmm."

"What do you mean?" I prompted him.

"I can just *see* it in you," Bill opened his eyes. "Somebody knocks you down, you just get right back up again." Then, he began saying things about me that he couldn't possibly have known. Bill was telling me things about myself that I'd put away, deep down inside. These were hopes and dreams that I'd always ignored or brushed aside. They were fantasies. Pipe dreams.

Bill Huston was my anchor in stormy seas and times of trouble. His great wisdom helped me through disasters both natural and unnatural.

"You're gonna do big things one day." Bill looked right at me, "and you'll be successful at it, too." He seemed so *certain* of it. I smiled politely. *That's nice,* I thought; but I wondered, *How can you say that? You hardly know me.* I'd always told myself that I couldn't really be the person he was describing. I wasn't good enough, or clever enough, or some other negative thing. I really wanted to believe what Bill was saying, but my self-esteem had taken a lot of beatings late-ly. Self-doubt is an extremely powerful addiction. *Why would he say such things about me*, I wondered. *Or even think them?*

"You really think so?" I asked hopefully.

"Honey, I *know* so," Bill replied firmly. Then, he began shar-ing Bible verses with me—but not in a preachy way. Bill just sprinkled them throughout the conversation. He was serving up a big helping of wisdom, and the verses were the seasoning that made everything go down just right.

I marveled at his ability to use the right verse at the right moment. He must have known the Bible inside-out, upside-down, and backwards. I felt a pang of guilt at my own casual acquaintance with The Book. *I really need to try reading it more*, I thought, my attention wandering. But then the conversation turned back to me, and my ears perked up again. (I can't help myself any more than anyone else can. When someone says nice things about me, I'm inclined to listen—closely!) With all of his musings and predictions, Bill had opened my eyes to new possi-bilities. *Maybe I am all of these things*, I thought. *Maybe I really can do all that I want to do.* I realized that I needed to pay close attention to this man.

An insurance physical usually takes about an hour. I think I was at Bill's house for about three and a half that night. I listened to him talk about God, and the Bible, and our purpose in life. It was just like being with Rita. Here we were, on the wrong side of town and a world away, yet it was like Bill and Rita were the same person. This charming older man, and the tragically young and lovely Rita, could have been twins separated at birth. They were so alike in mind and spirit. I feel certain that, were they to meet, they would greet each other like long lost siblings.

As I left Bill's house that evening, I was so peaceful and happy. I felt a rush of gratitude for the experience and I thanked God for that unexpected, wonderful visit. Had I allowed fear to stop me from showing up on Bill's front porch, I would have missed a night that changed my life. In my early days at The Lemonade Stand, Bill inspired me to forge ahead, to push on through the fear and uncertainty, and to get the job done.

Bill also believed that, if I were knocked down, I'd get right back up again. Now I was having serious trouble finding my feet. On the day that I found out what Kate and Karen had done, I was devastated. Almost completely nonfunctional. I didn't know which way to turn, or what to do. My family thought that the business was over. Helpfully, they suggested that I'd made a poor choice in trying to follow in Rita's footsteps. *Ah yes, thank you for that insight. I feel much better now.*

Self-doubt returned with a vengeance, as I told myself that I'd been foolish. I should never have started, because now I'd lost it all. Those two women had cleaned me out. After that, they bankrolled a real heavyweight operation that would steamroller right over my little shop. After crying, and berating, and pitying myself into exhaustion, a little voice spoke up inside me. The same one that told me to listen to Bill, way back when, was now telling me to pick up the phone and call him.

So I did. I dug through my old records, found Bills' number, and anxiously dialed the phone. It had been a while. The phone rang and rang, and—just when I'd begun to fear the worst—he picked up the receiver. I stammered out a greeting and waited for a reply.

"Honey, I've been waiting for you to call." he said, with a smile in his voice. I couldn't believe it. It had been a year and a half since I'd seen him last. And it seemed to me that I'd heard those words before, once upon a time.

As Bill began asking questions about what had happened, he told me to pull out my Bible. I continued whining and blubbering about my dire straits while I looked around for my copy. Once I found it, he interrupted and asked me to read Philippians 4:13. One of Rita's favorites, I knew it well.

I read it to myself, silently. "Aloud, please," he said.

"I can do all things through Christ who strengthens me," I read.

I opened my mouth to continue my sad soliloquy, and he said, "Read it again." I did. "Aloud please," he repeated.

I read it again. "I can do all things through Christ who strengthens me." I took a another deep breath, ready to resume my complaining.

"Read it again," he interrupted. I did. Aloud this time—and annoyed.

"Okay. Satisfied?" I griped.

"Nope," Bill quipped. "Read it again." So I did; and each time I finished he calmly said, "Read it again."

This wasn't getting any better. In fact, it was getting worse. I was practically biting off the words by then. "I. Can. Do! All. Things! Through. Christ! Who. Strengthens! Me." I was still crying, and getting angrier every minute.

I could hear the smile in Bill's voice as he tormented me. "Read it again, read it again." *He's actually enjoying this!* I thought furiously. I kept repeating and repeating it, and he was making me madder and madder.

Why did I call this man? I asked myself. *Why isn't he listening to me?* Bill told me to read it again and I finally snapped, "I don't get it. I'm saying what you want me to say!"

"No, *you don't* get it," Bill replied. "Read it again, *slowly* this time."

As I read slowly, I stopped crying. "I can do . . . all things . . . through Christ . . . who strengthens me." I calmed down. At that moment, I realized what Bill was saying. *Sharpest pencil in the cup? No, not always.* But I had finally gotten the message. Bill wanted me to see that I still had Christ on my side. I could do anything as long as He was with me.

Up to that moment, I'd thought my business was finished because of what these women had done. But I hadn't lost anything. Not really. It was all just material stuff that I was so worried about. Sure Karen and Kate might have all of the bells and whistles; but did they have the heart? "They may have money on their side," Bill admitted, "but do they have God?" He simply reminded me that nothing had changed in that regard.

"Besides this isn't about them," Bill said, urging me on. "It's about you." He told me to stop feeling sorry for myself and get back to work. People needed help, and God was still sending them in. So that's exactly what I did. I kept moving forward and I never looked back. Bill was right. I hadn't *lost* anything—and I still had a job to do.

It's not always easy to follow God, and to do His will. I was learning just how true that was. But it's when times get tough that you've got to know He's there beside you. If you understand that, you'll find that you have the strength to face anything. Obviously, I hadn't truly learned that on the day I'd stepped into Kate's shop. I was familiar with the idea, but I hadn't *known* it yet in my heart. If I had, my discovery wouldn't have been so devastating. Between Bill's little wake-up call, and the passage of time, I saw the truth of it. How you handle the rough times is what is most important. It's easy to have faith when times are good. It's more important to have it when things go bad.

Lean on God for support, and keep your mind clear of fear. Once that's done, you'll be open enough to see the signs and learn the lessons that God provides. That path leads away from trouble.

Several months later, a medical-services trade show opened up at St. Elizabeth's Hospital. The spaces were divided into a number of sections, each focused on a single medical specialty. Giant pharmaceutical companies showcased their latest innovations in expensive high-tech display centers. Small, local care providers occupied more modest booths. Everyone was there—big corporations, small practices, and pretty much everything in between.

Everyone, that is, except for me. I was too busy taking care of patients, on my own again. I simply didn't have the time to pull together a booth, or a bunch of marketing materials. Even if there were time, I couldn't have afforded it all. I was lucky to have business cards! While I couldn't be there as an exhibitor, I couldn't afford not to go as a visitor. With so much to see, there was sure to be something that could help improve my business. Who knew what I might learn? I was actually pretty excited about going.

The first thing I learned, upon entering the main floor, was that Kate and Karen had a booth for their business! A sudden rush of panic washed over me. As soon as I saw them, I started to feel that sick knot in my stomach. I wanted to turn and flee before they caught sight of me.

I almost did. I picked up a foot and was ready to go, when a voice in my head said, *"Forgive them."* I put my foot back down.

I was pretty sure that it was God talking—or at least, God prompting the thought. I don't think that I was quite ready to forgive anyone yet. Whether I wanted to or not, sometimes there is no ignoring that little voice in your head. *Forgive them,* it reminded me. *You'll feel better.*

Really? I wondered. *I don't know about that.* I stood there, debating to myself. *Do I have to do this right now? Couldn't I just go? Maybe do it some other time?*

No, the voice insisted. *Forgive them now,*

"Awww, man." I grumbled to myself. I took a deep breath and looked up at their booth. It was beautiful. Expensive. I felt small.

I turned away. *I know!* I thought, *Let's not, and say we did!*

Do it now, the voice commanded. I turned back. It all took place in the space of a breath or two; otherwise I'm sure I would have drawn stares. "Oh, look at the poor crazy lady talking to herself." People would have tip-toed past, "Shhh . . . don't make any sudden moves."

I took one last deep breath, and thought to myself, *Okay God, I'm going in.* And I did.

Kate and Karen were wearing their professional smiles for the passing crowd. They even turned them on me, as they noticed someone approaching. Then recognition dawned on them, and the smiles quickly fell away. They were replaced by a cool, emotionless gaze. No greeting, no nod, no "Hello, Gayle." Just a cold stare. Then, in unison, their eyebrows raised, half in curiosity, half in distaste.

"Karen," I nodded, "Kate." I paused and took a deep breath. "I just wanted you guys to know that I forgive you for everything you've done." They just stared at me.

Then they burst out laughing.

Ouch, I winced inside. I licked my lips and watched them for a moment. Then I gave a little shrug, and turned away. As I walked off, a wry little smirk crept up on my face. *Gee, thanks God. That was great. I feel so much better now.*

Not.

But with each step that little half smile spread wider and wider, until it reached all the way across. I realized that I really did feel great. It was like I had let go of all of the anger, grief, and fear. It all simply evaporated.

On the outside, nothing had changed. Kate and Karen were still the same low-down, dirty . . . um . . . *not-very-nice people* that they had always been. They had demonstrated as much when they laughed in my face. *Who cares?* I asked myself with a little smile. On the inside, it just didn't matter anymore to me. It was all okay. They could do their thing, and I would do mine. I felt free to go about my business and not think about them anymore. So I did. I spent a few hours exploring the convention center, checking out products or services that I thought might be of help. Passing out cards, and introducing myself to local service providers, I even made a few solid contacts that day. I felt *good* again.

When I returned to the shop, I hit the ground running. It was busy, things were hectic, there was too much to do. *It's all good,* I thought. Letting go lifted my spirits. Better yet, it opened me back up to God's positive signs and lessons.

I finally remembered a verse Rita and I had read together. "Do not judge, and you will not be judged. Do not condemn and you will not be condemned. Forgive and you will be forgiven." *(Luke 6:37)* One thing they forgot to mention there: forgiving does your heart good. It allows you to let go of pain; and it makes you feel better, too. Forgiveness gets you back on track. Try it!

Several months later, I heard through the grapevine that Kate and Karen had gone out of business. One might be inclined to exult at the poetic justice of it all. I took no joy in it. By then, I had enough perspective on the issue that I felt bad for them. Going out of business is always sad. It was certainly a surprise. It seemed like they had everything going for them.

I wondered if, perhaps, their hearts weren't in the right place. When they looked at the clients, did they see the "opportunity" before they saw the "need"? Could their customers then read that in their eyes? I don't know. I hope not.

A Helping Hand

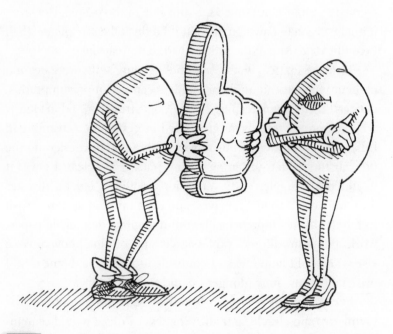

T hose first few years at Image Insights were chock full of challenges. There were up days and down days. Working there was like riding an emotional roller coaster, over and over again. It was true both personally *and* professionally. Losing a client was definitely a down day. About as down as they got. Having another client finish her last treatment, that was an up day. You haven't had a really good day until you've had a day like that. The ups and downs don't get much better, or worse.

Then, there were the ups and downs of the company itself. From all outward appearances, business was looking up. The shop was always busy, with patients coming and going all day long. But for all of that up-side, there was a down-side. With so many clients to attend to, I felt like I was *too busy*. I was managing, somehow, to help them, but I was spread really thin. I worked long hours to make sure their needs were met; but even as I carefully looked after my customers, I was ignoring the business itself. In order to survive, a business needs to be cared for, too. Somehow, that never seemed as important to me as taking care of the people. However, it finally began to dawn on me that if I didn't take care of one, then I couldn't take care of the other. I had to do *something*.

To make matters worse, my bookkeeping skills were beyond pathetic. In fact, calling them "skills" seems a bit presumptuous. Let's call them "bookkeeping efforts", or "struggles". I don't know what the proper term is for growling in resentment, screaming in frustration, then angrily pushing everything off the desk onto the floor, before collapsing in a sobbing puddle of defeat. I guess it would be "struggles". My office looked like a federal disaster area. My desk, cabinets, shelves, and even my chairs, were awash in a flood of incomprehensible, unintelligible, despicable paperwork. I couldn't afford a professional, and I didn't know anyone else who could help me; so I continued to struggle. Some days I wasn't sure how much longer I could stay in business.

Every once in a while, I found myself thinking about just giving up, and chucking it all. Whenever I did, I would remember the faces of my clients. Then I'd hear a little voice in my head—Rita's voice—saying to me: "Never give up! These people are counting on you." In my mind, I could see her frowning at me, "You promised me ten years, so you've got to get in there and fight. You can figure this out!" Then, in my imagination, her frown would fade into a smile, "You need to remember your

Philippians!" And then, there was the grin, "You can do everything through Him . . ."

One evening, after a very long day, I resolved to attack the
paperwork disaster head on. I decided to *organize it!* Of course,
all I did was rearrange a chaotic mess into an orderly one. But
once I did that, I picked up on a common theme in the chaos. Far
too many of those scraps of paper were stamped with the letters
I–R–S. As I surveyed my nice, neat stacks of notices from the tax
man, I thought, *This can't be good.* It looked like the IRS was paying more attention to Image Insights than I was. Every week
brought new and different tax forms to fill out and return. Thick
envelopes had arrived in the mail from them practically every day.
Some wanted money, others seemed to be forms for more forms.
If I ran into one I understood, I filled it in and sent it back. I foolishly hoped that a little show of effort might buy me some more
time. Naive? Yes. Foolish? Certainly. Desperate? Completely! I
simply didn't have the cash to hire an accountant, so I tried to
keep things organized as best I could. Apparently, the IRS didn't
think that sticking my head in the sand was good enough.

In my heart, I wanted to do everything right. I was willing to
follow the procedures that the IRS required. Unfortunately, my
head and my heart did not exactly see eye-to-eye, so to speak.
The spirit was willing, but the brain was unable. Even so, I did
not want to lose my company just because I hadn't met some
foolish paperwork requirements. But I had piles of bills and tax
forms that I simply did not understand. Clearly, if I failed to clean
up the mess, losing the business was exactly what would happen.

One afternoon, after much fussing and fretting, I disappeared into my broom closet. I had a big problem that I just
could not get my head around. It was time to do a bit of praying
and have a little talk with God about it. "Okay, God. I don't
know what to do with all this stuff," I said aloud, "but I don't
want to lose my company because of it. It can't be *that hard* to
work with the IRS, can it? I need you to guide me." If I had to

face the IRS, it seemed like a good idea to have a little backup from above.

By the time I emerged from my closet chapel, my plan had come together. It was the perfect solution. I would pack up every form, letter, or scrap of paper from the IRS and stuff it into one great, big box. Then, I'd haul it down to the IRS and ask *them* what to do with it. I had to talk with them before they shut me down. So my brilliant strategy was to *voluntarily* enter the dragon's lair, armed only with a cardboard box, I would stride boldly in, stand my ground, and in a loud, firm voice, say, "P-P-P-please . . . help me?"

The next morning, I arrived at the shop to collect my box. I told the staff "I'm on my way to see the IRS. Hold down the fort until I get back." Heads popped up all around, eyes wide with shock. The blood drain from their faces and they looked at me like I was nuts. It was as if I'd said, "I joined the circus and I'm off to stick my head in the lion's mouth! Be right back."

Everyone stared at me, too stunned to speak. Then, they all began talking at once. "Are you crazy? The IRS won't help you. You can't go over there. They'll eat you alive!"

"Does anyone have any alternatives?" I asked. "Any helpful suggestions?" All I got in reply was silence. I heard a cricket chirp. "Well?" I raised my eyebrows, "Anyone?"

Nothing. No one had a better solution. Neither did I, but I was pretty sure it was the right thing to do. "Come on you guys," I smiled and spread my arms wide, "Everything is going to be just fine." Then I paused, lowered my head, and bit my lip. When I looked up again, I said somberly, "If they put me in jail," I sighed heavily, "let my boys know where I am." I stopped and sniffled, "And take care of them until I'm out again." With a forlorn little wave, I shuffled out the door—and held a straight face until I was out of sight. Once they could no longer see me, I grinned. *That ought to keep them fretting.* I thought I was pretty funny.

t didn't seem so funny a short while later.

When I arrived at the IRS office, I started having serious second thoughts. I was losing my nerve in a big way. *Is this really such a good idea?* I asked myself. *Should I be calling attention to myself like this?* An old saying occurred to me—something about the nail that sticks up being the one that is hammered down. *On the other hand,* I tried to tell myself, *the squeaky wheel gets the grease.* Hefting the box up on one hip, I took a deep breath and pulled open the door.

The room I entered was gray and empty. A few chairs sat along one wall, beneath the room's sole decoration—a cork bulletin board. On the board were a few terse warnings concerning *Government Property* and *Proper ID* and *Fines or Imprisonment.* The waiting room was silent, and I felt a little chill shiver up my spine. A real friendly place—the office had all the warmth and coziness of the post office, or the DMV—or maybe an insane asylum. A linoleumed hallway stretched away to my left; to my right was a split door with the top half cracked open. From beyond the door, a stern, faceless voice reluctantly asked, "May I help you?" It didn't really *sound* much like he wanted to help.

The door opened a little more, and a face appeared. It didn't really *look* much like he wanted to help, either. I took another deep breath, summoned the last of my courage, and opened my mouth to speak. When I did, the words rushed out in a torrent, like I was afraid he would slam the door in my face. "Yes, sir. I'm in desperate need of help. I have this box of papers from you. I own a small business that I dearly love, and I want to stay in business. But I'm not sure, from the sound of your letters, that that's going to happen unless I get some help. I can't afford an accountant, and I'm terrible with paperwork. I'm a reasonably intelligent woman, but I can't understand what any of this stuff means!" I paused for a quick breath, and continued. "All my friends and family laughed at me when I said I was coming down here. They said you wouldn't help me, that you'd rather just lock me up and throw away the key. But I really want to make this work, I want my business to be completely legitimate. I just don't know where to start. There is so much to do and I can't begin to understand this stuff. If you won't help me, I don't know what I'll do." I finished with another deep breath.

He looked at me kind of funny, kind of frowny, with one eyebrow down and the other one up. *Great. He thinks I'm nuts.* He stared at me for what felt like forever. He didn't say a thing, just blinked a few times, looked at my box, looked at me. Finally, he ducked away and shut the top half of his bi-level door. *Thump, click.* "On, no," I sighed. "I'm going to jail."

A moment later, the whole door opened and he actually gave me half a smile. "Come on in," the man said. "Let's take a look at this box of yours." The agent relieved me of my burden and pointed me to a chair. "You're not going to jail," he said as he sat down. Then he opened the box, and growled, ". . . Yet." My eyes widened and I swallowed nervously. "Sorry. Agency humor," he laughed sheepishly.

I smiled weakly at his joke, and offered up a sad little, "heh, heh." *Funny guy,* I thought sourly. He finally picked up on my discomfort, because he extended a hand and, with a real smile, introduced himself as Bob. "I appreciate it when someone is open and honest with me." he said. "I'd be glad to help you out." I blew out a big breath—and a lot of tension—and smiled back at him. *Now we're getting somewhere,* I thought.

Over the next few hours, Bob and I painstakingly went through every last scrap of paperwork in that box. He was so kind and, to my surprise, even caring. Bob patiently explained to me what each and every thing was. As we went along, he paperclipped together the things that belonged with each other. Once we were well and truly organized, he made up a diagram for me. "This is a chart of every form that needs to be filed, and by when it should be done. It also shows you everything that needs to be paid, and by when." Bob lowered his gaze and warned seriously,

"You need to hold back enough money for each payment, when it comes due." I nodded; it sounded ominous. At that point, everything was still way over my head; but if Bob was willing to help, I was willing to do whatever he said.

After several hours of paper shuffling, I felt like I was beginning to get a handle on things. Bob gave me the chart and pointed out when the first item was due. "Keep this out where you can see it," he said. "And call me if you have any more questions." I thanked him for his help, and told him what a blessing he had been to me. Bob opened his door for me, smiled warmly and said, "Good luck, Gayle." And just like that, I was on my way out of the lion's den—still breathing and with all of my limbs intact.

What a relief! I'd lived in fear for so long, regarding my taxes, that I had paralyzed myself into inaction. Not knowing what to do, I hadn't done *anything*. Afraid what I might find out, I hadn't asked anyone. It was a sure-fire way to get nowhere. At times, my anxiety got out of hand, and my imagination went into overdrive with dreams of black helicopters, men in dark suits and sunglasses, and a private suite on Alcatraz Island. Whatever a taxpayer's worst nightmare is, I had it.

Now, all that was gone! What a surprise it had been to find actual human beings at the IRS. Bob helped lift the fog of confusion and anxiety that I had operated under. Once I could see clearly, I could do what had to be done. *All I had to do was ask for help,* I marveled. *Why didn't I think of it sooner?* Once again, the dramas of life had clouded my vision. All it took to clear things up was a little quiet time with God.

Leaving Bob's office, I felt like I'd laid aside another heavy burden. Yes, the taxes still had to be paid, and there were too many of them. But the fear was gone, and in its place was knowledge. I felt like I'd opened myself up to God and He'd provided a way. Don't get me wrong; I know Bob at the IRS isn't exactly the Angel Gabriel. What amazed me was the truth of Rita's words. Whenever I stopped and opened myself up to God, I found a sense of peace and clarity. There, I often found the answers that eluded me in the chaos and clutter of normal life. Even if, upon reflection, those answers sometimes seemed a little obvious.

While Bob may not have stepped off the stairway to heaven, for an IRS agent he was pretty angelic. A few days after my visit, he called to follow up. "I'm going to call every time something is due," Bob said. "I'll call the week before, so you can set aside the money you'll need. I'll give you a due date, and you make sure it gets paid." He held my hand and walked me through like that for an entire year. Bob made sure that things went smoothly until I understood them on my own. He also signed me up for an IRS class for small business owners.

The solution to my problem had been so simple. Just ask for help. Ask honestly and openly. I'm not much smarter about taxes now, than I was then. I don't understand as much as I should; but I know that there are others who do. *We can't all be good at everything,* I realized. *My weaknesses are someone else's strengths.* I was learning that, if I let others use their strengths, it was as good for *them,* as it was for me. It was a lesson I would learn over and over again.

Ask for help. It seems so obvious, doesn't it? Yet somehow it is all too easy to forget. "For everyone who asks receives; he who seeks finds; and to him who knocks, the door will be opened." (*Matthew 7:8*) I don't think they're referring to tax advice—or to winning the lottery, for that matter. But, "ask and you shall receive" does seem to apply when your motives are pure. Whether it's called "doing good", "doing the right thing", or "doing the Lord's work," there are always others who are ready to help. All you have to do is ask.

O f course, what's good for the goose is good for the gander. As Image Insights grew, I was constantly learning about new products, organizations, and other resources that could help my clients get through their treatments. I want-

When life gives you lemons. . .

Set up a support network!

Find professionals you can trust. Spend time in places that make you feel comfortable. Recognize that friends may be good for different times. One person may be great to celebrate with, but lousy at the grieving process. Ask people to share what they're good at.

ed to know as much as possible. There was a lot of help available for our people. All they had to know was who to ask.

One organization that was invaluable to cancer patients was the American Cancer Society. This vast network of volunteers worked together to raise money for research into cures for cancer. In addition, they were a library of information. If there was anything I or my clients wanted to know about cancer, the ACS could tell us the state of the art. From causes to coping, and treatments to cures, they were up on all the latest developments. With the help of the ACS, I learned again that if you ask for help, you'll get it.

One afternoon, I was preparing for my next client, when in through the door came three well-dressed people. They spent a few minutes looking around the store, then they approached me and politely introduced themselves as representatives from the American Cancer Society. We talked, for a little while, about the services that Image Insights provided. I mentioned offhand that I'd worked with some of their colleagues once before.

When I was first training with Rita, she and I did a little demonstration on a local cable television show. In truth, Rita did most of the demonstrating, and I helped out just a bit. During our segment of the program, we walked through a typical rebuilding process with Rita acting as the demonstration model. While she put herself back together again, I talked about how The Lemonade Stand worked. On the program with us was an ACS volunteer. When the host turned to her, she outlined the services that the American Cancer Society offered. That was the extent of my interaction with the ACS.

Coincidentally, one of my visitors remembered Rita and me from that show, so long ago. In fact, that's what brought them into the store that day. "We'd like to invite you to breakfast one day next week," one of the volunteers offered brightly.

"Well, that sure is nice of you," I accepted. "Mind if I ask why?"

The volunteers glanced nervously at each other. Then, one of them asked if I would bring along a list of names. They wanted to know who I might recommend as a candidate for the president of their local chapter. I was fairly new in the field and didn't know any big shots at that point. "I don't know if I can be much help," I hesitated. They looked chagrined. "But I can try," I offered helpfully. That brought on a big round of smiles. I figured I had nothing to lose, and the businesswoman inside of me realized that this was an organization I should know more about. Besides, *they were buying.* I was going to pass up a chance for someone to buy me breakfast?

The big morning arrived, and I had a wonderful time at breakfast. It was so nice to just sit and relax, and to chat with someone for a while—even if we were talking shop. It's not like I got out a lot. My life was pretty much work and home, work and home. If that sounds like a complaint, it wasn't—I loved my shop, and I loved my boys. But this silly little breakfast meeting was the closest thing I'd had to a social life in quite a while. Like a castaway, I was starving for some social attention. I was enjoying just being out of the store, so I was probably a little chatty.

We talked about the challenges I'd faced at Image Insights, and about all of the clients we'd helped. We talked about the many ways that the American Cancer Society could help my patients. We talked and talked, and I was having such a good time. That's when they told me that they were about to close the doors of the Kentucky branch forever.

"Why!?" I asked, stunned. "Why would you do that?"

"There just isn't any volunteer interest," one of them replied. "You're sitting with *the last three volunteers* in all of Northern Kentucky." *Unbelievable!* I'd always imagined the ACS as a juggernaut—unstoppable, rolling along flush with money and volunteers. Instead, I'd found out that there was no cancer society, at least not in our region of Kentucky. Nope; for us, the mighty American Cancer Society consisted of three lonely, worn-out volunteers. *That's it,* I thought sadly, and I shook my head in dismay. *That's all there is, there ain't no more.*

Even in this sad state of affairs, they were still believers. They refused to give up on their mission. Each of them had been touched by cancer, through a family member or friend. They didn't want to see the doors closed. Over the years, they'd done as much as they could as volunteers, but still the organization was dying on its feet. Unsuccessful at recruiting more volunteers, this sad trio was on the verge of total burnout. Now that I understood their predicament, I could see it in their faces. *How did I miss that?* I thought. *No wonder they seemed a little edgy.*

Besides running out of volunteers, they were running low on funds. The branch couldn't afford to hire a full-timer to take over. They desperately needed new blood; but they were short on money, short on help, and short on time. "Holy cow," I said. "You guys are short on everything!"

I could feel the pain they felt at the thought of their operation closing down. If something wasn't done soon, the ACS would be gone in Northern Kentucky—and with it, any extra local help for my patients. "Okay, let's go over my list of names," I said, but I warned them, "I haven't been in business long enough to have any serious connections. I do have the names of a few good possibilities, though." I smiled optimistically, "It can't hurt to ask."

I started down my list then, describing the relative strengths and weaknesses of each candidate. After a few minutes, I realized that nobody was talking. They weren't kibitzing with me, there was no back and forth. No objections, no agreements, no questions. Only silence. They were just staring at me and smiling. I stopped. "What?" I asked. All three started grinning.

"We were thinking . . . *you!*"

I stared at them. *Didn't see that one coming,* I thought, surprised. *Should have, but didn't.* I folded my hands on the table and stopped to think. *No such thing as a free lunch, uh, breakfast, is there?* They had caught me completely off guard, I really didn't see how I could do it. I was struggling night and day to keep my own store afloat. Where would I find the time for this?

Then I realized what had just happened. *Ask and you shall receive.* They asked. Just like I'd done with Bob at the IRS, the people at Colaplast, Bonnie at Ava Gabor Wigs, and countless doctors and nurses; they had asked for my help. *I didn't even buy Bob a cup of coffee,* I thought, with a twinge of guilt. *How can I say no now?*

I shook my head and gave a rueful smile. They had me over a barrel. An hour and a half later, I was the new president of the American Cancer Society in Northern Kentucky. Maybe it was a sugar rush from the maple syrup, but I even agreed to an open-ended one-year commitment. I don't know what I was thinking. In time, that open-ended year turned into three.

I t was even worse than I expected. Our local branch of the ACS was a mess. There was so much paperwork that needed to be done. Everything was in disarray, and I was left with a ton of work to catch up on. We had no office support staff, I had no mentor to lean on, and there was no money to hire help. *Funny. This is just like my business,* I thought. *No wonder they came looking for me!*

The Northern Kentucky branch of the American Cancer Society was in such a sad state that it hardly deserved such a grandiose name. There was so much to do that I felt like I'd been saddled with a second full-time job. I was busy enough working overtime on the first one. It was too much for one woman to handle. As far as I could see, the only way to make the operation work was to recruit more volunteers. I knew I couldn't do it alone, so I began recruiting. *Just ask,* I thought. *It worked for me—and then it worked on me.* It was worth a try.

I made the rounds of hospitals and doctors' offices again, just like I'd done when I first opened Image Insights. I told everyone who would listen that I needed volunteers—and I needed them *badly.* I was on a desperate mission to save our branch of the American Cancer Society. "All I need is just a *little bit* of help," I told them. "If we don't do something, it will be gone." I think it was that "little bit" that did the trick. People started responding to my pleas, and one-by-one our list of volunteers began to grow. If we could get a little bit from a lot of people, we would be okay.

The first order of business, for our new recruits, was to organize fundraisers. We had to bring in desperately needed donations; without them, nothing else could happen. Our first big fundraiser began as a five-mile walk for cancer survivors, and anyone who supported them. We called it "Making Strides." Our hope was that it would not only raise money, but also recreate a sense of community where it had long been missing. A local radiation oncologist, Dr. John Sacco, and a wonderful woman named Eileen Stern, who was a cancer survivor, helped me organize the walk. In fact, Eileen did such terrific work that I put her in charge of our new breast cancer support group, too. It would become another role in which she would shine. As we spread the word about the walk, our initial response was good;

so we decided it had to be even bigger. Our five-mile walk-a-thon evolved into a five-mile mass migration, by any means necessary.

Dr. John Sacco gave a great deal of his free time to help me save our local branch of the American Cancer Society.

Our participants walked, power-walked, jogged, and ran. We even had some crawling babies. Wheels were allowed too. Participants used bikes, wheelchairs, skateboards, and roller skates. We were up for anything. Whatever it took, it was fine by us. I didn't care if people used stilts or pogo sticks. The big event was held in Fort Thomas, Kentucky, on a day that could not have been more perfect if I'd ordered up the weather myself. Everyone had a great time, and all were proud to be a part of our first big volunteer activity. Adam and Nicholas, Saundra, my mom and Evelyn were all such a great help. They took care of everything, from registration and organization, to passing out water to thirsty walkers. The event was a great success—not only in money, but in spirit. Even more important than the funds we raised, was the goodwill we generated. People were excited to be part of such a lively social occasion, and they would come back again for more. Some of them would even return as ACS volunteers. I couldn't have been more thrilled with our first success, and my enthusiasm seemed to be contagious.

Our list of volunteers grew steadily larger, and so did the number of events and services that we offered. Dr. Michael Zinda, another local radiation oncologist, joined us to help. In addition to being a busy practitioner, he was a generous volunteer. Cheerful and intelligent, he made all of that extra work a lot easier to endure. Together, we arranged door-to-door fundraising, we began a breast cancer support group with Eileen, and organized many other special fundraising events. By the end of that first year, we'd recruited more than 1,600 volunteers to our local branch of the ACS. All this, after beginning with only three burned-out volunteers.

At the time, our goal was to raise $150,000. This would keep the doors open and the Northern Kentucky branch in existence. If we could raise that much, it would put the branch solidly on its feet for the year ahead. By the time we finished tallying up the results, it was shaping up to be a very good year. We not only met our goal, we raised over $190,000. Not too bad, for a bunch of rookies in their first season. With the excess, we were even able to hire a paid staff leader. This insured the survival of the branch. The success and future of the staff leader were tied directly to that of the branch itself. Her job was to continue the growth. She would prosper and thrive only if our branch of the ACS did. It was a good first year. Our chapter of the American Cancer Society was alive and well, and standing strong again.

I continued to serve as the branch president for three years. It was a lot of work and there were plenty of trials along the way, but the experience was more rewarding than I would ever have guessed. During my time there, I met a lot of amazing people. What a blessing it was to watch that failing organization come back to life. It wouldn't have been possible if not for our generous donors and volunteers. Those people gave selflessly of their time or their pocketbook. It turned out just as I'd hoped. A little bit at a time, from so many, added up to a great big beautiful thing. Ask and you shall receive, indeed.

On the other hand, there is some truth to the old Longfellow saying. If "into every life a little rain must fall," then I must have been due for an April shower. Several years after we'd put our local ACS back on its feet, I was presented with an unwelcome surprise. That very same staff leader—the one our fundraising had put in place—actually accused me of stealing. To be precise, she accused me of selling American Cancer Society products to my customers at Image Insights. When an attorney called to ask me about these accusations, I was floored. It was ridiculous! Of course I was able to prove where my products came from. Once I did, the attorney apologized for the organization. He seemed sincere enough, but the hurt feelings were difficult to bear. *Why do these things keep happening to me?* I wondered. *Do I have "stupid" written on my forehead?* Maybe it wasn't written there, but sometimes I was treated like it was. After all of the long hours and dedication, after all of the wonderful things we'd accomplished, it was painful to have it end that way.

As I often did, when the going got rough, I thought of Rita. I would recall some of the counsel she had given me. Rita told me that there would sometimes come bad with the good. There were days when it seemed like you couldn't have one without the other. When those days came, it was important to have God on your side. She told me that His support would give me the strength to bear the bad times.

Why had the woman at the ACS made her accusation? I never found out. It seemed best to let sleeping dogs lie. I did know that I had to put it behind me. I couldn't let it ruin what had otherwise been an amazing experience. If I sat down with my Bible, I thought I would find the strength I was looking for.

Sure enough, I did. "We work hard with our own hands. When we are cursed, we bless; when we are persecuted, we endure it; when we are slandered, we answer kindly." *(1 Corinthians 4:12-13a)* In other words, it was time to turn the other cheek. And so I did—forgive and forget. I put it behind me and stayed busy at the shop. If the ACS needed help, I pitched in and did my part. As Bill probably would have said, "It doesn't matter what *they* do. All that matters is what *you* do."

It was so comforting that, even though Rita was gone, I still had the legacy of her wisdom to draw upon. She had given me so much—a new role model to follow and a new source of strength. With that, came a whole new outlook on life. I hadn't even *asked* for that; but she'd given it to me anyway.

CHAPTER 10

My All-Volunteer Army

As Image Insights continued to grow, I began to see more positive results in the lives of my clients. Thanks to ongoing research, better medications and more effective treatments were available for patients. Education, and more frequent screenings, were catching some cancers at earlier stages, when they could be treated more effectively. As a result, a growing percentage of patients were surviving—and more often than not, they weren't as sick as they'd been before. People were recovering faster, and they were living longer.

This improvement in their fortunes became a double blessing to me. Many of the people we had helped over the past few years now came back to help us at Image Insights. Even though our store was just a brief rest-stop on their journey, they returned to show us their appreciation. It wasn't only our clients who turned up; often, their family members pitched in to help, too. They all understood how important it was to help others who were just beginning their struggle with cancer. These former patients felt that it was crucial that new patients should know what Image Insights had to offer. They wanted to help spread the word. Apparently, we'd been important enough in their lives, that they wanted to share us with others.

It was an incredible feeling to see our old clients looking so well again. What an exciting change! Rather than *leaving* our shop looking and feeling great, they were *coming in* that way! Once upon a time, Rita said that I would be her legs. Now these people were *my* legs—at least a centipede's worth. They spread The Lemonade Stand spirit far and wide. They took Image Insights flyers and business cards around to hospitals and doctors' offices. Even better, they took their positive personal experiences—their testimonials—with them. It was a powerful combination. Others came into the shop to help us send out our mailings. They spread the word far and wide in a way that my small staff and I never could have.

My mom, and her friend Evelyn, also came in to help. They would make these cute little candy favors by wrapping lemon drops in purple mesh. My dad would help to make them, too. They would tie it closed with a purple ribbon and attach one of our business cards. We would pass these lemon favors out to clients, hand them out at seminars, or leave them behind wherever we went. Many doctors' offices and hospitals began keeping them on hand, to pass on to patients who would need our services. Then, they would call the shop every few weeks to ask for refills.

We still make pink lemon favors to this day. We've made thousands of those silly little things.

So many wonderful people were willing to help, and they made me stronger than I would have believed possible. If ever I doubted myself, this was living proof that we were doing something that made a difference. Otherwise, why else were these people coming back? Besides being so helpful in word and deed, my returning clients knew the power of prayer. They understood that it was a daily struggle just to stay in business. Besides giving away their help, they prayed for me. For that, I'm most grateful.

Things were growing rapidly at Image Insights. With the constant flow of patients, the array of new products we were handling, and the army of volunteers that joined us, it wasn't long before I realized that we needed more space. There was a bigger building, across and just down the street, that looked like it would suit us nicely. It was a long way from opening a second location, but it was definitely a step up. The word got around fast. When people heard that I was moving the store, volunteers arrived from miles around. They came in to paint the new store and move all of our furniture. They helped stock the shelves and counted up the inventory. They cheerfully swept, and mopped, and cleaned, and wiped, and did whatever else had to be done.

It was like the SeaBees had rolled in. With their "can do" spirit, my volunteers *could* and *did*. In the space of a few short days, we rebuilt Image Insights, bigger and better than ever. A project that had taken us weeks to accomplish our first time out, seemed to come together almost overnight this time. It was truly a beehive of activity. Hammers banged, saws whined, paint splashed, and furniture moved. Boxes were packed, hauled, and unpacked. A hundred things were happening all at once, each with drive and purpose.

Along with my volunteers, my family was there for me again as well. Adam and Nicholas even brought along a few of their friends to help carry boxes. That gang of young men worked up a real sweat, too. Doing the work of twice their number, the boys were almost a blur as they shuttled back and forth across the street. Their energy seemed almost limitless. If it flagged at all, a quick application of junk food—pizza or burgers—quickly returned them to active duty.

Adam, Nicholas, and their friends worked like real troupers. Competition and teamwork went hand-in-hand as they encouraged each other with jeers and good-natured insults. "C'mon you wuss, is that all you can carry?" went the challenge. "Yeah, yeah. Any slower and my grandma's going to lap you," came the reply. On and on it went, back and forth; the more rude or colorful things got, the better. They might have been noisy, hauling their loads back and forth, but those boys could really get the job done.

After a while, their chatter and insults became the background music to our work. It even rubbed off on the rest of us, and some of our more "mature" volunteers started egging each other on. It was a noisy, hectic day, and we were all in good spirits. That's why, when the noisy chatter finally died away, I had to wonder what was up. It was suddenly so quiet.

The move was nearly finished. Only a small stack of boxes remained. But the boys were nowhere to be seen. I hunted around the old store. "Have you seen Adam or Nicholas?" I asked, over and over again. The answer was always the same: a puzzled frown and a surprised negative. *This is odd,* I thought.

I didn't see any of the boys on the street between the old store and the new one. Feeling a twinge of worry, I hustled over to the new shop. In through the front door I rushed, and . . . nothing. *Where are they?* Now I was concerned. Looking around the new location, I fought down a surge of panic. The boys were nowhere to be seen—not a one of them. By the time I reached the back of the store, I was beginning to feel real fear. *Where have they gone?*

When life gives you lemons. . .

Play!

When you're feeling blue, fill your personal space with a million reasons to smile. Draw on walls, write love letters, collect teddy bears, entertain your inner child. The magic of play is a healer.

Then, I heard hushed voices. They were coming from the storeroom at the back of the building. I strode down the hall, determined to find out just what was going on. I rounded a corner and stepped into the doorway. Hands on my hips, I took a breath and was just about to demand, *What in the . . . ?*

I backed out quickly, without making a sound.

In the storeroom, surrounded by half-open boxes. The boys stood in a tight little group, their backs to the door. Someone had made an important discovery. The boys had discovered breasts. Or, to be more precise, *breast forms.* Apparently someone had gotten curious about the contents of the boxes they were carrying. This discovery demanded further exploration. After all, this was virgin territory to these very young men. It was the undiscovered country.

Breast forms of every size and shape lay scattered about, as the boys compared and contrasted their finds. They were so engrossed in their studies that they'd never heard my approach. There was valuable information here, to be grabbed by the handful. While they were busy getting their share, I quietly slipped away.

Retreating to the front door, I silently pushed it open and ducked out. Waiting a beat, I re-entered the shop—noisily this time. I picked up a few boxes and dropped them loudly to the floor. "Boys?!" I called out, "Adam? Nicholas? Anyone here?"

After a few moments, and a little noisy repacking, they emerged in a ragged train. "Hey, Mom!" Adam and Nicholas greeted me, almost in unison. Eyes bright and smiling, they sauntered past with a cheery, "Almost done!" No fools, those two; they had perfected the art of acting innocent. Not that anyone had done anything wrong, really; but they weren't about to let on. The other boys weren't as good at it. They shuffled past with an assortment of mumbled greetings and nods. Once they were all out the door, I let my poker face slide into a wide grin. I could act innocent, too.

In my years at Image Insights, I was blessed with help from so many wonderful volunteers. In a perfect world, I could tell every one of their stories. Unfortunately, one book is too small a space to fit them. To tell them all, this would have to be a multi-volume set: *The Encyclopedia Samaritanicca*. For every story told, there are dozens more left unmentioned. Some volunteers made a difference to hundreds of people. Others mattered to only a few. But what matters, is that they *made a difference*. They were important in someone's life. My volunteers mattered, and they are remembered.

I remember them all. One might think they'd tend to blur together after the first fifty, or hundred. They don't. It's easy to remember the people who have acted as angels in my life. When you are suffering under a heavy burden, and someone does something to lighten your load, you don't forget them. My clients haven't forgotten these angels-on-earth, either. When you're in dire straits and someone throws you a lifeline, you remember them forever.

It's a good thing to be remembered fondly. But consider that old maxim: We're remembered not by what we get, but by what we give. I know I'm not the first to say it, but that doesn't make it any less true. My volunteers are remembered by thousands of patients, and their families, across the country. And my volunteers are remembered by me.

One of those very special people was a woman named Saundra Strunk. One of my very first clients, Saundra came to see me after she had a mastectomy. Like Rita, she had also lost her hair to cancer treatments. Saundra was in need of a complete makeover—wigs, prostheses, and bras. A warm and wonderful Christian lady, she reminded me so much of Rita. Patient, loving, and kind, it was always such a pleasure to work with her. Saundra had a great attitude and as I got to know her better, I came to know what a beautiful woman she was, inside and out. Saundra endured her treatments, and their serious side effects, with grace and optimism. After a rough session, she would straighten up and carry herself tall, as if to say, "Okay, what's next?" And no matter how badly she felt, Saundra was always positive and encouraging to me. Her strength inspired the same in others, myself among them. I'm pleased and proud that she remains my best friend to this day.

After Saundra finished with her treatments, she returned to Image Insights to answer phones for me. Always generous and thoughtful, she would often surprise me by bringing me lunch. I was usually so busy at work that I developed the bad habit of skipping meals and running on adrenaline. Saundra noticed, and did her best to put a stop to it. "You need to take a little break once in a while," she chided me. "If you don't take care of yourself, how are you going to take care of us?" I would nod thoughtfully in reply, as I munched on a sandwich, and then I'd promise to try to do better.

Saundra was always ready for anything. No matter what I needed help with—answering phones, running errands, or helping with clients—she would take on any assignment and complete it efficiently and with good cheer. With her energy and enthusiasm, she outshined all but the brightest of my employees. It never ceased to amaze me that volunteers, like Saundra, would do so much and ask for nothing in return. It was all the more remarkable that they did so even as they were suffering, either from their illness or the debilitating treatments.

As if all that hard work weren't enough, Saundra was also good for my spirits. She was so encouraging, and she believed strongly in me and my mission. Saundra truly understood the Lemonade spirit, and she wanted to see us help others just like her. I was able to confide in her about anything; and I did, about almost *everything*.

My best friend, Saundra, and I. In matters of inspiration and perseverance, she picked up where Rita left off. Words don't do her justtice.

I told her how I thought I ought to be helping *thousands* of people, rather than just dozens, or hundreds. I felt like I could never get enough done. Somehow I had to grow the business some more.

Saundra knew about the constant financial stress I was under. At one particularly bad time, I was in serious trouble. If it went on much longer, the business would collapse. Saundra asked her mother, Eleanor, to lend me $25,000 to help the store stay on its feet. Eleanor was not a wealthy woman, but she believed in Saundra. And Saundra believed in me. Their trust, and financial help, kept Image Insights alive. In time, I was able to make good on everything; but I never could have done it without them.

The business always had its ups and downs. Sometimes everything operated smoothly, and we were temporarily flush with cash. Other times, things were rocky and finances became unbearably tight. An insurance provider could change the rules on us, or slash some types of coverage. When that happened, we were out of luck. The work was already done. The patients had been helped and equipped, but there would be no more reimbursements. Or maybe only a partial payment. The merchandise we dealt with was painfully expensive, so it hurt to be left holding the bag. But I couldn't really pass my extra expenses along; most of the patients could afford it even less than I could.

Even if the work *hadn't* been done, and the rules were changed—what was I going to do? Tell a patient who needed help, "Sorry. Can't help you. The rules changed last week." No, not gonna happen. There were times when patients came in without any coverage at all. How could I tell someone who was fighting for her life, "No. You can't have a wig."? I couldn't. So I bit the bullet, and helped them as much as I could. Then I'd try to figure out how to pay for it all later. Yes, I was taken advantage of, now and again—but it was rare. For every bad apple who tried to play the system, there were a hundred good people in genuine need.

If it wasn't a rule change playing havoc with my business, or coverage lapse, then it was something else like it. Suddenly those flush cash reserves were all gone and I was back in trouble. When it happened again, Saundra recruited the help of her brothers. We even discussed the idea of going into partnership with them. Logically, it seemed like a good idea. But then, left on my own to think about things, I began to worry again. I knew I could trust Saundra's family. They were like my own. I had known her brother, Steve, for a long time—he was the one who usually took Saundra to her treatments. So, of course I could trust him. But the potential for loss of control made me very nervous. I was afraid that if the business were run by somebody else—someone who didn't have Rita's vision—then the mission might change. Episodes like those with Kate and Karen, or the staff leader at the Cancer Society, didn't make it any easier to let my guard down. Above all, I was afraid of disappointing Rita.

While the partnership was an attractive offer, I just couldn't make the leap. One day, they might crunch the numbers and find that they had a difficult financial decision to make. One that would take Image Insights in a different direction. I couldn't let that happen. The business was not about *money;* it was about *people,* doing the right thing, and serving God. When I turned them down, Saundra's brothers seemed to understand. Even though I did say no, they continued to offer valuable suggestions and clever ideas as long as I was in business.

It was because of Saundra that her brothers were so willing to help me. They believed in her and understood all that she'd been through. Because Saundra had so much faith in me, they believed in me, too. People like Saundra come along once in a lifetime. Yet God has seen fit to introduce me to more than my share of people just like her. I'm blessed to have Saundra, and her family, as a part of my life. In fact, Saundra *is family.*

Early one morning, I got a call from a nurse at one of the hospitals. She had a "very important person" who needed a wig, and she was referring him to me. I sounded suitably impressed, and I thought, *this is shaping up to be a pretty good day.* I was honored by the referral, because it meant I'd come up in the world. The hospital had begun to treat me as the "go-to girl" for wigs and prosthetics. In our clients' eyes, we were the authority on the subject. If there was *anything* they needed, they knew where to look for help. I was proud to know that the doctors and nurses saw us the same way.

The nurse on the phone told me, "This patient is a big shot, so do your best for him."

"I'll do exactly that," I replied, while knowing inside that he would get the same treatment that everyone else got. *Of course it will be my best,* I thought. *What else would it be?*

According to the nurse, this man was a vice president with the Xerox Corporation. Ron had just been transferred to the

Midwest from New York, but from the buildup she had given him, he must have been hot stuff. I was securely confident as I prepared to meet him; but as the day wore on I started to get a little nervous. I knew it was silly. It's not like he was royalty or anything; but suddenly I was worried about making a good impression. I wished the nurse had simply told me that a man needed a wig. That would have been quite sufficient.

When Ron came in for that first visit, he brought his wife with him. He really was the epitome of the successful business executive—meticulously dressed, polished, and coiffed. His wife, Janet, was a tall, elegant woman, impeccably attired in a tailored dress. She wore the kind of beautiful jewelry I'd seen only in the most expensive stores—but never outside of one. They obviously traveled in circles that I'd never *seen.*

Ron spoke clearly and eloquently, and he was very well informed about his condition. His more poetic turns of phrase left me feeling a little awkward whenever I verbally stumbled over one too many "umms" or "uhs". But with perfect manners, they pretended not to notice my slips or slang. It's a sign of class when people who are well-off don't lord it over others. They simply try to make those around them feel comfortable. Ron and his wife did just that. It wasn't long before I settled down and got over my nervousness. Ron and Janet were kind and patient, and that finally put me at ease. *What is it about people with money that makes us so nervous?* I wondered. *Why do we want so badly to make a good impression? They're just people. With money.* I smiled as the thought occurred to me. After that, I was able to treat them just like regular folks.

Fitting a man for a wig is not at all like fitting a woman with one. Right from the start, most men aren't comfortable having someone fuss over their appearance. But fitting a man requires a lot of detailed, close-in work. It also requires patience, which Ron had in abundance. We got along really well. Fittings take a long time, and can be very dull if there is no interaction. We chatted about everything—about our families and our work. At one point, he complimented me on a gold cross necklace that I was wearing. It was nothing, just a clean, simple cross on a thin gold chain. He admired it for its clarity and purity. So I expressed admiration for the beautiful cuff links he wore on his shirt. They were subtle and elegant, and probably from a store I wouldn't dare to set foot in. They were also a clear indicator of his classical tastes. Ron was refined, not ostentatious. While I guess I can't really call him a "regular guy," Ron was a good guy, with a great attitude and an engaging personality. What could have been a long, tedious wait for him, and a demanding job for me, turned out to be a pleasant afternoon of time well spent. Nearly three hours later, we finished the fitting and I felt like I made two new friends.

Ron and Janet came back a week later to pick up the wig we had ordered. We had a good, long conversation about dealing with cancer, as he patiently sat through another long session in the chair. After cutting and thinning the wig, Ron and Janet agreed that it looked perfectly natural. The careful work paid off, and Ron's wig was indistinguishable from his natural hair. It made him feel more comfortable that, as an executive, he could continue to work without people knowing that he was losing his hair. Watching the boss' hair fall out was not likely to secure the confidence that his employees had in him. Maintaining his normal appearance helped to keep Ron centered.

About four weeks later, Ron called to ask if he could stop by to talk. This time, he arrived dressed much more casually than before. He also came alone. We talked about his treatments, and about how his cancer was progressing. Things were difficult, but he was bearing his burden stoically and with good humor. Ron spoke again of the cross I was wearing the day we'd met. "Clean, simple, and elegant," he called it. I joked that the cufflinks he'd worn weren't exactly a match for the track suit he had on that day.

Changing subjects, Ron suddenly said to me, "You know, Gayle, you're the best little-known secret I've ever heard."

"What do you mean?" I half smiled and half frowned.

"I probably don't have to tell you what a roller coaster my life has become." Ron paused for a moment to collect his thoughts, then he continued. "Meeting you has been among the greatest experiences I've ever had. You've done a terrific job with me. Under the circumstances, you've made me feel better than I ever thought possible." I smiled and shook my head. I wanted to tell him that mine was the easy part. He was the one with the hard work to do. But before I could say anything, he continued. "There is only one thing wrong. More people need to know what you're doing here. You need more exposure."

"That would be nice," I nodded ruefully.

"Do you have a marketing brochure?" he asked seriously. "Maybe we can make some improvements."

I gave a short, sad laugh. "No." I shook my head. "I can't really afford any of that. I'm lucky to keep my business cards stocked." Brochures involved all kinds of things that I knew little about, and couldn't pay for anyway. A good brochure required writers and designers and printers. Even a bad brochure needed a printer. It would be a stretch to pay for that—and what good would a bad brochure do me? I told Ron as much.

"Well, now you have me," Ron replied. "That's my specialty with Xerox, and I'm going to help you put together a brochure." So just like that, I had a marketing manager—one who was definitely out of my price range. Ron hadn't needed anything that day, he'd simply stopped by to volunteer his time and expertise. He was determined to create marketing materials for Image Insights—all while he was going through his treatments. And he wouldn't take "no" for an answer. Which was good, because my answer was an emphatically grateful "yes".

When Ron returned the next week, he was in a wheelchair. Only seven days had passed and already things were going badly for him. It was heartbreaking. This once well-groomed, articulate, and intelligent man could barely speak now. He didn't care anymore if he wore his wig or not. It was painful and disheartening to realize how quickly his cancer was progressing. As painful as it was to see, it must have been devastating to live through—but Ron would have none of it. He was as determined as ever to create an effective brochure for me, and somehow he found the energy to gather the information he needed.

Suffering as he was, this former Fortune 500 executive worked diligently to create a sales brochure for my tiny little company. Over the next few days, Ron wrote the copy, commissioned the art, had the layout designed, and made arrangements for the printing. I was torn. Part of me wanted Ron to stop working so hard and get some rest. The other part knew that the work was keeping him energized. It was giving him purpose and providing fulfillment. In any case, it didn't matter whether I felt torn or not; there was no stopping him. Ron was on a mission, and he would not stop until it was accomplished.

When it came time to finish the brochure, I had to go to Ron's home. By then, it had become too difficult for him to go out. As we went over things together, I could see how much pain he was in. Ron, however, was single-minded and remained focused on the job at hand. We applied the finishing touches and got the project ready for the printer. The brochure was beautiful. It had a friendly, open, appealing look to it and even expressed a sense of humor. It was sure to cheer people up, even as it provided them with much needed information. It was just what we needed.

I told Ron how much I loved the final result, and that I was grateful for his hard work. "Words really seem so inadequate," I told him, "but I truly could not have done this without you." He shrugged off my praise and my thanks, but I continued. "Your hard work is going to make a difference, Ron. It's going to help lots of sick people feel much better." He smiled at me and nodded sleepily. His efforts had worn him out and he closed his eyes for a rest.

A few weeks later, Ron's wife, Janet, called to tell me that he was in the hospital. The doctors had scheduled yet another operation, but this time the brain cancer had spread so much that it was inoperable. Ron wasn't doing very well and his time was growing short. I wanted to do something nice for him, to show him how much his help meant to me, and to make him feel better, if only for a moment. *But what do you give the man who has everything?* I wondered. *And what do you give him when he knows that everything means nothing?* I couldn't afford anything fancy; and flowers don't usually mean much to a man. I said a prayer for Ron and asked God if He had any ideas. *I'll let you know,* was the reply. On my way to the hospital, I realized that I was wearing the same cross that I'd worn on the day we met.

It was evening when I arrived at the hospital, and Ron was asleep. I didn't want to disturb him, so I waited for a while, hoping he might come around. *Maybe a nurse will come in to bother him and wake him up,* I hoped—sort of. He continued to sleep peacefully, and I couldn't bring myself to wake him. After an hour or so, I took the cross off and put it in a little box. I set it on top of a note that asked Janet to give it to him.

When she called the next day, Janet was crying. She asked me how I knew to give Ron the cross. It had made him so happy. Janet said, "When I pulled it out of the box, he saw it and his face lit up. He held out his hand to take it . . ." Janet stopped and bit off a ragged sob. "He had tears streaming down his face." Then, she took a deep breath and continued. "He held it in his fist and brought his hand to his lips. 'That's hers, that's hers,' he said softly, and he just closed his eyes and cried quietly." Late that night he passed away.

I did some crying myself as I talked to Janet. I told her, "I tried to listen to God, knowing He'd brought us together for a reason. It wasn't just because Ron needed a wig. There were reasons that we may never understand." I paused to wipe my nose and steady up a bit. "Ron talked about that cross before. He seemed to like it. It wasn't even a fancy crucifix, just a simple cross—especially compared to your beautiful things." I smiled at the memory. "For some reason, he was taken with it. When you told me he wasn't doing well, I knew I was supposed to pass that cross on to him. Then God would take care of it from there."

I think about Ron often. What a special man he was. Even as he was dying, struggling painfully through his last days on earth, he was determined to help me—and my patients. Even as he saw his own end approaching, he thought only of others. What a miracle it was that he would spend some of his last precious days on us. He gave me some of the last moments of his life, working to insure that Image Insights would continue to live and breathe and prosper.

"Even though I walk through the valley of the shadow of death, I will fear no evil, for you are with me; your rod and your staff, they comfort me." *(Psalms 23:4)*

Ron was buried with my cross, an honor that still brings tears to my eyes.

CHAPTER 11

Lemonade Stand, Live!

One quiet afternoon in the shop, I met a sad, lonely woman named Colette. When she came into Image Insights, I could see that she was undergoing treatment. From the look of her, she was having a very difficult time of things. She walked with her shoulders slumped and her head down. When I greeted her, she met my eyes briefly, and did most of her talking while looking away. She lacked even the confidence to look me in the eye. *This is one sad woman,* I thought. *She looks almost ashamed to be in here.*

As we began our consultation, Colette was mostly quiet and withdrawn. I asked her the same questions I usually asked. I was trying to get a feel for her likes and dislikes; but Colette's answers weren't very illuminating. Her replies were usually only one word—and often just one syllable. She would mumble her answers and I had to listen closely to hear. I continued to prod gently and, little by little, she began to let me in. After a consultation that lasted a good deal longer than most, she finally began to shed some light on her preferences.

When I had what I needed to begin, I reached out and took her hand. "Let's get started, Colette," I said. Then I stood up and led her to a salon chair. "When you walk out the door today, you're going to feel like a new woman," I promised. I squeezed her hand and she closed her eyes for a moment. When she opened them I could see that her eyes were wet with tears.

Two hours later, Colette was smiling and laughing and looking beautiful. She was indeed a new woman, and not just on the outside. As we finished up, I took her hand again and gave it a squeeze of encouragement. "You look great," I smiled at her. She teared up again immediately. "Are you going to be okay?" I asked.

Colette smiled at me then, and looked me right in the eyes. She said, "Gayle, you have no idea how much it meant to me when you first took my hand."

I looked at her quizzically. "Why is that?"

"My family is afraid to touch me," Colette sighed. Then she continued softly, "I've been feeling very alone for quite some time now."

I wanted to cry. This wonderful woman was starved for affection. She was feeling lost and alone, because her family didn't know any better. Did they think cancer was contagious? I was always stunned to learn that there were people who still thought that way.

Or, it could have been that, fearing loss and pain, they were withdrawing from contact with her. Either way, they were failing her when she needed them most. By withholding contact, they were doing her harm. Emotionally, she'd been beaten down. That would make the physical trauma of her treatments much more difficult to bear.

What Colette needed was to be held, tightly and often. She had to know that she was loved, and even more, she had to *feel* it. I could only imagine the anguish she must have felt at being emotionally abandoned by her family.

I walked Colette to the door, but before I let her go, I gave her a big hug. "You are not alone," I told her softly. Then, I stepped back and took both of her hands. Gently but firmly, I gave her an order. "Whenever you feel that way, you come see me." She promised to do just that and, with a grateful smile, she went out the door. As I watched Colette leave that afternoon, I realized sadly that there was still a lot of education that had to be done.

In general, people were becoming better informed about the medical aspects of cancer. Unfortunately, most people did not truly understand the emotional turmoil that patients suffered. Even some doctors were guilty of that. Many of them believed that, since their patient was alive, that should be enough to make them happy. Simple as that, right? Alive equals happy.

At the time, the great majority of these doctors were male. They did extraordinary work. They were creating new treatments and making miraculous advances to the state of the art. These doctors were saving peoples' lives, every day. Unfortunately, there was one minor detail that most of them overlooked. They weren't women. Their perspective was off.

That didn't mean they weren't doing good work. They were. But this was all about point of view. Not being women, these doctors didn't know what it meant to *be* a woman. They didn't really understand what the treatments did to a woman's self-esteem. Usually, there was no "self-esteem" left. Often, there was not even a sense of "self" left over. These women literally had to rebuild themselves from the inside out.

The doctors worked hard to be sympathetic, but they could never really *know* how the women felt. They had no idea what it was like for a woman to look into a mirror and see a stranger looking back. Had they ever woken up to find that they were bald? I don't mean 40 years old, "Oh no, my hairline is receding" bald. I'm talking about going from the golden mane of Farrah Fawcett to naked as a cue ball, almost overnight. Yes, these women were grateful that the cancer was gone, but they still missed the way they had been before.

The clearest way to put it would be to ask a man to use his imagination for a moment. Stop and imagine that you wake up to find yourself *completely* bald—right down to the eyebrows. Now imagine that half—but only half—of your "package" is missing. Now try going about your day feeling like your old self. Can't do it, can you? It doesn't matter that you're still you—and that you're no less a man than you were—you don't *feel* the same anymore. *That* is how these women felt. Their beautiful hair was all gone. They were missing a breast, sometimes both. After that, it would be hard for them to feel normal again. Unless a woman had an iron will, she was probably going to need a little help. That's where we came in.

Every day, I saw first hand what these women lived with during and after their treatments. Once the medical work was done, I was left to deal with the "human" side. I believed that the doctors and nurses needed to see this side more clearly. *It's not enough to put Humpty back together again,* I thought, *if all you have left is a hollowed out shell.* These people had to be put together again on the inside, too. So while an oncologist is not a psychologist, if he understood the problem, he could send the patient to another professional who would finish the work he had begun.

Just as Rita had done, I began holding seminars at the hospitals. There, I'd talk to doctors, nurses, technicians, and anyone else who would listen. Saundra always volunteered to come along as my model. She was a good sport, always willing to remove her wig in public to let the audience see her bald head. Saundra would proudly unveil her shiny scalp before huge groups of people. She knew it was making a difference, and that somewhere, someone would benefit from it. When Saundra did her "reveal", you could almost see the audience cycle through their emotions. At first, they were taken aback by the sudden change in her appearance. Then they were amazed by her openness. Finally, they were impressed by her bravery and fortitude.

I really admired Saundra for her boldness and willingness to share. When other women heard about what we were doing together, they practically lined up to volunteer. I found that there were a bunch of my clients who were all just as willing to do the same. We formed a kind of strange theatre troupe, these women and I, as we traveled around to put on our seminars. We were definitely "off Broadway"—way, way off.

The first few seminars must have touched a nerve in our corner of the medical community. A flood of interest quickly developed, and we began to get phone calls asking for our presentation. On request, I put together a full-fledged education seminar for a panel of doctors. I brought along eight brave women, each of whom had undergone different types of breast cancer interventions. In front of this crowd of physicians, one by one, they each bared their chests so that the surgeons could see and understand. It was important that they actually see a woman before them. Not a patient, but a woman. These weren't abstract, anonymous patients requiring medical treatment. They were speaking, breathing, warm-bodied, beautiful women. And they voluntarily shed their polished exteriors to stand half-naked in front of the doctors, with all of their scars revealed. I thought they were so brave.

Again and again, I saw the same thing. Some of those doctors were under the impression that it didn't really matter to a women that she didn't have a breast anymore. They thought that their female patients were just thankful they no longer had cancer. I wanted those doctors to see that this kind of thinking was not entirely accurate. It may have been true, but it was not the whole picture.

Yes, these women were grateful to have been spared, but now they faced a whole new set of challenges. Simply put, they were left feeling lopsided because a breast had been removed. Their clothes no longer fit properly, and the women felt unattractive, or worse, unfeminine. They understood, intellectually, that they should be counting their blessings; but emotionally, these women felt anything but blessed. They felt bruised and battered, as if their core female identity had been stripped away.

Deep down, almost every woman has one little thing in common. It may not be fashionable to admit it, and some won't want to hear it; but that doesn't make it any less true. Way down inside, once you peel away the posturing, almost every woman wants to be one thing—even if only for a moment. To put it bluntly, they want to be a princess.

Most women want to be seen as beautiful, to be looked upon with admiration. Against all common sense and education, most women want—at least once—to feel pretty and to be looked at that way. Of course, standards of beauty vary, but my battle-scarred female clients were afraid that they no longer fit within the standards at all. While you don't have to be Barbie to be beautiful; in their hearts, they were afraid that their princess days were over. Intellectually, they knew it was not true; but emotionally they were not so sure.

The women battled daily with these conflicting emotions; but the doctors seldom saw that part of the struggle. Our seminars were a chance for these women to stand up and be heard. For the doctors, it was an opportunity to learn what these women experienced, to understand the emotional trauma they faced after the surgery was complete. With information, comes understanding. A physical cure does not necessarily mean that the patient is all better. The emotions have to be healthy, too. The doctors were learning that there was a need to bridge that gap. My volunteer women were instrumental in helping them to understand that.

Dr. Peter McKenna was one of the first surgeons to take action after one of our early seminars—at least, action directed towards me. Our audiences were always warm and appreciative, and no doubt many of our guests gave our presentations some serious thought. Some probably put our suggestions to use. But Dr. McKenna was one of the first to open a direct dialogue with us.

Dr. Peter McKenna is a plastic surgeon who liked the idea of making patients "whole" again. When he sent in clients, I knew our message was getting out.

A bright, young plastic surgeon, he specialized in reconstructive surgery. He saw the truth of what we were trying to express—that the care wasn't over once the cancer was cured. He was excited to find that there was continuing treatment available for his patients. He liked the idea of finishing with a patient who felt whole again, rather than just patched up.

In a complimentary letter, he said, "You do a remarkable job of covering the misfortunes of some of our patients. I was especially impressed with the sensitivity that you have regarding their deformities." His letter asked for contact information, which he promptly put to use. We began to see some of his patients almost right away. While I was pleased to have the business, I was more excited to have concrete evidence that our message was being heard, and understood.

The seminars gradually grew larger in scope. On one occasion, we held a fashion show at Northern Kentucky University. The event was part education, part entertainment, and part fundraiser, and it was a big success on all counts. One of the local department stores generously donated all of the clothing. A wonderful lady who worked there, Charlene Wynn, helped me organize the whole thing. She helped each woman design a gorgeous ensemble, with

Charlene Wynn turned a bunch of my clients into runway fashion models. A stunned audience soon learned that they were all cancer patients.

beautiful lingerie, swimwear, or evening gowns. Then she added jewelry, and every accessory imaginable to give each woman a look that suited her perfectly. Charlene really knew her stuff. Every one of those women looked stunning—they really were princesses for a day. What a tremendous ego boost it was for them, after all they had been through.

During the fashion show, no one in the audience had any idea that these women were cancer survivors. In their minds, they were enjoying a fashion show filled with beautiful models of all ages. What could be better than enjoying a night out, eyeing pretty girls? And it was all for a good cause.

At the end of the show, each woman took a few minutes to tell her story. They gave brief accounts of their struggles with breast cancer. Throughout the room, the smiles and laughter died away and mouths fell open in astonishment. The audience was taken completely by surprise. The room was utterly silent and no one moved, unless it was to wipe away a sniffle. When the last woman finished speaking, a thunderous applause rose

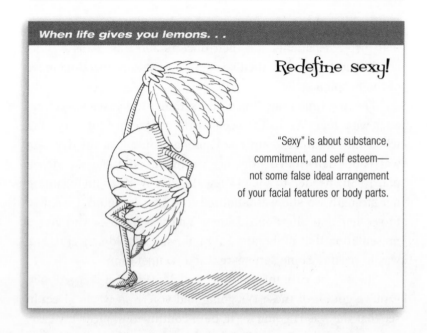

When life gives you lemons. . .

Redefine sexy!

"Sexy" is about substance, commitment, and self esteem— not some false ideal arrangement of your facial features or body parts.

from the audience. As they came to their feet, I saw many of them wiping tears from their cheeks. It was an amazing experience; my eyes were as wet as anyone's, and I'd known what was going on from the start. The smiles those girls wore could not have been any bigger. They were so pleased to see that no one had caught on. Nobody realized they were missing their own hair or breasts. It was a resounding affirmation of their feminine identity. Yes, they realized, *we are still women.*

As much as I'd like to take credit for them, the seminars weren't my idea. I was still following in Rita's footsteps. Her Lemonade Stand had been as much about education as my Image Insights was. Even when she was laid up in the hospital, Rita still held seminars for other patients. Just because she was temporarily off her game, that was no reason for the education to stop. With IVs hooked up to what seemed like every part of her, Rita would roll out of bed and make her way down to the hospital's main auditorium. There, she would hold a seminar that inspired patients and their doctors and nurses, as well as family and friends. By then she'd become an unofficial member of the hospital staff.

The first time I saw Rita hold a seminar was just a short time after we'd met. We hadn't been working together for very long when she had to close up The Lemonade Stand for the day. Rita was badly dehydrated from her treatments and she was doing poorly. She needed to spend a few days recovering and regaining her strength, so she was admitted to Christ Hospital. I went in to see her that afternoon. I knew Rita was supposed to give a presentation that night, and I thought she should cancel it. She was in need of some serious rest and recuperation.

"Let's just call this off for tonight, Rita." I begged her, "You've got all of these IVs going and you're so weak." I could see that she wasn't going for it, but I continued to plead my case. "I'm worried about you. We need to cancel tonight's speech. You really need some time to rest."

She was shaking her head before I'd even finished. "No, honey, we can't cancel," she said firmly. "I'll be okay by tonight. You'll see. You finish getting things ready for me, and I'll be there."

When the time came, Rita made her way downstairs, pushing her IV caddy along before her. Just off-stage, she unclipped, unhooked, and unplugged all of the tubes and leads she'd been wired with. Then Rita took to the stage wearing a brown robe and a turban, and without a speck of makeup. She looked worn out and beat up. As she always said, Rita looked "just like a POW."

For me, it was painful to watch. She should have been in bed, not shuffling onto a stage to give a presentation. I had seen her all wired-up to her hospital bed upstairs. Rita had looked so tired and frail. It broke my heart to see her walk out onto that stage so carefully. I could see how much pain she was in, and my eyes welled up with tears. I couldn't believe how that woman just poured her heart out to help other people. She was relentless. I don't think Rita had a self-centered bone in her body. She was always thinking of others.

On the stage waited a chair, a makeup table, and a mirror. Rita sat down at the table, introduced herself, and started to tell her story. With her cosmetics close at hand, she tilted the mirror to the proper angle and began to put herself back together again. As she worked, she spoke. Rita told the audience all about her battle with cancer, and how it had affected her life.

As her story progressed, Rita seemed to come back to life right before the eyes of her audience. While they watched, she transformed herself. Once she had finished her makeup, she put on her wig, and added earrings and a necklace. With a final look in the mirror, she stood up and peeled off her dull brown robe. Underneath, she wore a sharp navy-blue skirt and a striking lemon-yellow jacket. Even her shoes glowed a citrus gold. The change was amazing and it took my breath away. As I looked out at the audience, I could see that they were just as astounded. Only moments before, Rita had looked as if she were on her deathbed. Now, she looked absolutely radiant.

Then, even though she could barely walk a few minutes before, she casually strolled over to a piano that we'd rolled on stage for her. I had seen the beautiful baby-grand in her home, but I had never heard her play. Rita sat carefully down at the piano and began to play. True to form, she played and sang the *Lemonade Song*. And she did it beautifully.

> And he sings I, I got all I want
> 'Cause I've got my love
> And one day I'll be sittin' up in heaven on an easy chair
> Sippin' lemonade, love lives there

Within minutes, everyone in the audience had teared up or was openly crying.

Rita had that effect on others. She simply wanted people to "get it." She wanted them to know the power of God as she knew it—or at the very least, to feel a breath of His presence. Watching her, I don't know how they could not. After witnessing her passion and certainty, I think even the most cynical non-believer would have to ask himself, "I wonder if maybe there is something to this God stuff?"

Rita never pulled her punches. She didn't dance around the subject of spirituality. She was right up front with it. She wanted people to know that there is a Lord and Savior for every one of us. She thought, if people could see *her* belief, they might not be so afraid to try a little for themselves. What harm could it do, to try a little believing? None, as far as Rita could see. And it worked. It took me a few years to really understand it; but now, looking back, it is clear as day.

When you "get it" on the inside, it shows on the outside. You will be radiant in your personality and people will want to know why—they'll want some for themselves. That's the way it worked with Rita. She wasn't preachy or pedantic; she simply radiated positive energy and attitude. It rolled off her in waves because it came from inside. Then others simply let it wash over them. And the more you learned about her, the more amazing and powerful it became.

Rita was open, honest, and up-front with her faith. She wasn't pushy, but she didn't hide it away, either—and that attitude did *a lot* of good. Through her belief in God, and the good work it inspired, Rita affected the lives of more people than she ever knew.

Our seminars, and special events like the fashion show, were helping people understand what life was like for a cancer survivor. The seminars always went well—there was *never* a bad one—and the audience always left well-informed and impressed. But as good as they were, these events never reached more than dozens, or maybe hundreds, at a time. I wish I'd thought of it first, but it was a face from the past who pushed me to take the next step. It was time to take it to a higher level. The next big step was to take Image Insights to TV.

Taffy was a television producer in Cincinnati. She put together segments for a talk show that aired on a community access channel. Taffy remembered an early seminar I had done with Rita and the American Cancer Society, and she had a sudden insight. Taffy called and asked, "Why don't you come down to the station? You could do a "before and after" on one of your clients and we could put it on the air."

Wow, I thought, *that could be good.* The chance to get more exposure was too good to pass up. I knew that her show would reach far and wide, and it would inform people who were well outside of my range. I knew, from personal experience, that there were lots of people who withdrew from the world once they were stricken with cancer. Some of them were so devastated by the bad news—or even ashamed—that they stayed inside and hid. They folded up and lived the life of a shut-in.

Some patients mentally "gave up" early. They were simply waiting for the end. Others had more fight in them; but they were hiding out until the battle was over and they were "normal" again. Either way, it was no way to live. If things went like I hoped they would, then Taffy's show might reach a few of these forgotten souls. Maybe it would help bring them back into the world again.

Taffy must have taken my moment of thoughtful silence as a sign of hesitation, or even fear. "C'mon, I know you can do it. It'll be just like your seminars," she prodded me. "It'll be easy."

I made some tentative responses, but I was stalling. My mind leaped ahead to imagine the scene. I saw myself standing in front of the cameras . . . and I realized that maybe this wasn't such a hot idea after all. It wasn't so much fear at work as it was vanity. I was growing more reluctant by the moment because I was a touch self-conscious about my weight. I'd heard that the television adds an extra ten pounds or so. Or, was it the camera that added it? I wasn't sure. *What if they both add ten pounds!?* my mind raced, *What if there are two or three cameras!?* So I said, "No way. I'm not ready to do this yet. I need a little more time!" *Maybe I can hit the gym for a few weeks,* I thought.

Taffy wouldn't take "no" for an answer. "You'll be fine," she prompted. "It'll be great." In the end, guilt got the best of me and I promised to give it some thought. I told Taffy that I'd call her back.

That night, I prayed for a little guidance on the matter. God reminded me of the wonderful opportunity that it was. The show would be a great way for me to get our message out. There were people at home, living in reclusion, who could see the show. They had no idea that there were products and services that could help them. I felt like God was telling me that I should stop worrying about myself, and *think about them.* It was important that I go down there and do it.

The next day, I called Taffy and said, "I'll do it—as long as you'll help me through." Then I warned her, "It's been a long time since that show with Rita, and I didn't really have much of a part. I'm good at fixing up patients, but I don't know much about talking to a camera."

"Oh, please," Taffy reassured me. "Everything will be fine." *Famous last words,* I thought.

The big day arrived and I took one of my clients, Lynn Smith, down to the studio with me. Lynn had been one of my nursing school instructors, from way back when. At the time, she had driven me crazy. As the pharmacology instructor, she was strict, and tough as nails. Her class was very difficult, but considering the subject, she was as hard as she should have been.

Now, Lynn was dealing with cancer, and she was in need of nursing care herself. She needed the special kind of care that we offered at Image Insights. Because she knew how special that care was, Lynn eagerly volunteered to join me. Remembering her class, I teased her about going on television with me. "For all those times you put me on the spot, now it's *my turn!* You know what they say about paybacks . . . ." Truthfully, I was glad to have her help.

Once we were in the studio, I began to get a little nervous. This wasn't ordinary stage fright—after so many seminars, I was actually pretty good about getting up on stage. My audiences were usually open, friendly, and forgiving. If I tripped over some words, or made a little

Lynn Smith was my hard-nosed nursing instructor, but when she came to me for help years later, she became a generous volunteer and a good friend.

mistake, it was okay. If I let on that I was somewhat less than perfect, they were usually ready to go right along with that.

Real people are one thing, cameras are another. You'd think that it would be easier; but I could relate to people. Those cameras though, they just stare at you with that cold, unblinking eye. There aren't any knowing nods or forgiving smiles if you make a verbal stumble. The camera just stares at you—like you're an idiot. It's recording everything for posterity, so it demands perfection.

We got all set up to begin the shoot. The props and furniture were arranged, our tools were organized, the lights were adjusted, and the cameras lined up. We took our places. At a wave from the booth, the cameras were rolling and we were "on".

I blew my intro three times.

At my growl of frustration, Taffy smiled, "Don't worry about it. We'll cut out the bad stuff."

Oddly enough, that hadn't occurred to me. I forgot that there would be editing involved. Mentally, I'd been approaching it as if everything had to go right on the first pass. I thought I had to be perfect. Taffy's reminder helped me to relax a little.

"Don't talk to the cameras," Taffy offered next. "Just talk to me." As she moved around the set, I did talk to her. It helped a lot. I'm not so good with technology. I work better with people. Taffy's comments were just what the doctor ordered. She really did walk me through, just as I'd asked.

Of course, Lynn did a fabulous job the whole time. The cameras didn't seem to bother her at all. Like Sue, and Saundra, and so many of my patients, Lynn was a real trouper. She was willing to appear at less than her best, if it would help others. An affront to her vanity was a small price to pay if it offered others the chance to find themselves again. Lynn was naturally beautiful, and she looked great in anything I put on her. I was lucky to have her there. Between her quiet confidence, and Taffy's helpful suggestions, the taping of the show actually went off without a hitch. Once we were finally rolling along, I kind of fell into the role. I tuned it all out and worked as if I were back in my own shop.

The taping went well, but when we were finally finished, I was more than relieved. Rolling up a power cable, one of the crew passed by and said, "You handled that like an old pro."

"Beginner's luck," I replied, laughing nervously. He rewarded me with a wry little grin. All of my nervous energy returned in a rush, so I began cleaning up our supplies, and silently thanking God—over and over—that we were done. That TV stuff is a lot tougher than it looks. Over the course of several long hours, we had taped two half-hour shows. It was hard work, but it had gone well, and I was just so happy that we could all go home. *At least it's over with,* I thought. *Now I can get back to normal life again.*

Before we could get out of there, a producer's assistant approached me. "Okay, Gayle," he said brightly, "Next month— when do you want to do this again?"

I just looked at him. "Again?" I shook my head, "Oh, no. I don't think so. This was just a one-time thing," He held up his hands, as if to slow me down, but I continued. "I'm just happy that it's all over, and that I didn't foul things up for you. Now, I'm outta here."

The PA lowered his hands and raised his eyebrows, looking at me in a way that said, *Oh, you poor naive child.* "No," he shook his head slowly, "I'm pretty sure you'll be back." Then he grinned at me.

I didn't know what the poor man was talking about, so I walked off to find Taffy. I looked all around the studio, and checked the control room, but Taffy was nowhere to be seen. The assistant quietly followed along, confident in the knowledge that he was right. When I ran out of places to look, I stopped and he sidled up alongside me. "Taffy's word is law," he said softly. "And my understanding from Taffy, is that you're going to be here once a month to host and produce your own show."

I turned to look at him. "You're kidding," I croaked. Wearing a little smirk now, the PA just pursed his lips and shook his head. Then he walked away. *Nope, not kidding,* I realized, with some astonishment.

So now I've got a TV show, I thought, bewildered. *Who'da thunk it?* At first, I wasn't sure if it would be a blessing or a curse. It was, of course, a blessing. Before I knew it, I was hosting and producing my own little television show—with a lot of help from Taffy's staff. They were the true talents, I was just the pretty face, so to speak. After a while, I did get pretty good at it. By then, I'd learned to enjoy the tapings almost as much as I did our live seminars.

The show turned out to be a wonderful vehicle for inspiration and education. Cancer patients and their doctors could hear about successful therapies and cutting-edge treatments. We demonstrated products and techniques to help patients in their struggles with cancer, or through their successful recoveries. Since it was community access, the shows ran several times during the month—and at pretty much every time of the day. It gave us a lot of exposure, and I would get comments and compliments almost everywhere I went. It was The Lemonade Stand, Image Insights, and our seminars, all rolled into one. Our little show reached out to help or inform thousands of people scattered across several states. It was something that my little shop could never have done on its own.

A few months before, I'd told Saundra that I wished I could help, not hundreds, but thousands of patients. In truth, my little store simply was not equipped to do that. My few employees and I were not capable of it. But even if I couldn't help every patient, one by one, our show would direct them to others who could. Taffy and her production team were helping to make my wish come true.

Nobody was going to get rich working hard on a show like this. After all, this was "cable access". Some of the crew were working as a community service. Others were young people learning the ropes before trying to go pro. But whatever their motives were, I was grateful for their help. The word was getting out, and people were getting help. That's all that mattered.

"Comfort, comfort my people, says your God" (Isaiah 40:1). I hope that's what I was able to do. Between Taffy's crew, and my volunteers and employees, there were a lot of people working very hard to get the message out. If the television program and seminars helped even one person, then it was worth it. But I'm pretty sure that we did better than that.

CHAPTER **12**

It's Better to Give Than to Receive

I know it's a cliché, but making a difference to someone we know and love is its own reward. Whether it is our children, our family, or our friends, we give to each other. We help each other and do things for one another. Usually we are blessed, and our loved ones return the favor. While it's good, it's also very safe. There is no real risk involved. We don't give to those we love expecting "even Stevens" or "fair's fair." But we usually know that we're going to get it.

Giving to an acquaintance, or even a stranger, is something else entirely. Giving without expectation of a reward is difficult. But there are other things in life besides real, or immediate, rewards. How many people get to know the extraordinary feeling of truly affecting another's life? Not just family or friends, but strangers. Helping someone outside our circle of loved ones is strangely, spiritually rewarding. It makes you feel good about yourself. It provides a sense of accomplishment for a job well done. When you help someone in need, you feel like you've made a difference in the world, even if it was just a small one. It is an *honor* to help others—and it's something we should all try to do.

I was truly fortunate; Image Insights gave me that honor every single day. I did everything I could to take care of the people God sent to me. And like clockwork, He kept sending people to help me in return. I was astonished by the number of volunteers I had that were clients at one time. I was even more impressed by the volunteers who were clients still. The selflessness of these people, when they were at their absolute worst, was something to behold. I so admired their strength and devotion.

Another one of those exceptional people was a woman named Annie. One of my first clients at Image Insights, Annie was a young, single woman tragically afflicted with breast cancer. She should have been out meeting people, building a career, or starting a family of her own. Instead, she was struggling just to stay alive. When other young women were graduating from college, getting married, or moving into their own home, Annie was battling cancer. She was facing the fight of her life, when she should have been chasing her dreams.

Annie was a lost soul, left to deal with her trauma all by herself. She didn't really want to be alone, she didn't even *like* to be alone; but she was. The family she had was scattered far and wide.

Her mother had died when she was a young woman, so Annie's core pillar of support was long gone. She had been the apple of her mother's eye, and their relationship was very close; so the loss devastated Annie. She felt like she'd been left all alone.

Annie did have a sister in Cincinatti, but Mary was a working mom, with two little children of her own to take care of. Although she tried to be helpful, the added responsibility threatened to overwhelm her. Unwilling to be a burden to Mary and her young and struggling family, Annie kept her distance.

Annie's father was still around in northern Ohio, but he kept his distance. A brother stayed far away in Alaska. She'd had an argument with her father years before, and feelings were hurt on both sides. Annie hadn't spoken with either of them since. For a long time, they didn't even know about her cancer. After they did learn about it, so much time had passed that they didn't know how to reconnect. Annie couldn't even remember what the argument had been about. Either that, or she was unwilling to admit it. I don't

Annie was beautiful, generous, and painfully troubled. I was honored to have a part in helping her find her way, and proud to be her friend.

know what caused their falling out, but it was heartbreaking to see what stubbornness had done to this family. Now, to Annie's way of thinking, it was too great a divide to be bridged. She refused to burden them with her illness. She would go it alone.

"Call them," I urged her one day. "Just say you're sorry. Who cares whose fault it was?"

Annie looked away from me and shook her head sadly. "I can't," she whispered, "It's too hard. Too much has happened."

"Okay, if that's too hard, just tell them that you miss them." I begged her. "Then see where it goes from there." But Annie just

couldn't do it. Because of that, she was left to fight for her life
without the support of her family. Annie chose to go it alone,
facing her end without knowing she was loved. Because she had
no one at home, she turned to others for companionship.

No matter how sick she was, Annie would come down to
Image Insights and ask me to let her help answer the phones. It
seemed to make her feel better, being out and working, so I told
her I was glad to have her there. She did whatever she could to
help out around the shop. I hoped that helping others might
improve Annie's sense of well-being, and even raise her self-
esteem. Seeing that she was loved by people at the shop might
give her the confidence to reach out to her family again.

As time went by, it became apparent that Annie's condition
was not improving. As she became even more ill, Annie asked if
she could move a hospital bed down to the shop. "That way," she
explained, "I can keep on answering the phones for you." As it
was with Ron, I was torn. On the one hand, I thought she ought
to get some rest; on the other, I knew that her work with others
was what kept her going. If I told her to stay home, she would do
it. But she would be miserable and alone, and her condition would
deteriorate faster. We made arrangements for her to continue to
come in. Annie was so pleased. "The only time I really feel good
about myself is when I'm helping other people," she explained. "I
need to be here. I need to do *something* good in my life."

This is more than just a family squabble, I realized. *She thinks
that she's a bad person. She thinks that she's unworthy.* Annie was
laboring under some heavy guilt and pain. I told her, quietly,
"Annie, if you ever need to talk, you can tell me *anything*." I
shrugged, "Or nothing." I smiled at her and took up her hands,
"Maybe, if you talk it out, you'll find that things aren't as bad as
you think." I pressed her hands tightly for a moment and let her
go. I didn't want to push her.

Eventually, Annie did open up; but only just barely. It was
like I had knocked on her door, and she'd cracked it open

enough to peer out—but she wasn't going to open it enough to let anyone all the way in. I learned that when Annie lost her mother, she spun out of control and engaged in a lot of self-destructive behavior. She thought that these were things that God could never forgive her for. Afraid she was going to hell for her misdeeds, Annie was terrified of dying.

As her cancer progressed, Annie knew that the end was inevitable; but still she kept fighting on. Sadly, Annie was not fighting to *stay alive*. Instead, she was fighting to delay death. I don't think Annie believed that she had anything left to live for. She was not proud of her track record and she was certain that God had a low opinion of her. Annie was pretty sure that heaven was not in her future. While staying out of hell might sound like a good idea—it doesn't really give you much to *live* for, does it?

I knew she would find forgiveness, if only she asked. After all, how could she be forgiven if she were unwilling to ask? Oh, she could, certainly. People turn the other cheek, and forgive and forget all the time. But it couldn't mean anything to Annie until she asked for herself. Asking is a sign that you own up to your mistakes, that you want to do better, and that you're ready to move on. It's also the first step to letting go of the past.

It's probably the single greatest example of "ask and you shall receive."

I tried to tell her that, whatever it was that bothered her, she could learn to let it go. All she had to do was ask. But Annie was not so sure. She didn't think that she deserved it. Because of her pain and shame, Annie couldn't see what a special person she really was. She saw only her own perceived flaws and failings. I wanted to help Annie deal with her cancer, but I realized that part of it would be helping her to deal with her spiritual crisis. How would she find a reason to live if she didn't think she deserved to? Annie had to learn that there truly was forgiveness for her, but she wasn't hearing it from me. It was time to bring in the big guns.

Annie had been raised Catholic, so I took her to a Catholic priest for counseling. He tried his best to convince her that she was a good person. The priest pointed out that we all make mistakes. We all do bad things, at one time or another, in our lives. "But the glory of it is that, when we ask for forgiveness, God *will* forgive us," he promised her. "God will keep on loving us, and encouraging us to do better." He made a fine argument that day. When we left, *I was certainly convinced.* Annie was not.

As I drove her home, I could see that Annie was exhausted. Her strength was ebbing, but still she wanted to talk. Annie danced around her subject, skirting at the edges; she wanted so badly to unburden herself. Inside, she truly wanted to find some forgiveness; but no matter what she did, she thought she would never earn it. "There's too much, Gayle," she admitted. "It's not that I made a few dumb mistakes when I was young." Tears slid down her cheeks and she wiped them away. "There was more to it than that." She sat quietly for a long time after that.

I wasn't sure what to do. *Should I draw her out?* I wondered, *or just wait for her?* I thought it might help to talk it out, but, "What did you do?" didn't seem like an appropriate question. It felt more like snooping. *Should she be spilling her guts to me?* I wondered. Obviously, these were serious matters to her—I wasn't sure that it was my business to ask for her confession. In the end, I waited for her. Annie could tell me as much, or as little, as she needed to.

"I haven't been a good person, Gayle," Annie said softly. Then she almost whispered, "He can't forgive it all. Not everything." With that, Annie leaned her head back and closed her eyes. We rode the rest of the way in silence. I wanted to tell her that she was *wrong*, that she *could* find forgiveness—but arguing with her just then did not feel like the right course of action. She wasn't ready to hear it from me. My voice wasn't powerful enough to her.

I drove on quietly, my heart aching for this sad, beautiful young woman. She was convinced that her soul was lost. *Well,* I thought, *if that priest couldn't convince her, maybe the next one can.* I squared up my shoulders. *If we have to see every priest in Kentucky, then we'll just keep on trying.* Annie may have given up on herself, but I hadn't.

Every week, I took her to see a different priest. It always went the same way. Annie listened politely, but she wasn't buying it. With results like this, I was afraid that she would give up and stop trying. But as thin as it was, Annie never lost her thread of hope. She *wanted* to find someone who could help her to believe; so we continued to try. We went through four more priests before Annie found the right one. I'm not sure what he said that was different from the others, but this time it clicked. The light came on and she got it. Annie finally believed that God would forgive her, and I could see it in her face. She actually looked like a great weight had been lifted from her shoulders. Annie walked a little taller, and she smiled a lot more. At last, she was coming to terms with her past, and Annie was at peace with herself.

Christmas was approaching fast, and Annie's health continued to deteriorate. While she had won her spiritual battle, her body was losing its physical one. Even so, Annie bore it well. I knew she didn't have too many days left— Annie knew it too—so I convinced her to call her sister. It was important that she reconnect with her family while she still had time. Annie called, and the conversation with Mary did her spirit some good; but it was quite a physical drain on her. By then, even the smallest chore could be exhausting.

Annie didn't want to be alone that night. She knew her time was growing short. She was on oxygen by then, and she was afraid that she might die in her sleep, with no one there beside her at the end. With no family of her own, and her loved ones out of touch and far away, she truly was all by herself. My boys and I packed our things, and went over to Annie's house to spend the night with her.

We decided to make a holiday slumber party out of our overnight stay. Adam and Nicholas hung Christmas lights all around the living room, and we decorated a tiny tree. After preparing a snack, we all settled in to watch Annie's favorite Christmas movie. No matter how many times she saw it, she couldn't help tearing up. I felt the same way. Together, we all watched Jimmy Stewart and Donna Reed in *It's a Wonderful Life*. We laughed, and cried, and stayed up late. Then we fell asleep on the floor around Annie, and she slept soundly and peacefully on the couch. It was a good night for her, and for us.

Annie spent the month of January in the hospital; but after several weeks there, she'd had enough. If she was running out of time, she wanted to spend her last days in familiar surroundings. Annie hadn't been home long, when she called and asked if I would bring her Communion. I packed up my things, stopped by the church, and headed over to Annie's house. I knocked softly on the door and started to let myself in. Before I could push open the door, it swung open and I found myself face-to-face with a strange man who looked like he had been up all night. Anxiously, I introduced myself. "Hello," the man almost whispered to me, "I'm Annie's brother." Over his shoulder, I could see another man in the room, an older man, but one who was definitely cut from the same cloth.

"How's she doing?" I asked, hoping for the best but expecting the worst. As I walked through the door, I saw that Annie's bed had been moved into her living room. Her strength was failing rapidly and she could no longer climb the stairs to her bedroom.

"She's in and out." Annie's brother tried on a half-hearted smile, but it died on his lips. "She's . . ." his words trailed off and he simply shook his head. It was worse than I'd feared.

Annie's brother took me over to meet their father. I offered my hand and introduced myself again. Annie's father smiled gratefully at me. "Good to know you, Gayle," he squeezed my hand. "Annie told her sister, Mary, all about you. Then Mary told me." He took my hand in both of his and said, "Thank you for everything you've done for my daughter." Beyond them, in the living room, I could see Annie lying in her bed; a priest stood at her side, speaking softly. I recognized him. It wasn't just "a" priest, it was "the" priest—the one who finally convinced Annie that God had a place for her. I realized then that I wouldn't need my Communion set.

"Please don't thank me," I replied. "It's been my pleasure to spend time with Annie. It is my honor to be her friend. She's really a wonderful lady."

Annie's father chewed on the inside of his lip as his eyes welled up with tears. "I can't believe she's dying . . . " He shook his head as he looked down at the floor. ". . . I didn't know." Tears rolled down his cheeks, and he whispered, "I *should* have known. We left as soon as I found out."

The three of us moved close to Annie then, so that I might see her; but she was in and out of consciousness. Now that we were closer to her, I recognized the priest's soft words. He was giving Annie the Last Rites.

We waited quietly until he had finished, and then we sat down close to Annie's bed and waited for her to come around again. I told Annie's father about our last few months together— about the help Annie had given me at the shop, and about our quest for the perfect priest. I explained what little I knew about Annie's feelings of guilt and unworthiness, and told him of her search for forgiveness. "Annie found it," I finished, "she really seems to be at peace with herself."

I wasn't able to give Annie her Communion that day, but her father gratefully took it from me. Then he bared his soul to me, and confessed his regrets. He was so sure that he'd been a bad father. I don't know everything that happened between them, but Annie's father was as full of guilt and shame as Annie herself had been. Like her, he didn't believe he deserved forgiveness.

"It's all okay," I told him, "because Annie has forgiven you. And she knows that you forgive her, too." He lifted his head at that, and I could see the faintest glimmer of hope in his eyes. "The past doesn't matter anymore," I encouraged him. "All that matters is today." He seemed to draw a little strength from the words, so I asked, "Would you like to tell her how you feel?" He nodded.

Annie still lay resting with her eyes closed; but Annie's father stepped over to her bed, and stood beside her. He took her hand and was, for a moment, unable to speak. Finally, he choked out, "Annie . . . girl?"

Her eyes opened and immediately filled with tears. Annie had not been completely coherent that day, though her response suggested that she was all there now. From the other side of the bed, I leaned in. "Annie, your dad is here. He wants to talk." I asked her, "Do you know why?" There were more tears then, but she nodded and gave a tiny smile. I smiled back, "Did you hear what we were talking about?" Her smile grew a little wider then, and she nodded again. "Good," I told her, and stepped back to give them some room.

Annie's father whispered soft words to her, and I could see her tiny nods and barely-breathed responses. Whatever their troubles had been, she forgave him that day. Over the course of the day, the rest of Annie's family arrived to share her last moments and offer what comfort they could. While it is a tragedy that it couldn't have happened sooner, a lot of old wounds were healed that day. Annie spent her last hours here knowing she was no longer alone.

It snowed a lot that day and there was a lot of fresh powder on the ground. At a break in the storm, most of the family went outside and laid down in the snow. They covered the front yard in snow angels. When they went back inside, one of them told Annie what they had done. "The angels are here now." A few minutes later, she was gone.

Annie was a sweet, beautiful, generous girl. I saw how good she was, as she helped others at the shop. Even as her strength was failing, she was forever giving. I hope Annie finally realized just how wonderful she truly was. I tried to let her know.

Suffering so much pain, physically and spiritually, Annie thought she might find redemption in helping others. It makes me proud to know that I was a help to her—that I had a part in guiding her to that redemption. How many people can say that they actually walked through the life of another in such a way? It was a joy to see her lay her spiritual burden aside. I watched her leave her pains and fears behind as she took her first steps into a new life with Jesus. I miss Annie, but I know she's doing far better now than when she was here. It was a painful time. It was also a rewarding time. I know Annie felt the same way.

Not every story involved such pain and sadness. Not every story involved a patient, either. One of my most dedicated volunteers was a man who had no connection at all to Image Insights, until he stepped through our door. Neither a client, nor a relative of one, Jerry came in one day, tagging along behind an accountant. I had finally scheduled a meeting with a real professional, to see if we could straighten out the mess.

Our volunteers came from all walks of life. You name it, they did it. Except for one thing—accounting. I never ran into anyone who could teach me about bookkeeping. And boy, did I need it! To say that I had no head for numbers would be putting it kindly. Numbers frustrated me. They pained me. They aggravated me beyond the capacity for rational thought. Naturally, I hid from them.

So there I was, still taking care of clients by the boatload— and still drowning in a sea of paperwork. Intellectually, I understood how important the bookkeeping was; but it never *felt* as important as taking care of my clients did. And there were *always* patients to take care of. So I was forever "getting by," doing just enough to keep my head above water. It was no way to do things. I was probably making all kinds of mistakes that were costing me money. I knew I needed an accountant to help get my records in order. A professional would get things ship-shape and working smoothly; but I knew it would cost me. Still, what had it cost to *not* have one?

I cracked, and called in a pro. The accountant came down to my office promptly, bringing along Jerry to help evaluate my sit-uation. Jerry, it turned out, had a head for numbers *and* a head for computers—something else I was woefully unsuited for. I showed them where everything was—basically, I pointed to the mess—and apologized for the condition it was in. It was really quite embarrassing. "Don't worry about it," the accountant said, shaking her head; then she shrugged, "I've seen worse." As she and Jerry went about their business, assessing the sad state of my affairs, I returned to work.

That afternoon, I sat down with the accountant and Jerry, and we discussed what had to be done. Image Insights was a mess. It was worse than I thought. It would take a lot of work on their part—and it was going to add up. I blew out a big sigh as I tried to decide what to do next. It was the end of a long day, I was tired, and this would be a painful and unpleasant decision.

Who knew that business was so full of Catch-22s? If the shop was ever going to start making money, then I had to hire an accountant. But hiring an accountant would cost me more than a pretty penny. *I should make the smart decision,* I thought. *Bring the pro on board.* But I was worried. What if the extra expense cost me an employee? What if I had to cut back on service to my clients? What if I had to say "no" to someone in need? But I couldn't go on faking it as a bookkeeper. I had to make a decision.

I was literally saved by the bell. A woman rushed through the door and into my store. She apologized, breathlessly, for showing up at the end of the day. Her husband had surprised her with an invitation to dinner that evening—dinner with his boss. She wanted badly to make a good impression, but she was a wreck. I could see how important it was to her. She was half

When life gives you lemons. . .

Comfort yourself!

Set aside time each
day to give your body a
chance to relax and
restore itself.

excited, half frantic, and another half terrified that her illness
might ruin the evening.

"I know it's a lot of work for so late in the day," she pleaded desperately, "but I'm not looking, or feeling, my best these
days." She looked small, mousy, and bedraggled. The only
impression she would make would be that of pity; her treatments had badly beaten her up. "I just don't think I can handle
it on my own," she finished bleakly. Then she fixed me with an
extraordinarily sad, hangdog look. I've seen Basset Hounds that
looked more perky.

It was my call to action—a patient needed me.

I directed her to a chair, and turned back to the accountant.
"Thank you for looking things over," I said, "but I don't think I
can afford your help just yet. I'm so sorry that I wasted your time
today." Nodding, she shook my hand, wished me a good night,
and left. I expected Jerry to tag right along with her. Instead, he
got up and returned to my office. I was a little nonplussed by

that, and felt a tad uneasy. After all, I didn't really know who Jerry was, or why he had stayed. But I did have a client to attend to, so I got down to business.

By now, I was pretty darned good at my job—even if I do say so myself. I put that nice lady back together again like there was nothing to it—I could almost have done it blindfolded. With a whirlwind of make up and brushes, my client was looking sassy, stylish, and sophisticated in very short order. She went from shell-shocked POW to glamorous VIP in just twenty minutes.

Jerry emerged from my office just as she was preparing to leave. Holding her head high, she flashed him a dazzling smile, tossed her hair, and said, "I hope you both have a *wonderful evening.*" Jerry almost tripped over his tongue. She looked *goooood.* In fact, she looked spectacular. That woman was glowing, inside and out. Jerry just stared at her, and his mouth opened and closed a few times—almost like a goldfish. Hands hanging at his sides, he watched her walk out the door. Once she was gone, Jerry finally managed a whispered, "bye."

Still staring at the door, he asked me, "Was that really the same woman who came in here a few minutes ago?"

I couldn't help smiling at the stunned look on his face. "Yes, it was," I laughed. "One and the same."

Jerry remained silent for a long time. "Wow," he finally said. "Amazing."

Then he turned away from the door and looked at me. "I'll be back in the morning, Gayle," he said. "It's time you stepped into the 20th century and got computerized. It'll help you to be better organized."

I shook my head and smiled. "I appreciate any advice you can share, Jerry; but I can't afford to pay you." I snorted a little laugh. "I certainly can't afford a *computer.*" Besides being horrifically expensive back then, I hadn't the faintest idea how to use one.

Jerry smiled back and said, "I'll see you tomorrow, Gayle."

As promised, Jerry returned the next day, carrying a keyboard, a monitor, and a computer. I was suitably impressed. They didn't exactly give away computers in those days—not like they do now. I was also a tad intimidated. Technology and I had never been best friends. Ours was more of a feuding relationship, a little Hatfield and McCoy. I expressed my amazement, then told him, "Jerry, I don't even know how to turn one of those things on!"

"Don't worry about a thing," Jerry said, as he set down his burden. "I'll enter everything into the computer." I started fretting about money then, but he raised his hands to stop me. He shook his head, "This isn't going to cost you a dime. I'll have you running a modern professional business soon." I tried to protest, but he continued, "Just like that lady last night, we're going to do a makeover." He grinned, "Of course, this one may take a little longer." I was so taken aback by his kindness, that I didn't know what to say. After all, *we'd only just met—yesterday!* It was my turn to stand there, stunned and amazed, looking like a goldfish, while Jerry gathered up his equipment and headed for my office.

Jerry kept coming back, day after day, for three weeks or more. At first, it was to organize and enter the information into the computer. After that, he spent his time teaching me how to maintain an effective record-keeping system for the business. I didn't understand why he was putting so much time and money into Image Insights. *How does someone do that?* I wondered. *How can he afford to be here, giving away his time and talent like this?* Jerry never explained why he continued to return; but every day he was there, hard at work.

It wasn't until much later that I understood. I was his version of the American Cancer Society. Even though he was busy—and how could he not be, a man of his talents?—he came in anyway. Image Insights was in disarray, and in desperate need. He had the skills to help. We were his charitable cause. As far as I know, Jerry hadn't lost anyone to cancer. He had no direct, emotional connection. He was simply doing it because it felt like the right thing to do. How blessed I was to have Jerry's help, and how grateful I remain. One day, he drops in, backing up an accountant to do a damage control assessment. The next day, he is single-handedly updating and modernizing the entire business. It was amazing.

Several weeks later, Jerry pulled me aside and said softly, "Gayle, I swore I'd never get back into the medical business. It's just too stressful." His voice rose, "I *promised* myself I'd stay out of it." He paused for a moment, and a corner of his mouth lifted into a wry grin. "But for some reason, I know I'm supposed to be here to help."

I smiled and was about to offer my thanks, when he frowned. "The thing is," he continued, "I've been reviewing your records. You shouldn't even *be in business* right now, Gayle. Everything is in such a financial mess that I don't know how you've kept the doors open as long as you have. It seems impossible!" He finally noticed my growing look of alarm, because he stopped laying it on so thick. "You provide a wonderful service to these people, but I'm just not sure how you manage," he finished politely.

And I'd thought I was doing pretty well! I sighed, *I guess not!* Yeah, I knew that things were a mess; but I'd thought I was making progress. Okay, sure, I was forever struggling to pay my bills, and I never took home a paycheck. That's not so good. And yes, I was constantly robbing Peter to pay Paul, juggling checks and bills to stay afloat and risking everything to get my clients whatever they needed. So maybe things weren't exactly rock solid, but Jerry hadn't told me anything I didn't already know.

He was just trying to help, I knew that. But when someone, who knows what he's talking about, tells you that you're a financial disaster—that's when you really start to worry. I had worried plenty before, but now it was official. According to experts, I had good reason to stress out!

Is the glass half-full, or half-empty? I had always been a glass-half-full kind of girl. I'd always tried to walk on the sunny side of the street. I took lemons and made lemonade. I looked for the silver lining on a cloudy day. So I reviewed Jerry's comments in my head, ". . . shouldn't be in business . . . Everything is a financial mess . . . don't know how you've kept the doors open . . . it's impossible." *Well, where is the silver lining in that?* Talk about blowing the wind out of your sails, I suddenly felt like I'd been paddling hard and going nowhere.

Jerry left with his customary, "I'll see you tomorrow," so I began closing up and turning off the lights. I sat there for a moment, in the near dark, and looked around the shop that I loved so much. I thought about all of the people who depended on me. "This does not look good," I sighed to myself. Keeping the doors open *was* a daily struggle, and I wondered again how much longer I

Jerry Decker is a truly kind man, as talented with numbers and computers as he is generous. Incredibly, unbelievably so.

could hold on. Nothing like a bad report card to sap your self-confidence. I was exhausted when I finally locked the door and headed for home.

verything always looks better in the morning, I thought. Still, I wasn't sure what to expect when I went in to Image Insights the next day. *What kind of bomb will Jerry drop on me today?* I wondered. I had been on the verge of losing the store since the first day I'd opened the doors. It was a way of life to me. But I was still there.

I knew Jerry thought that I was crazy to hold on to a business that wasn't making me a cent. But he didn't understand what drove me to continue. I decided that I would explain to him that I wasn't in it for the money. I was in it to help people, simple as that. If scraping by was the best I could hope for, then that would have to do. One way or another, I planned to stay on the job for as long as God wanted me to.

I spent the morning building up a little speech in my head, running over the words until I was ready to explain it all to Jerry. I had it all planned out. I would tell him *why* I was still in business. I'd show him that I would *stay* in business. My spirit and fire would surely triumph over his niggling financial details. They *had* to. I had people to take care of.

When Jerry came into the shop, I squared my shoulders, took a deep breath, and strode over to confront him. *No time like the present,* I thought. "Jerry," I said, "I just wanted to tell you . . ."

As soon as I started to speak, Jerry calmly interrupted me. "I'm going to donate $45,000 to Image Insights to keep you going."

My mouth fell open, and my words died in my throat. Out came some small, unintelligible sound. "I . . . uh . . . " *Did I just hear him right?* I licked my lips and took another breath to try again, "I . . ." But nothing else came out—not from my mouth anyway. Tears started flowing then and I began to cry instead. I was overwhelmed and didn't know what else to do!

After a few minutes of this, I finally calmed down enough to try to express my appreciation. "I had a big old head of steam worked up," I laughed, "and I was going to *convince you* that I could keep this thing going. That somehow, I would get past this, and . . ." I paused for a breath, ". . . and then you come in and do *this* . . ." I started crying again. Blubbering, really, as I told him, "You can't know what this will mean for our patients. How many people this will help . . ." I sniffled and wiped my nose. "I don't know how I'll be able to repay you."

Jerry gave me a hug, as much to calm me down as to hide his embarrassment. He had teared up too, at my reaction. He said, "I don't really want the money back. What you do here is important, Gayle. I want to help you keep on doing it."

I was speechless again, and quite out of breath—*talk about your emotional roller coasters!* Jerry gave me a little pat on the back and pulled out a chair for me. I took it gratefully. Then he walked back to my office and got to work.

What can you say about that?

If it seems like I spent a lot of time with my mouth hanging open in astonishment, it's because *I did.* People were constantly amazing me. You might think, after a while, that I would have become a little jaded. After so much had happened, both good and bad, nothing should have surprised me anymore. But just when I thought I'd seen it all, someone would surprise me again.

The future of Image Insights would have been completely different if not for Jerry. He not only provided the funds that kept the company alive, he also stayed on for two more years, organizing and computerizing everything. Jerry brought our office out of the Stone Age and into the Space Age, and helped us to grow into a more professional organization. His work allowed Image Insights to stand on a firmer foundation than ever before.

Up until then, Image Insights was a one-woman show—with a lot of help from the staff and my generous volunteers. But I had to be there every day. Otherwise, it would be like the *I Love Lucy Show* without Lucy. Yes, there were a lot of people there to help; but if I were sick, or out of action for more than a short time, there would be nothing left to do. By creating a more orderly and efficient structure, Jerry freed me up to spend more time with my customers. So while Jerry's financial help had been staggeringly generous, it was all of his hard work that proved truly priceless. The company would not have survived, and thrived, without him.

As if that weren't enough, Jerry proved that he wasn't afraid to get his hands dirty either. No task was too big, or too small. Even though we'd just moved into our larger office, it quickly became apparent that we were outgrowing our space again. With Jerry leading the way, we were able to move into another location. This one had more room for us and better parking for the clients. And just as before, an army of volunteers formed up to get the job done.

Jerry also convinced much of his family, especially his father, Carl, to get involved in the store. They worked tirelessly to help me remodel and repaint. They installed new shampoo bowls and even moved walls. If something needed fixing, they fixed it. If it didn't, then they made it better. They were such a blessing to me.

Sometimes I wondered what drove people like Jerry to do as they did. My volunteers would go so far beyond the call of duty; and they worked without expectation of reward. They accomplished miracles, great and small, as they worked to help those who were suffering. Day by day, I depended on those generous people, and I could not have run Image Insights without them. In the end, I always understood that it was just as Rita said. I continued to help the people that God sent; so He continued to send the people that I would need. I kept my promise, so He kept Rita's. I thanked God everyday for their help. I wonder if my volunteers understood that they were the answer to my prayers—literally, the answer to my prayers. I hope that they got as much out of the bargain as I did.

You know that old saying about it being better to give than to receive? It's a Bible verse; the Apostle Paul was quoting Jesus Himself. "In everything I did, I showed you that by this kind of hard work we must help the weak, remembering the words the Lord Jesus himself said: 'It is more blessed to give than to receive.'" (*Acts 20:35*) I'm not sure I can say which is better. I kept on trying to give, but there was always a volunteer who was ready to one-up me. Not by design, they did it purely out of generosity of spirit. No matter how much I tried to do, there was always someone willing to give a little more. But I guess that's the point, isn't it?

13

Lemon Blossoms

Things were humming along fairly smoothly for Image Insights. With help from so many generous people, how could we not? Oh, we weren't rolling in dough, or anything; but Image Insights was getting the job done. We were taking care of more clients than ever before, and I was able to do it without fretting over so many financial details. The new, larger shop accommodated a larger clientele, and I had a good, solid staff to help them. We were maxed out, but in a good way. The only way we could help any more people would be through additional locations. To reach more clients, we would have to cast our net a little wider.

Only one problem, new locations are expensive. It had taken a long time to get this one on its feet. There was no way I could afford the overhead on yet another store. *Well,* I thought, *if I can't afford another shop, then I'll have to get by with the one I have.* We'd survived this long by making-do, so we would just have to wing it a little bit longer.

In the beginning, the majority of my clients were locals, mostly from the northern Kentucky and greater Cincinnati area. They came down to the store to get their wigs or prostheses, with a doctor's promise that we would take care of all of their needs. If the doctors were going to promise, then we had to deliver—and we did. As time went on, and our reputation grew, I began to see clients from farther and farther away.

A lot of these people were really sick. Many of the patients had two daily treatments to undergo. They would come into the shop, between their appointments, with their emesis basins and cold washcloths in tow. That way, they were properly equipped if they found themselves needing to throw-up, but without a convenient restroom nearby. *Can you image feeling that sick? All of the time?* Things may be better now, but in the late 80s and early 90s, this is the way things were done.

It was always hard to see people feeling so poorly. I know, when I'm sick, I want nothing more than to go home and go to bed. When you feel bad, there's nothing better than being pampered or getting some much needed rest. These folks didn't have that luxury. Instead, they were sitting in one of my chairs, struggling bravely through a fitting, and hoping that they didn't need to use that bowl. This was not like a stop at the salon for a quick cut or manicure. They were often long sittings, and many of the clients felt miserable during the entire process. Even so, they were glad to be there, and they tried their best not to let their suffering show. I understood how much pain they were in, and found their stoicism inspiring, and heartbreaking, at the same time.

Often my poor, worn-out clients would have to come back again a week later to pick up their wig. If the wig was not one that we kept in stock, then the first visit was only for fitting and ordering. Then, once the wig arrived, they had to come back to pick it up. At that point, we would also take care of any trimming or adjusting that was needed. However, that could also mean a long second session in the chair, as well as the additional trip. I hated asking them to do that. After all, our job was to make things easier on them, to save them the extra trips.

As time went by, I found myself caring for lots of patients from next-door Indiana. Many of these people lived way out in the rural areas. They had a long trip to make to get into my office. When you are that sick, having to make the trip twice is a tall order. Since I plainly couldn't afford another store in Indiana, I cobbled together a compromise. *Who needs another shop?* I thought. *We'll go mobile.*

The idea occurred to me after one of my clients asked for a favor. She wondered if I might meet her at a convenience store that sat just over the border, in Indiana. I knew this would make it a lot easier on her, so I agreed. It was a nice drive, and a welcome break after a week of being cooped up inside the store. We passed the word to our Indiana clients: on Saturdays, I would make the drive into Indiana a regular part of my schedule. My Indiana clients could pick up their supplies at the quick-stop just across the Indiana state line. I didn't know my way around the state, but I did know where that little store was. Since it was easy to find, the parking lot made as good a meeting place as any.

The trade-offs had to be on weekends—our meeting spot was 40 minutes away. The insurance companies were not about to pay for a delivery service, and to go during the week would rob my other customers, and the store, of my time. So, every Saturday, when I finished with my clients, I would pack up any products that were going to Indiana and I'd hit the road. After a little while, I'd pull in to the convenience store parking lot and pop my trunk. I'm sure the people inside that quick-stop thought I was crazy. We probably looked like drug dealers—or moonshiners handing out cases of hooch.

I had visions of someone thinking just that, and calling the cops. Singing to myself, "Bad boys, bad boys. Whatcha gonna do?" I would imagine myself surrounded by wailing police cars, bathed in flashing red and blue light. A bullhorn blares, "Police! Put *down* the box! Step *away* from the vehicle!" Then I'd imagine the surprise on their faces when they jimmied open the trunk to find nothing but wigs and prostheses.

Waiting in a parking lot can be boring.

Of course, no one ever called the police. My clients would drive up and I would give them the things they needed. They were happy and grateful. Then they turned around and drove home. Other than in my head, there was no excitement; but it was a good arrangement for all of us. It made things easier on my customers and I felt better for taking good care of them.

y clients and I did our little drive-by wiggings for quite a while, but eventually the word got out on the street. I was busted.

Late one day at the office, the phone rang. In a no-nonsense voice, a secretary informed me that she had a call from the head administrator of the Dearborn County Hospital in Indiana. "Hold, please," she ordered tersely. *Uh oh!* I thought, *she sounded serious.* While I waited, my mind raced. *I've never been there, don't know anyone there . . . I wonder what this guy wants?*

I didn't have to wonder long. "I think we need to talk, Gayle," the administrator said sternly, when he came on the line. "We need to make you legal."

You got the wrong girl! My imagination fired, *I never set foot in Dearborn! I've been framed!* What can I say? It had been a long day.

The administrator began speaking and I focused in. He calmly introduced himself as Mr. Dean. *Oh, how appropriate,* I thought in another momentary lapse. Administrator Dean had simply called to schedule a meeting with me. I did have a lot of patients from Indiana by then, so I assumed he was looking for more information about Image Insights. *I'll have to put together a package for him,* I thought. I agreed to see him, and he gave me directions to the hospital. We set up a time for the following week.

"I've heard a great deal about you," Mr. Dean said, when he welcomed me into his office the next week. "You know," he continued, "there are patients all across southern Indiana telling their doctors about the *drive-by wig woman.*" I started grinning as he went on. "It seems that she's

Russell Dean headed up Dearborn County Hospital, where he offered me free office space to help us reach out to his patients.

meeting with patients and helping them with their products—right out of the trunk of her car! At a quicky-mart no less!" He folded his hands and raised his eyebrows. "You wouldn't know anything about that, would you?"

I started to laugh. *Busted.*

"I thought so," Mr. Dean smiled. "I'm gonna make you an offer you can't refuse." And then he did exactly that. Mr. Dean asked if I'd like to have an office right there in the hospital. It was connected directly to their cancer center, and he was willing to give it to me free of charge.

"Did you say *free of charge?!*" I asked, stunned.

"You bet I did," he grinned back at me.

I started babbling excitedly. Since the office was connected to their cancer center, the patients could get help right away. In privacy. And they wouldn't have to drive 40 minutes to get it! Mr. Dean just smiled and nodded patiently, as I told him everything that he already knew.

I remembered Rita telling me, "When you don't feel well, you don't want to run around to a bunch of different places to get the things you need." There was no one-stop shop for the people in Indiana. They didn't have a Lemonade Stand or an Image Insights nearby to turn to.

Well, they did now.

When I walked out of that hospital, I was walking on air. *I can't believe this,* I thought. *I have a new office! A brand new office! A FREE brand new office.* I started laughing out loud. *No more parking lot drop offs. No more drive-by wiggings!* I couldn't believe my good fortune, and I said a quick prayer of thanks.

I hadn't even been looking for such a place. Dreaming, sure, but not looking. Yes, I wanted another shop; but I *knew* it wouldn't happen anytime soon. I knew it for sure. There wasn't the money for it. If I had to do business out of the trunk of an old Chevy, then so be it. Just goes to show you; I guess I didn't *know* so much after all.

It sure helps to have people say nice things about you; because just like that, I opened up my second location. Mr. Dean handed me a wonderful opportunity—one my competitors would gladly have paid for. Yet, he'd given it to me for free. He called it "community service." I thought it was a miracle. God truly works in strange and wondrous ways. One day I'm dealing wigs out of the trunk of my car. The next day, I have a second location at the Dearborn County Hospital.

I began spending a half day every week at the Dearborn County Hospital, taking care of my Indiana clients. With staff people like Bill and Christie, and volunteers like Jerry, to rely on, I knew that the main store was in good hands. The shop could get by without me for a little while. As time went on, things got busier and busier at our little shop in Indiana. Every week, Bill and

Christie would pick a day to drive in and help me take care of our people out there. I couldn't have managed it without them.

Sometimes, over the days ahead, I still couldn't believe how we'd been blessed. I'd almost have to pinch myself. Two stores. Wow. Who'd have thought it was possible!

It would probably surprise most people to realize it, but even after being in business for seven years, I still had not made in onto Easy Street. We were doing better than ever—the business was growing and we were always busy—but somehow there was still never enough to go around. One might think, with the generous benefactors, my hard-working volunteers, and the two store locations, that my family and I would have been living the high-life by then. But if there ever was a road to Easy Street, I never found it in my *Thomas Guide*.

We had added another zero to the numbers in the income column. The trouble was, we'd added that same zero to the numbers in the expense column, too. Every time our fortunes picked up, it became an opportunity to help more clients—especially those in dire need. If we had a good month, most of our income went right back into helping customers, some of it went into the business, and if there was anything left, some of that went home. Oh sure, things had picked up a little for me and the boys. We had moved out of the apartment and rented a little house; but it was nothing fancy. There was certainly no Mercedes sitting in the driveway. We were just one more little family, working hard and getting by.

After seeing so many patients, one thing I'd learned was that they were people, just like us. They were working for a living, and getting by; living their lives as the parents, grandparents, brothers, sisters, friends, or little children that they were. Then, all of a sudden, they're told that they have cancer. One of two things was going to happen: they would either get through it, or die from it. And if they got through it, it would probably happen only after a lot of pain and struggle.

How's *that* for a wake-up call? Talk about throwing a monkey wrench into the works.

Besides being sick, many of these people would lose their hair, eyelashes, and eyebrows. Some of the women would lose a breast. Or two. Sometimes, as a complication, a patient would experience an incredible swelling in their arms or legs, known as lymphodema. It is painful and very debilitating. Frightening things were going to happen to their bodies; things that they'd never dreamed of. This was all going to happen *in addition* to their normal daily struggles of life. It's hard to be concerned about the laundry when your hair is falling out. It's hard to worry about the cable bill when you've just lost a breast.

A fair percentage of my clients had no money left to pay for our services. It was all gone. They had no way to pay for wigs, breast prostheses, bras, or other post-surgical products. Their treatments had wiped them out—physically and financially. There was usually little or nothing left for "recovery". Few insurance companies would even consider covering these "non-essential" items. If they did, they paid only minimal amounts.

Although I was ostensibly running a business, that business also involved mercy. I often found myself giving of my time and energy for free. That, I didn't really mind, it was *my* time and energy to give. The difficulty came when I had to give products away. Not that it was difficult *to do,* it wasn't. It was difficult to *reconcile* financially. Add in the day-to-day costs of operating a business, and the result was that funds were usually in short supply. Helping my customers was very rewarding, spiritually; but balancing the books was *never* any fun. I suppose a "by the numbers" kind of businessman would have questioned my priorities. That may be, but I thought my priorities were fine just the way they were. In the end, it really didn't matter what anyone thought, because I knew in my heart that I was supposed to be doing this.

My family would try to warn me, "You're never going to stay in business; you give too much away." But they weren't standing there when the patients came in—completely bald, nothing left of their self-esteem—looking desperately for a little help. A thin ray of hope had led them to me. They needed my help; and if I had a way to do it, I wasn't going to deny them. How could I?

One rainy day, I was asked to meet a woman at Children's Hospital. I drove across town through the rain. When I arrived, I found my way to the patient's room. There, I saw a little five-year-old girl playing happily away on her bed. Her mother was on the phone, so I waited patiently and watched the little girl make up stories with her toys. She seemed so happy in her imaginary world. As I watched, I could hear her mother telling someone about how her daughter was sick all the time now. As I listened, I learned the truth of her condition. This sweet, beautiful, happy young child had only a few more weeks, maybe a month, left to live.

I hadn't even spoken to the mother yet, when it dawned on me why I was there. Basically, I'd been asked to come do a wig for her funeral. When I realized that, it utterly and completely broke my heart. I bit down hard on the inside of my mouth to prevent a sob from escaping my lips. It wouldn't do that little girl much good to see the nice lady suddenly burst out crying. *How does a mother have the strength to make such arrangements?* I wondered, *How could she even bear to look that far ahead?*

That little five-year-old was so happy and playful. She didn't have a hair on her head, but she didn't care. Her world was so small. All she wanted to do was play, and learn, and spend time with her mommy. That's all she needed. What difference did a little hair on her head make?

But it mattered to her mother; so we did our fitting right there and then. In those days, there were very few nice wigs made specially for children. (That there should be any at all is a heartbreaking thought.) I had to special order this one. I knew that this family didn't have the money to pay for a wig like that.

It was expensive. But that didn't matter. The finished product was gorgeous and it looked beautiful on her.

How on earth do you walk away from something like that? How do you say, "No, I'm sorry. I can't help you." Or, "No, it's not covered."

Times like that, money didn't seem very important. So, despite the voices of my family and friends pleading with me to stop giving products away, I did it anyway. It's not that they were being cold-hearted with their advice. They had my best interests at heart. After all, how could I continue to help people if I went out of business?

Logically, their advice made sense. But it seemed like, the more they said it, the more God sent in people who couldn't afford the things they needed. I couldn't just turn them away. Their problems made mine seem pretty darned small. So I listened attentively to the advice that everyone gave. Then I continued to do what I knew was right.

A few months later, I got another important phone call. This one came from a lady by the name of Helen. She was one of my successful competitors in Glendale, Ohio— basically, on the other side of town. Helen told me that she would be closing down her store in Glendale soon, for personal reasons. I expressed some sympathy, and was about to wish her luck, when she dropped her bomb on me. Helen asked if I would be interested in buying her store!

Interested? Of course I'm interested! I thought, *but "interested" and "able" are two different things.* "As much as I'd like to say 'yes'," I told her, "I don't have the money to buy another business."

"Let's talk about it first," Helen said. "Come on over, and we'll see what we can cook up."

I drove up to meet her that very day. Helen's store was about 40 minutes away from my Covington location, so I was there before lunchtime. I'd never been to Glendale before, but it turned out to be a beautiful little town. *I could stand to spend a little time here,* I thought. We met at the shop, and Helen took me to a nearby restaurant for a bite of lunch. There, we could talk about our respective situations, and see if we could come up with a solution that suited us both.

Helen had to get out of her business immediately; but she was very concerned about her clients. She wanted to make sure that they were well cared for. It seems that Image Insights had developed quite a good reputation; so she knew that she was safe in calling me. Helen had been a competitor, as dedicated to her business as I was to mine. Now that she had to leave it, she was saying that she trusted me with her clients. She couldn't have paid me a higher compliment than that. Once again, I was amazed at how God had brought us together. I actually dared to hope that we might work something out.

We talked about business for a while, so Helen knew I wasn't making any *real* money at Image Insights. She understood why, too. Helen knew what it was like to give away products or services when someone was in need. She knew what it did to the bottom line as well. Perhaps that's why she made the decision she did. In the end, Helen agreed to sell me her client list for $1,500. She also allowed me to take over the space pretty much as it stood.

Helen had been up and running in Glendale for several years. She had a strong client base in place, and she was practically handing me a working operation. It was smaller than Image Insights, but it was already operating smoothly. I wouldn't have to build it up from scratch. There were also two nice ladies who worked for her in the store, and both wanted to remain. However, as good as Helen's deal was, I wasn't any richer now than I'd been when I walked in. My pockets were nearly empty and my accounts were not much better. Sadly, I realized that I couldn't afford to keep them both. The best I could do would be one.

Right then and there, Helen and I wrote up an agreement by hand on a piece of paper. We agreed that I would buy her client

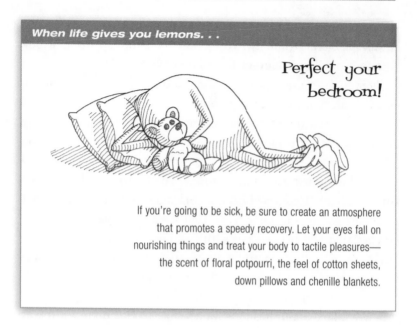

When life gives you lemons. . .

Perfect your
bedroom!

If you're going to be sick, be sure to create an atmosphere
that promotes a speedy recovery. Let your eyes fall on
nourishing things and treat your body to tactile pleasures—
the scent of floral potpourri, the feel of cotton sheets,
down pillows and chenille blankets.

list for the price she asked. We also agreed that, within the next
few weeks, I would take over her shop so that she could move on.

We left the restaurant and drove back to her Glendale store.
It was snowing so hard you could barely see your hand in front
of your face. It may have been freezing outside, but I felt warm
and toasty on the inside. I marveled once again at the hand of
God in everything. Here was my competitor, driving me back to
her old store—and *my* new one! Helen had been around these
parts long before I had, she was the old pro; but she'd come to
me for help. Out of the blue, she had called, looking to make a
deal. By helping to solve her problem, I suddenly had a *third*
location! It was hard to believe that it was really happening.

We pulled up to the Glendale store to find a woman standing outside. With her nose pressed up against the glass, she was
peering in, looking for someone. Helen got out of the car, and
asked, "Can I help you?" As she did, she unhooked an extra key
from her keychain.

"Hi, my name's Edna," the woman replied. "I heard this shop was getting ready to close, so I came to see about buying it." As it turns out, she owned a competing business on the far side of Cincinnati, and she was looking to expand. Helen and I looked at each other. I raised my eyebrows, not sure what would happen next. Helen just smiled and handed me the key. Then she said to Edna, "Well, I'm sorry. I just sold this business."

I'm pretty sure that Helen would have made more money if she'd sold to Edna instead. In fact, I *know* she would have. But she was a woman of her word, and clearly wasn't in the business just for the money. It was important to Helen that her clients were well taken care of. It had to be by someone who would care for them as much as she did. I'm proud to say that she'd decided that person was me.

The changeover went smoothly and quickly, and before I knew it, I had a *third* location of Image Insights in beautiful downtown Glendale, Ohio. The employee I'd been able to keep was a wonderful lady. She had been with Helen for several years, and did a really fine job with the patients there. She was a natural addition to Image Insights, and everything fit together like it had been planned that way from the start.

There was one thing that Helen had done differently, and as time passed, we knew we would have to make some changes. Up until then, the Glendale store had provided only breast prostheses and bras. They did not carry wigs, or provide makeup and skin care. Well, Image Insights was about more than just selling products. We were there to provide care—full service, from top to bottom, inside and out. Clients were supposed to leave Image Insights looking like a million bucks, and feeling even better. They were not supposed to leave the way they came in, with nothing but a shopping bag in their hand. It was time to convert Glendale into a full service shop.

By late spring, remodeling had begun in earnest. Jerry and his father, Carl, once again went beyond the call of duty in their extraordinary efforts to get the job done. Also there to help was Saundra, my best friend and constant companion. She was still engaged in her own war with cancer, so I was forever inspired by her ability to find the

Jerry Decker's father, Carl, was another wonderful, generous man. The old saying is all too true, the apple doesn't fall far from the tree.

strength and energy to help me. *Saundra, Jerry, Carl . . .,* sometimes I wondered, *What did I ever do to deserve such friends?* They were such angels, in the truest sense of the word. And there were many others like them.

After one particulary long day of hammering, painting, and moving furniture, Saundra and I were driving home in my old car. It had been a hot and humid summer day and my tired Chevy had no working air-conditioner. After all of the work we'd done, I felt dirty, sticky, and sweaty. I could think of nothing finer than a cool shower and some clean, fresh clothes.

My Chevy was still equipped with good old 4/65 Air. It was a long drive home, so I turned it on. We rolled down all four windows and I stepped on the gas and goosed it up to 65 miles an hour. I felt a little better after that; but Saundra was still roasting under her wig. "Gayle, do you mind if I take this thing off?" she asked, one hand on either side of her head.

"The whole thing?" I replied, "Or just the wig?" Saundra smirked at me. "Of course not," I said, "go right ahead." She removed her wig and laid it on the seat between us. Then Saundra leaned back in her seat, closed her eyes, and sighed as the breeze cooled her scalp.

After a little while, Saundra lifted her head and asked, "Would it bother you if I took off my prosthesis? You wouldn't believe how warm these things can get."

I shook my head. "It's okay by me." I knew all about prostheses, and I could imagine how she felt. Having something akin to a big water balloon lying against your skin all day was bound to be uncomfortable, especially during the hot, humid summer. Saundra removed it from her bra and laid it on the seat between us, next to the wig. At the time, Saundra was not the petite woman that she is now. That breast form was a triple D, so it took up a fair chunk of room on the seat!

We rode in comfortable silence for a while, gradually cooling off and looking forward to showers and supper. That 4/65 Air was doing the job, except for one thing: I was running it in a 55 mph zone. *Apparently, the highway patrol disapproves,* I sighed to myself, when I saw a set of red and blue lights flashing in my rearview mirror. "Aww, man!" I whined, as I began looking for a place to pull over. Saundra sat up and looked around, puzzled. "Busted," I said, and nodded towards the rear. She looked back and watched the cruiser as it followed me off the road.

I pulled out my license and registration and we both sat up straight in our seats. I looked in my mirror to see the uniformed patrolman approaching, all somber and serious. I took a deep breath and blew it out. The gravel crunched as he came up alongside my door. I tried on a small smile and glanced up as he leaned down to look through the open window. Those reflective sunglasses gave away nothing. "Hello, officer," I tried cautiously.

He took a moment to survey the situation with that mirrored, expressionless gaze. One sweaty female driver. One bald female passenger. One wig on the seat between them, and something that appeared to be one very large fake breast.

I had just opened my mouth to offer an explanation, when the officer said stonily, "You ladies have a nice day." Then he walked back to his cruiser and pulled away.

We laughed about it all the way home. I can't imagine what he must have thought. But then, probably, neither could he.

he new Ohio store came together relatively quickly. It took a lot of hard work to get it done, but by then we had had a lot practice.

Two of my best cosmetologists, Bill and Christie, each offered to make the drive to Glendale to expand the services that we offered there. It really was above and beyond the call of duty for them; but they were both thrilled to be part of building out the new location. I knew they could be trusted to run the store in my absence, so I happily accepted their offer. They became the hub around which that store was built. Every day that we needed a hand in Ohio, they drove an extra 40 minutes to give it. I knew how tough it was. They made the trip as often as I did, if not more. Just as they had done in the original store, Bill and Christie brought all kinds of life, and talent, to the new shop. And, of course, the clients loved the extra care.

As had so often happened before, it wasn't long until we realized that we were terribly short on space. We'd built out the Glendale store, but as business picked up, we found that we were tripping all over each other. Once again, Jerry and his father came to the rescue. It seemed like we'd hardly settled in at Helen's old shop, when they were packing things up and helping us move to Springdale, Ohio. There, we settled into an even bigger location. It was a wonderful expansion and it allowed the Ohio store to offer all of the services we'd gotten so good at in Kentucky.

We were so busy by then, that I hardly had a moment to think. It was always go, go, go. But every once in a while, I'd stop to take a breath and reflect on all that had happened so far. *We're helping patients in three states now!* I would think to myself in amazement. I knew Rita would be proud.

O ne beautiful, late summer evening I attended a sort of fundraising dinner party. It was a wonderful night to be out, but I didn't really know any of the other guests. I was just sort of milling around, a single woman trying hard not to look out of place. I wondered how long etiquette demanded that I stay. I was feeling a little lonely and beginning to have second thoughts about accepting the invitation. *What was I thinking?* I asked myself. *I don't really fit in. I'm like a third wheel here—or the 33rd wheel!*

I was just about ready to pack it in, when one fine gentleman approached and introduced himself as Brother Giancarlo Bonutti, SM. Then he asked who I was, and what I did. I was grateful for the attention, but I also knew he'd probably just bitten off more than he could chew. I tried to warn him off. "It's a *long story*," I said. "A *very* long story."

"Maybe you can give me the abridged version," he replied with a smile.

I told him I'd try; but in my mind, all that did was reduce it from an epic to a novel. I couldn't help myself, but for some reason, I told him everything—the whole tale. Probably too much coffee and not enough social life. I told him all about Rita, and how she had led me to Jesus. I spoke about what a beautiful, courageous woman she was, and how she understood that she had a purpose to fulfill before she died. I told him about how hard Rita worked to live up to her goal, and how she had passed it on to me. Now my job was to continue her mission. Giancarlo listened attentively. I gave a brief history of Image Insights—our successes and struggles—and briefly told him of some of our generous donors and volunteers. I mentioned some of our tragedies too, like the little baby girl that I'd just met. I tried so hard to be brief, but there was too much to tell. There were so many people to remember and I didn't want to leave anyone out. The whole story just came tumbling out.

I couldn't believe I hadn't bored him, or frightened him away. Just the opposite, in fact. Giancarlo was constantly inquisitive, prompting me further with questions, always wanting to know more. I was eating up his entire evening, and was beginning to feel embarrassed that he'd asked, but he was just wonderful about it. When I finally caught up to our present day,

I couldn't believe I'd devoured an hour of his time. I said to him, "I'm so sorry, I didn't mean to take up your whole night."

Giancarlo shook his head dismissively and replied, "Gayle, that is the best story that I've ever heard."

Two weeks later, Giancarlo called and asked if he could drop by my office. Of course he could; he needed no invitation, and I told him so. When he arrived, Giancarlo explained that he was with a large church in Cincinnati, and that he'd told my story to some of his friends and fellow board members. I was surprised to learn that many of these people had already heard of me. I had even taken care of a family member of one.

Based upon what they already knew, and what Giancarlo had told them, a motion was offered and seconded. Then they took a little vote. As Giancarlo told me about the minutes of the meeting, he presented me with an envelope.

"The board voted unanimously," Giancarlo continued, as I opened the envelope. "They voted to start a foundation to help the people who can't afford to pay you." I nodded politely, vaguely following along. *What's a foundation?* I wondered. I looked down at the paper that I'd absentmindedly pulled from the envelope.

It was a check for $25,000!

I was so overwhelmed that within seconds the tears flooded out and I started crying like a baby. It was like he'd turned on a faucet, or a firehose.

Giancarlo shushed me and got me settled down again. "This will act as a reserve," he explained. "It will grow on its own—and it will attract new donations." I wiped away tears and tried to calm myself as I listened. "Now, when someone comes to you for help, but can't afford to pay, this fund will reimburse Image Insights." Giancarlo smiled at me. "You'll get paid, and you won't have to stop giving things away!"

I started crying again.

I couldn't believe it. I'd been warned not to "give" my way into the poorhouse. Even so, I'd continued to do what I thought was right, and once again God continued to provide. As always, He did so in new and unexpected ways. Thanks to Giancarlo and his church, I had $25,000 in my hand. With it, we would start a foundation to help the people who couldn't afford our services. To me at least, that was a new and unexpected way.

As I understand it, most people start a foundation by selecting a board and its members first. Then, they do the necessary paperwork and file it. Finally, they go out and raise the money they need to fund their project. Leave it to me to do it all backwards!

In memory of Rita, I decided on the name *The Lemonade Foundation.* I'd always wanted to do something special in her honor. Rita was so important to me; she had changed my life in so many ways. I wanted her legacy to be out in front again, where everyone would see it and know it. I hadn't taken The Lemonade Stand name for the business after Rita passed away, because I wasn't sure that I could. While I'd doggedly stuck to her mission, and had continued to live with her Lemonade spirit, that little fact had always bothered me. Calling it The Lemonade Foundation was like putting her stamp back on things. It gave us the good old Rita Snider Made-in-the-USA seal of approval. Everything felt right again. People would know that our work was a part of Rita, and Rita was a part of our work. And what better way to honor her, than to offer help to those who needed it most but could afford it least.

The Lemonade Foundation became a reality just a few months later. Many people wanted to help, either by donating, or through service on a committee or the board. Now that the foundation was formally established, we were quickly able to begin helping people. And with that, suddenly money started pouring in from dozens of different sources. A group of attorneys, whose former colleague I'd taken care of, donated $10,000. The families and friends of many others I'd helped did the same. Without a single word of advertising or promotion, the funds started pouring in. This was good, because I still had a lot to learn about promoting a foundation. But once again, I knew it was God at work in my life.

From all outward appearances, we were beginning to look like a real success. Image Insights had grown to three locations. While this supposedly "for-profit" company had yet to show real profit, we were helping thousands of people across three states. In addition, we had The Lemonade Foundation, a non-profit entity to take care of those who could not afford our products or services. What a tremendous blessing the foundation was. It truly helped to steady up the business by making good on a constant drain on our financial resources. Best of all, it allowed me to continue to do what I thought was right. I could continue to give help to those who needed it. If they were truly unable to pay, I could take care of them and then send them gladly on their way, knowing that my business would still be okay. The board would review the details of the case and make good on the loss.

From the outside anyway, I was finally starting to look like a sharp, successful businesswoman. Of course, anyone who knew the inside truth—and there were a lot of them—knew that there was no savvy business sense involved. No, just a lot of hard work, and a lot of prayer. Looking back, it should have been impossible; but we did it anyway.

Every day, my staff and I did our best and tried to do what was right—no matter what the cost to the company. It was not done carelessly or cavalierly. There was much worrying and fretting. But we always did right by our clients. We relied on hard work and prayer to get us through, and somehow God always provided us with another generous soul to fill our needs. Whether it was a volunteer to help with the chores, or a benefactor to keep open the doors, somehow He always provided.

Rita had a verse for that. She had a verse for everything. "Blessed is he who has regard for the weak; the Lord delivers him in times of trouble." (*Psalms 41:1*) We had some times of trouble, all right; and we received more than our share of deliverance.

14

Making the Most

Thanks to The Lemonade Foundation, my burdens were becoming lighter. The foundation served as a guardian angel for the business. There were lots of people who wanted to help us continue our work, but not everyone could volunteer. However, they were able to help financially. The foundation gave them a safe, secure way to make their donations.

Then, the committee screened our applications for reimbursement, and decided which cases were eligible. We didn't want to
waste a cent of those generous donations, so we were careful with
our submissions. Even so, I don't think there was ever a rejected
case. We were there to help people, and they were there to help
us. By pulling together as a team, we were able to do a lot of good.

Knowing that The Lemonade Foundation was there made
my job much easier. If a customer came in for help, but didn't
have the means to pay, I could give them what they needed, just
as I had always done. The difference was that I didn't have to
worry anymore. There was no more stressing about whether I
would make the payroll, or cover my overhead. It was amazing
how much pressure it relieved. I was spending less time worrying about every nickel and dime, and more time doing what I did
best—taking care of people.

The foundation came with its own system of record keeping,
screening, and reimbursements. For the first time, I could see in
concrete terms just how much I had been giving away over the
years. I was more than a little surprised. In fact, I was a lot surprised. *No wonder things were always so tight!*

In addition to the donations that came in to the foundation,
people began to include knick-knacks with a lemon theme. If it
had a lemon on it, somebody sent it in. There were lemon pins
and brooches, lemon mugs and pitchers, lemon pillows and
stitched lemon samplers. There were glass lemon ornaments of
every size and even lemon stained glass. *If this keeps up,* I
thought, *I'll be able to open a lemon museum.*

Making the foundation Rita's legacy was a big part of what
made it so successful. Her story was the foundation's story.
Bringing back the Lemonade name made it more accessible to
people. Reminding them of her story made it more real. It also
made it easier for them to give. Image Insights had always done
the work, and we'd done it well. We lived and worked by Rita's
lemonade gospel. But The Lemonade Foundation just clicked

with people. As soon as they heard the name, they understood the idea. The donations proved it.

Late one night, I was driving home after a seminar in Columbus. The day had been a long one, and I was tired. There was still a good deal of road left to travel, and I was looking forward to a nice hot shower and a warm comfy bed. I was traveling down I-71 when I got the strangest feeling—it was a sudden impulse to exit. Taking the off-ramp to Smith-Edwards Rd., I wondered, *Why am I doing this?* As I pulled to a stop at the light, I saw the big Joseph Beth bookstore just down the road. *I need to go in there,* I thought, though I wasn't sure why. I wasn't craving anything to read, there was no sudden urge to pick up a mystery, or a romance. The only things I craved were my shower and my pillow.

The store was closing soon, but I made it in with a few minutes to spare. *Now, why am I here?* I wondered. I began to roam around the store, but I felt aimless. *Okay, God,* I said to myself, *if I'm here to find something, a little direction would be nice.* It was a big store, I was tired, and I wanted to go home.

A moment later, I found myself in the cookbook section, which was not my usual stop. I liked to cook as much as anyone—but who has the time? If I cooked, it was usually whatever was quick and easy—although I usually burned it. *I don't want a cookbook,* I thought, as I gave the shelves a quick once over.

I was about to give up and go home when something caught my eye. It was a bright yellow spine, way down low. *The Lemon Tree Cookbook. Oh, okay. Lemons. I get it.* I grabbed the book and headed for home. At the very least, it would make an addition to the lemon memorabilia collection. *I'll look at it tomorrow,* I thought, as I tossed it onto the back seat. Then I got back onto the freeway and headed for home.

It wasn't until the end of the next day that I opened the book and flipped through the pages. It was a cookbook devoted to lemon recipes. At the bottom of almost every one was a drawing of a lemon. But they weren't normal cookbook lemons—they were silly, scribbly, lemon cartoons. Lemons, with arms and legs, doing things that most lemons don't do. Like walking. When I saw the recipe for Lemon Doodle Cookies, I smiled. There on the bottom of the page was a cartoon lemon, in bare feet and a diaper, scribbling on the wall with a crayon. I looked through a few more pages. When I saw the Lemon Custard recipe, I laughed out loud. It had a lemon in cowboy boots and a cavalry hat, and it was all shot through with arrows—a lemon Custer. Those silly cartoons really clicked with me, and I got an idea.

We had started to make small gift baskets to sell at the shop. They were full of little luxury items and treats for the patients. The baskets were intended as little pick-me-ups that family or friends could buy for their loved ones. I thought it would be nice to add a card with one of these funny little lemon cartoons to each basket. On each card, we'd add a note saying "pamper yourself for a day," or "try something new." It seemed like another good way to spread the lemonade spirit.

The next day I contacted the cookbook's publisher. I explained what I wanted to do with the cartoons, and asked if I could contact the artist. They kindly put me in touch with him, and he created a new set of cartoons to go with the cards, and into a brochure. Those little lemon people generated smiles all around. Eventually, they became our little mascots.

The baskets were warmly received, so we set aside a corner of the store to display them. A small gift shop within the shop, we christened it The Lemonade Stand. Those little baskets went over pretty well with people, but the part I liked best, was seeing the name up in lights again. Rita's "Lemonade Stand" label had come full circle. Since her family never did use the name, I was happy to put it back to work. Rita's Lemonade touches were all over Image Insights again, just as they were supposed to be. And the foundation we had created in her honor was doing so much to help people. I wish she could have been there to see it all.

J ust as Rita had done, The Lemonade Foundation was making lemonade out of lemons. It was getting help to people in need, and restoring their dignity and sense of self. One of the special patients the foundation did its work for, was a bright young girl named Sarah. She was only 14 and had been diagnosed with a terminal illness.

Imagine that. I could still remember 14. I could not imagine how she faced it.

Yet, Sarah stood up to things so bravely that remembering her still takes my breath away. Her mother, Kim, was just as brave, and far more courageous than I could ever be. Sarah's mom was always by her side, and she was cheerful and happy without fail when the two of them were together. I would watch them play around, and stand in awe of their relationship. Kim knew that her 14-year-old child was about to undergo

So bright and sunny, Sarah made the most of every moment she was given. She inspires me to go on, no matter what the odds, every day.

an ordeal more punishing than anything the rest of us will ever live through. She made the most of their time together. I honestly don't know how she did it. I had a great relationship with my boys; we were a happy family. Imagining myself in her shoes was an almost unbearable idea.

Sarah and Kim were always smiling. They were happy together and were simply making the best of a very bad situation. From the moment they walked in the door at Image Insights, I was impressed by this young lady and her mother. As I began to work with Sarah, I quickly realized that her mother didn't have the money to pay for a really nice wig. Yet, Kim was determine to do the best she could for her. Being a young high-school girl, it would be tough on Sarah to attend classes with no hair. My job was to help this young lady the best way I could. I really felt for this girl, so money was not an issue. If I'd had to pay for the wig myself, I would have. We chose a beautiful wig for Sarah, one that was a perfect match for her real hair.

It was always helpful when people came in before they started to lose their hair. That way I could see their natural look and create a match that was close to perfect. It was possible to get a match by looking at a photo; but real life was always better. Sometimes, the pictures people brought in were 10 years old, or more! That was when it became a real challenge. After all, there aren't very many of us who want to wear a style that's more than a decade out of date!

Sometimes, during a fitting session, a friend or family member would try to cheer up a patient by encouraging them to throw caution to the wind. "If you have to get new hair anyway . . . blondes have more fun!" Urging them to be creative, they would say, "Long or short, blonde or brunette, red or black; try 'em all! Now is your big chance," they would say. "You can do whatever you want."

That always *sounded* like a lot of fun. But truthfully, there are few souls hardy enough to make changes like that during such trauma. The rigors of dealing with cancer make losing your hair a good deal less than fun. When reality sets in, and the hair is all gone, most people aren't looking for a big change. They've had enough change. Most of the time, a patient simply wants to look like her old self again. For the majority of my clients, we stayed close to their natural style and color.

That's not to say that my customers didn't experiment. Once they'd grown accustomed to the changes, many of them came back for new wigs. It happened all the time—for some more quickly than others. Sarah was one who adapted to the changes well. She was young and flexible. Once Sarah got through the initial challenge of wearing a wig, she decided to go all out, just as Rita had done. We tried every color and style on her, and had a really good time doing it. But even Sarah had to be ready for it first.

Through all of our visits together, Sarah and I had become very close. She was around so often, that the boys had a lot of opportunities to see her. She was only a couple of years younger than Adam and Nicholas, so it really hit home with them to know a client who was so close in age. Such a young girl, Sarah was truly living every moment. That made a big impression on Adam and Nicholas. They were struck by her ability to "make lemonade" out of such lemons.

Sarah was my friend; so I told her, "if you ever need anything, you call me. Even if I'm at home." One day, she did. The following morning would be her first day back to school, and things weren't timing out right. Her wig would come in late, but school began early. Even worse, Kim couldn't get the time off from work to bring her down to the shop, fit the new wig, and still get her to school on time. The first day back at school can be tough. For Sarah, it would be doubly so. She would be facing the same responses that adults faced, but magnified in the pressure-cooker environment of high school. I told Sarah that, if it was okay with her mom, I'd come to her house and we'd prepare her wig there. Then I'd drop her off at school on my way in to the shop.

Kim happily agreed, so first thing in the morning, I packed up Sarah's wig and my supplies, and prepared for another drive-by wigging. When I arrived at Sarah's home, she was bubbling over with excitement. We set to work and she could hardly sit still in her chair. Sarah was thrilled to have her new wig, and it looked beautiful on her. I showed her how to pull it back in a ponytail, or pull it up in barrettes; she could be just as creative with it as with her own hair. But since this was her first day back at school, Sarah wanted it to be as close to normal as possible. We left it long, and put a few clips in it, and Sarah looked just like her old self again—gorgeous.

When I dropped her off at school, she gave me a big hug and practically bounced out of the car. The big smile on her face stretched ear to ear, as she waved goodbye. Such a simple little thing, Sarah was so happy just to have hair again. When she walked toward the front doors, she had so much spring in her step that she was practically skipping. Wearing a wig, and walking into a school full of kids who knew the truth, takes a good deal of courage. Sarah had that courage, and a whole lot more. She was such a cool young woman.

As Sarah continued to take her treatments, she had good days and bad ones. We stayed in close contact, because I wanted to take good care of her, and supply her with wigs for as long as she needed them. It was important to me that she always felt good about herself.

A few months later, we were doing a fitting, trying on a few new looks. While we were chatting, Sarah told me that she would really like to be on the Rosie O'Donnell Show one day. At the time, this was the hottest afternoon talk show on television, and Rosie's bubbly personality really appealed to Sarah. In fact, she adored Rosie. Sarah's dream was that one day she would work in television, too. Even though she knew in her heart that she did not have forever to live, Sarah was determined to make the most of the time she did have.

Sarah really wanted to meet Rosie, and she told me that she had the perfect plan to catch her eye. She was going to send Rosie some pictures of herself, modeling all kinds of hats, scarves, and wigs. But first, she would decorate a box to put them in. She planned to cover it with every single picture of Tom Cruise that she could find. Sarah knew that Rosie had a crush on Tom, and she was sure that such a box would get her attention. Then, once Rosie had opened it, she would find Sarah's pictures and letter. After seeing that, how could Rosie refuse?

How, indeed? God love her, Sarah had it all figured out. I said, "You're absolutely correct. How could Rosie refuse?" The next day, I called my television crew and asked if they would be free to do a taping at the shop. I had an idea, and didn't want to do it at the studio. I thought we could help Sarah put together a video letter, but I didn't want it to look like a professional television set. When I shared the idea with Sarah and her mom, they were delighted that so many people were willing to go all out for Sarah.

On the big day, the camera crew began setting up at the shop. As they did, Sarah sat with her sister, Stacy. They munched away on french fries as they watched the crew at work. Once everything was ready, Sarah began trying on wigs—timidly at first—while the crew taped her. After a few minutes, she warmed up to the guys and began to "let her hair down." I think Sarah tried on every wig and accessory in the store. Being the focus of such lavish attention, Sarah had a terrific time. She had no fear of the camera and was completely unselfconscious. A little fashion blender, she swirled together hats, scarves, and wigs of every color, stripe, and flavor. Sarah whipped up combinations that were by turns sharp and stylish, or hilarious. Fearlessly, she paraded every one before the camera with the proper sense of drama or slapstick. Her energy was infectious, and the camera crew had a good time, too. When we were finished with the tape, we gave Sarah a copy and she sent it off to Rosie.

As it turns out, the Make-A-Wish Foundation also knew of Sarah's dream to be on the show. Their good work and Sarah's enthusiasm must have been an irresistible combination, because they actually made it happen in short order. A few weeks later, Sarah was live on the Rosie

Sarah Zepernick had her moment in the sun on the Rosie O'Donnell Show, followed by a fabulous night on Broadway at The Lion King.

O'Donnell Show, where she got to play the announcer and introduce Rosie on the air. Sarah was also a guest on the show and was accorded the full VIP treatment. After the taping, Rosie took her backstage for a special surprise. There, the cast members of *The Lion King* were waiting to meet her. The Broadway show had just opened and was the talk of the town. After introductions, some chatting, and photos, Sarah was presented with souvenirs and tickets to the play. So

When life gives you lemons. . .

Laugh!

Scientists have discovered that laughter will trigger the brain to release certain chemicals—endorphins—that can block pain and give you a sense of well-being.

after a thrilling day in the world of television, she had a spectacular night on Broadway. It was truly a night to remember.

Such a wise and wonderful young lady, Sarah was so full of God's spirit. She knew the score; but she wouldn't let it get her down. She took full advantage of every moment available to her. We should all be so smart. Most of us take for granted something Sarah was given too little of. But our time is limited, too; it won't last forever. So young and full of fire, Sarah made the most of her time here. Her time was much too short.

Over the following years, Kim created a foundation in Sarah's name. Called the Sarah Zepernick Childhood Cancer Foundation, they raised a great deal of money for children's hospitals in the tri-state area. After several years of continued growth and success, Kim brought in a business woman to help manage the foundation.

As so often happens, the business person was driven more by money than by mission. She lost sight of their true purpose and it wasn't long before the foundation collapsed under poor management. But, taking a cue from her daughter, Kim refused to give up. She is now at work building Sarah House—a hospice home for terminally ill children.* Sarah's brave and fearless nature continues to inspire good deeds and change lives.

S pending so much time with Sarah was a reminder, if I ever needed one, time is precious. I had two boys that wouldn't be around forever—one day they would be all grown up. Before I knew it, they would be out of the house and off making lives of their own. I tried my best to make the most of my time with Adam and Nicholas. Being a business owner tends to demand a great deal of time. So does being a single mom. That's not an excuse for anything; no, it's just a recognition of the state of my affairs. I was determined that Adam and Nicholas would grow up to be responsible gentlemen. I knew it was my job to guide them, or see that they got the guidance they needed.

That being so, they spent a lot of time with me at the shop. One thing I'd learned, during those first seven years at Image Insights, was that I had two terrific sons. I'd already been pretty sure of that; but if I ever needed proof, they delivered it in spades. Adam and Nicholas stood by me through all of our struggles. Through all of our ups and downs, they never complained.

I thought it was important to make them a part of the business, and they were always willing volunteers. I don't suppose that they had a lot of choice—but it's far better to work with volunteers than draftees. The boys took turns cleaning the office, they helped sell the products, they answered phones, and ran errands. The two of them even gardened for me, planting seasonal flowers all around the shop. Whatever the job, Adam and Nicholas attacked each one with energy and a positive attitude.

My boys truly believed in me, and they showed it in so many ways. Day by day, I struggled to fulfill the dream of a woman

---

*If you are interested in finding out more about Sarah House, go to www.runforthegold.com

they had known only briefly, yet they supported me whole-heartedly. The boys gave up so much to stand behind me. Little by little, we were improving our financial situation; but things were always tight. There never was enough money for extras; we simply made do with the necessities. I was so proud of them, but as the boys got older, I began to worry. I was afraid that they might think this was all life would ever be—a never-ending struggle just to get by.

I wanted Adam and Nicholas to know that life could indeed be rewarding. I wasn't sure that they would understand "spiritu-ally rewarding," not at their young age. So I tried to show them examples of just plain "rewarding" instead. Every so often, we would hop in the car and go for a drive around the ritziest part of town. Pointing out the beautiful mansions and gleaming Porsches and Mercedes, I would say, "It can be this way for you, too. All you have to do is make the choice. Choose to work hard and do the right thing." Years later, I could see that they weren't really motivated so much by money. It seems that my boys understood spiritual rewards, and the rewards of family, better than I had imagined. As Adam put it, years later, "Mom, you raised us with morals, not money." They both grew into good, hard-working, responsible men.

My little "rags to riches tours" may have been a foolish stunt, but growing up in a single-parent household like they were, I was worried about them. There was no one at hand to show Adam and Nicholas the way to success. They didn't have a successful father figure around that they could pattern their lives after. Their father had been a good man on the inside; but alco-hol and prescriptions had taken that man away from us. Now, there was nobody to bring in the bacon but me. Even worse, there was no one around to show them how to be a man, a hus-band, or a father.

I had been a single parent for so long that the boys didn't remember it any other way. Each year, they gave me mother's day cards *and* father's day cards. That may have been good for me, but was it good for them? I was anxious about my sons not having positive male role models. I had to teach my boys how to become men—how to work with other men, and how to respect women.

At the time, all of their authority figures were female; my boys were being raised by a woman and they were being taught by women. Adam and Nicholas attended a Catholic school where the teachers were all either nuns or female instructors. I knew that my sons were sharp. It wouldn't be long before they figured out how to play the system. I didn't want them learning to charm or sweet-talk their way through things. It was important to me that they treat women with honor and respect. It was a skill that their natural father, unfortunately, had never learned.

I took them out of their Catholic school, with its all-female faculty, and placed them in a school that included male teachers and coaches. There is an old saying: surround yourself with the people you want to be like. It was as true for them as it was for me. Over time, they found a number of admirable teachers and coaches that they could emulate.

Besides looking for role models, I wanted my boys to learn about leadership. I wanted them to be strong and self-sufficient, not dependent upon others. While I understood that their coaches would be instrumental in that, I thought I had something to offer in that regard as well. I wanted them to know that there was a little leadership in their family tree, too. In the past, I'd never considered myself a leader. I would think, *Oh, I could never do that.* But over the years, I found myself put into positions of leadership over and over again. Between Image Insights, The Lemonade Foundation, and The American Cancer Society, it seemed I was a leader whether I knew it or not. Exposing Adam and Nicholas to the workings of business and small government might awaken in them an ability that had taken me decades to develop. At least, I thought so. I took them everywhere—to Foundation committee meetings, to community board meetings, and even to the television studio. I wanted them to see how adults treated each other, and I wanted them around every positive influence that I could find.

The business demanded a lot of my time. As the sole bread-winner, I wasn't home every afternoon for them. There is another old saying about idle hands, so rather than let them become latchkey kids, I kept them busy. If they weren't with me, they were doing *something*. Besides helping out at the shop, Adam and Nicholas were altar boys in church; and they were always involved in after-school sports.

Since we were so busy, we had to make a concerted effort to spend time with each other. I wanted to keep tabs on them, so every Sunday night, the three of us would sit down to dinner together and discuss what was coming up for the week ahead. I wish I could say it was a sumptious Sunday spread, but there wasn't always time for a home-cooked meal. We tried; but the odds were just as good that it was take-out. While the meals were important, it was the

Nicholas grew into such a fine man—both boys did. I like to think that I'm responsible for that, but I know it was more them than me.

time spent talking that really counted. We made plans for practices, games, school functions, or late nights at work. We also tried to work in a few evenings for quiet sit-down dinners during the week, but we *tried* more than we succeeded. When we did succeed, it was rarely "quiet", and sometimes it was barely "dinner". With the constant comings and goings and the always ringing telephone, it was easy to forget a pan on the stove. If dinner was only partially burnt, the boys were kind enough to gulp it down without complaint. If it was burned beyond recognition, we picked up the phone again—for pizza. It was chaotic, and we were always very busy, but we were happy together.

As the years went by, and the business grew, we began to see a change in our fortunes at home. Instead of pinching pennies all of the time, we actually had a little extra at the end of the month. It wasn't a lot, not by any stretch; but compared to what we were used to, it was a big deal to us. After so many years of hard work and sacrifice—at home, at work, and at school—things were starting to look up. I finally had a little extra money in my pocket—and the chance to do something nice for my boys.

Adam and Nicholas had always worked so hard at school, but we'd never been able to afford anything like class rings or yearbooks. So one winter, several years after they'd finished high school, I paid a visit to their old stomping grounds. At the administration office, I asked if there were any old yearbooks still in storage—specifically, one each, from the years that Adam and Nicholas had graduated. There was much in the way of shrugged shoulders and puzzled frowns, but some phone calls were made and I began to

I worried that I never provided for them well enough. Adam reassured me that they were content. "You raised us with morals, not money."

hope. Sure enough, we learned that extra copies, from over the years, were stowed away in the bowels of the building. Hopefully, there were still a few left from the years that I needed. Some time later, a dusty and disheveled teacher showed up with a pair of gleaming shrink-wrapped yearbooks.

Over the next several days, I tracked down most of the boys' old friends. Many were still in the neighborhood; others hadn't gone too far away. Those that I found led me to others. I told them what I was trying to do, and every one of them happily obliged. They filled those books with fond remembrances, wisecracks, rude remarks, and best wishes. In every place one of the boys appeared in a photo, it was surrounded by compliments and cut-downs, defaced and defamed in good fun.

They were remarkable little books, a curious mixture of wisecracks, sarcasm and sincerity. The yearbooks still fairly gushed with youthful optimism, but it was tempered by the maturity of people who had put high school behind them and moved on to other things. It was a blast of nostalgia for everyone involved, and it gave them all a chance to say things they could never have said when they were all so young. Needless to say, Adam and Nicholas devoured every page.

It was interesting to see how their friends had changed in just a few short years. Those yearbooks reminded me, not of a Bible verse from my days with Rita, but of an old Latin term from Catholic school

Tempus fugit.

Time is fleeting, alright. It races by, and we had best not waste it. Sarah's story would seem to demand as much. Her days were far too few in number; but there is not a one of us who will be here forever. It brings to mind another old Latin phrase. It may be a cliché, but that doesn't make it any less true.

Carpe diem. Seize the day.

CHAPTER 15

A Whole New World

Other than some time with my sons, I didn't have much of a personal life. But I was okay with that. I was focused on seeing Adam and Nicholas become bright, confident young men; and I was busy growing Image Insights. I worked hard to make my little company the best it could possibly be. But as I did that, I saw a lot of loving couples come through my doors.

Even under the weight of the fight with cancer, these couples had relationships that were stronger, and more loving, than any I had ever known. They reminded me just how solo I was.

The best loving relationships that I'd had with men were those with the men in my own family. My father, my brothers, and especially my sons; those were good relationships. But when it came to picking a mate, I seemed to have a knack for choosing attractive, fatally flawed men. So for the time being, the only men in my life were family men—my family. The problem was that time was running out. I also had to face that fact that, one day soon, Adam and Nicholas would want to move out on their own.

Whenever I saw one of those loving couples, it gave me something to think about. I would occasionally remind God that I was still a single woman. *Hello, God . . . remember me? All alone, here.* I was still committed to carrying out the mission I believed He had set before me; but I let Him know that I wouldn't mind a partner. And I did not mean a *business* partner. I thought I would be a good wife. However, I wasn't too confident in my own ability to choose a husband. I told God that, the next time, I'd like His help in picking the right man for me.

My first marriage had been terribly difficult—to put it kindly. My first husband was a Stone Age Italian, barefoot-and-pregnant, my-way-or-the-highway kind of guy. Except, to him, the highway was not an option. If the marriage was difficult, the divorce was doubly so. I had never wanted a divorce, but I'd really been left with no other choice. The only good things to come out of that marriage were my sons—and beautiful things they were. If I had to have the one to gain the others, then that's how it had to be.

Now that I had my boys, I wasn't looking to make that trade again. A few years had passed since the divorce, I found myself wishing for a partner again. This time, I wanted a *real* husband, and father, one who took his roles seriously. I wanted a partner who could offer love and respect all around. However, a husband required dating—which was not an appealing prospect. After my first experience with marriage, I was a little gun-shy about men. Needless to say, I was not a bright light on the social scene.

Besides, I had better things to do; I had two young boys to raise. Nicholas and Adam were only six and seven at the time, so they needed a lot of attention. I was happy being a young mother, and the three of us made a close, tight-knit little family. There were times when I thought it would be nice to have a partner; but I was pretty sure that a single woman with two kids was not a hot property on the dating market. *It can wait,* I thought. After my first husband, I wasn't so eager to dive in again, anyway.

When I met a man at our apartment complex pool about a year or so later, the whole thing just kind of snuck up on me again. We ran into each other a few times that summer, and I learned that Tom was a nice man. Eventually, he asked me on a date and I, with some hesitation, accepted. I was a little nervous about going out with someone I didn't really know, but we had mutual friends, and after dinner we would meet them for a little dancing. It seemed a safe enough bet.

We went to a beautiful, and expensive, restaurant. I was dressed in a long, flowing gown and Tom cut a fine figure in a dashing suit. He was going all out to make a good impression, and even ordered dinner for the two of us without even looking at a menu. Never having developed a taste for shellfish—even expensive ones—I was a little horrified by the giant prawns that arrived as the main course. He was trying so hard to impress, so I delicately picked at them while we talked.

We talked a lot, and I learned a great deal about him. For example, he was a nuclear engineer. He learned a good deal about me as well. It was an educational evening. I even learned something about myself.

For instance, before that night, I had no idea I was allergic to shellfish. Really, really allergic.

On our way to dancing, I had to ask him to pull the car over. There, on the side of the road, I proceeded to divest myself of my dinner, carefully holding my gown away from the flying bits of shellfish debris.

Tom was worried that he should take me home, but I thought I felt much better. We continued on to the dance club, and I ducked into the ladies room, where I crossed paths with another patron. She screamed, and cried out, "Oh, my God! What happened to you?!" In the brightly lit restroom, I could see that I was in trouble. My face was swollen and covered in welts. As I rushed back to Tom, I found I couldn't walk so well. I barely got the words out, "We need to go to a hospital."

At the emergency room desk, the nurse on duty didn't even bother to look up. She asked my name, and Tom had to answer. She asked my address. Tom answered. She asked my date of birth, and Tom looked helplessly at me. I slurred in response, "Ith not gonna mather in 'bout two minuth." She looked up at that.

In seconds, I was back in the emergency room, pumped full of meds. The date ended with me stretched out on a table, swollen, naked, and packed in ice. *I look like a spoiled blowfish at the butcher shop,* I thought to myself. Once the doctors had me stabilized, the nurse brought in my "husband" for a visit.

After that, I never saw him again.

Or, so I feared. Actually, he did come back again, and again. We started dating, and it was a royal courtship. He spoiled me with everything. There was lavish attention, luxurious gifts, bountiful shopping, and beautiful dates. Compared to my first marriage, I felt like a princess. Within a few short months, we were married.

We moved to New York and I settled in to what I thought would be an idyllic life. That is, until I made an important discovery. Tom was a good man, a good provider, and would make a good husband—for someone who had no kids.

He was a cold fish to my boys. Dismissive and completely uninterested. He'd been polite enough to them while we were dating, but I should have realized it then. He never wanted to do anything with the boys. Only with me. By rushing headlong to claim my prize, I had missed all of the important signs. Clearly, Tom had no interest in fatherhood. His own daughter, from a previous marriage, was treated no better.

Suddenly, Tom didn't look like such a prize. *I'm such a fool!* I berated myself. *What have I done?* My sons were *everything* to me. They were my world. They were my family. My greatest accomplishment and my greatest joy. And I had sold them down the river for a few trinkets. I was so ashamed. Hoping it would get better, I tried to make it work; but nothing changed.

After a year of trying, we were divorced. Compared to the first one, it was fairly amicable. We simply went our separate ways.

And this time, I really did never see him again.

Naturally, I gave up dating. Actually, I pretty much gave up on men in general. It's not that I had anything against them. I liked men. As a gender, they're great. But I was a lousy judge when it came to picking my own personal specimen. I'd been up to bat twice, and struck out both times. It was time to take myself out of the game. I didn't give up for life; I just decided to take a few seasons off.

I wasn't exactly a recluse. I had friends. I went to fundraising events. Dozens of people came through my doors every week. So it's not like I was a hermit. I was just . . . single; and I resigned myself to it. I knew that, with Christ in my life, I would be happy whether I married again or not. I was committed to taking care of Adam and Nicholas until they were adults and able to fend for themselves. After that, if God thought I was ready, maybe I'd step up to the plate again.

I stayed out of the game for the next decade. For the most part, I was okay with that. A partner would have been nice; but if God thought I had other priorities to attend to, then I would take care of those. I focused on my boys and I worked on my business. First it was my nursing career, then it was that hectic year with Rita. Now I was in my eighth year of triumph, tragedy, and turmoil at Image Insights.

The boys had just turned 18 and 19 when I was invited to a wedding. The event took place on a farm out in Maysville, Kentucky. It was beautiful there, so tranquil and picturesque. Two dozen wild horses roamed free on hundreds of acres of grazing land. The rolling meadows were dotted with forests and bordered by a shimmering, silvery lake. It was truly my idea of Eden. There was a charming old 1840's cabin there; and the wedding would take place between it and the lake.

I loved it there; and I said so to anyone who would listen. Two people who did listen were the owners. They were friends of mine, and knew all about my work. As I sung my praises of their property, one of them looked at the other. They nodded, and looked back at me. "Why don't you try living here, then?"

I was dumbstruck. I had only been fantasizing out loud. Not even that, I was just vociferously expressing my admiration. It was like they'd said, *Okay, then. Here, have your fantasy.* What do you say to that? I said nothing, I just blinked.

"Yeah! The horses need a friend." They continued, taking my silence for hesitation. "You could get away from it all! Give yourself a break." Then they tried to sink the hook. "It's so quiet here. You could write your stories down—turn them into a book!"

Before I knew it, I had moved in. It didn't happen overnight, but it did happen faster than I would have guessed. I actually did a lot of soul-searching about it. High school had wrapped up, but I felt like I would be abandoning my boys. Or, so I thought. If I moved out to the country and left Adam and Nicholas to fend for themselves in the city, it was like I'd be running out on them. Or, so I thought.

Of course, the boys were all for it. "You gotta go, Mom!" They would say, "It's your dream place! You can't pass this up." I didn't understand their motives at first; I suspected that they were just itching to be free of parental authority. It was some time later that I finally understood the truth.

They were already at that age anyway. Adam and Nicholas could take off whenever they wanted to. But for as long as the boys could remember, people had patted them on the head and said, "Now you boys take good care of your mom." And so they did.

For all these years, we had been an inseparable trio. Now that they were old enough to move out, they weren't sure that they should. Adam and Nicholas were worried about *abandoning me*. If I moved out to the country, it gave them tacit permission to head off on their own. Obviously, they needed this as much as I did. In the end, it would make us all stronger, and more independent.

A week later, the boys moved into an apartment with friends, and I moved out onto the farm. It was as peaceful and idyllic as I'd imagined. Paradise on earth, I could not have been any happier. I was also quite proud of myself for my mature decision.

Twenty-four hours later, I was scared to death.

"What on earth was I thinking?" I scolded myself, "I hate being alone! Why didn't I do a trial sleepover?" The only room in the cabin that had any power was the kitchen. The only heat was from an old stone fireplace where I burned coal for warmth. I skulked around all night by the light of a candle or flashlight. I was too terrified to go to sleep. It was pitch black outside, and eerily quiet. I kept thinking I heard strange animal noises, and told myself repeatedly, "It's only a horse. It's only a horse." I was talking out loud, just so I had someone to hear! It was a long night.

Eventually I did fall asleep, and everything was fine. The next morning was beautiful, like nothing I'd ever seen, as the mists rolled off the meadows and the sun climbed over the trees. I watched the horses gather at the lake for a drink. I was happy again.

In a short while, life out on the farm began to feel perfectly natural. The quiet was so very relaxing; and while the black nights could make me a little nervous, the blanket of stars was simply astonishing to behold. After a few days, the horses warmed up to me. We would spend the mornings together as I sipped coffee on the porch, and then went out to feed them bits of apples or carrots.

Work was as hectic as ever, and the drive could feel like a long one; but it was worth it. That rustic old cabin in the country really was a slice of heaven on earth. I never did get that book written; not on the farm anyway. But better things were in store for me there.

At a hospital one day, making my rounds, a radiation oncologist asked me a question that would change my life. Not that I knew it at the time. Dr. Michael Cross was a man whose opinion I valued and I had a lot of respect for him. He was highly skilled and extremely good with

Dr. Michael Cross connected me with many important people—from patients who needed my help to the man who would become my husband.

his patients. Dr. Cross was also very supportive of Image Insights. He knew what we did there and he showed that support by sending us many patients who would benefit from our help. He asked me, "So, you live in Maysville now?"

"Yes," I replied. "Why?" *Not exactly riveting conversation.*

"Do you ever see Dr. Zinda?" he asked.

"Dr. Zinda? No." *A little more interesting,* I thought, and asked, "Why? Should I?"

"He has a clinic there that he visits twice a week," Dr. Cross told me. "You've probably been passing each other, going in opposite directions, for months."

Now that is interesting. I hadn't seen Michael, er, Dr. Zinda, in probably three years or more. Not since we'd volunteered together at the ACS. "Maybe I'll drop in on him then," I said, thoughtfully.

I showed up at Dr. Zinda's clinic a few days later, hoping to catch him off guard at his lunch hour. I did. He was as surprised as I had been to find out that we were in the same neck of the woods. When I told Michael about life on the farm and my old log cabin, he said simply, "You're kidding."

"No, really," I assured him. "It's peaceful out there. Life stripped down to the essentials." Then, I invited Michael to take a look for himself.

He did come out to visit me on the farm. It was really quite comical to watch the big city boy pick his way carefully through the road apples. I had to smile as I watched Michael give the horses a very wide berth. He was going nowhere near those wild things. I showed him around my primitive dwelling, and when I finished, all he could say was, "You're crazy."

Over the course of the next few visits, he did warm up to the horses. Michael would join me, every few weeks, for a little breakfast out on the porch. Coffee and bagels for us, carrots for the horses. We spent most of our time talking about work or talking about our kids. I found out that Michael had also been through a divorce recently. As single parents, we both had a lot in common.

It was nice to have someone to hang out with. Every now and then, we met for lunch. After a while, Michael casually asked me to supper. It wasn't long before we started meeting once or twice a week for dinner and conversation. While on the outside it may have looked like we were dating, I probably would not have classified it as such. That would have been too presumptuous.

As far as picking men went, I had a lousy track record. My limited experience in dating had led to a pair of disastrous decisions. After that, I stayed off the market for so long that I'd forgotten what dating was like. I had serious doubts that my skills had shown any improvement. We had a nice, deep friendship going. It was the first really good relationship that I'd had with a man, outside of my family. I was not about to jeopardize it by making noises like "serious" or "commitment". Why ruin a good thing?

R econnecting with Michael put me in touch with a whole new group of patients that we had yet to reach. For some reason, it hadn't even occurred to me to reach out to the doctors around Maysville, even after I had moved there! In the early days, I was busy trying to get the word out around Covington and Cincinnati. Maysville was outside of our area. By the time I moved there, things were so busy at the shops that I hadn't thought about contacting the doctors in my new home town.

As soon as we'd met up with each other again, Michael began sending patients in to Image Insights. One of those patients was a tough, ornery woman, June Kilgus, who was about ten years older than I was. It turns out that June had had her eye on the good

June Kilgus was a woman made bitter by cancer, who later softened and became my "mom away from home."

Dr. Zinda for quite some time. "One day," she confessed to me, "when we get this all cleared up, I'm going to take that young man off the market." Truthfully, she didn't confess that idea until later. When we first met, she didn't like me at all.

At our first session together, I offered our usual professional service, and I did so with my usual good nature. But June had a stern, no-nonsense demeanor, and one withering look would say, "Why don't you just get the job done and keep the chit-chat to a minimum." I did; and I breathed a sigh of relief when she was gone.

The second visit went no better. Neither did the third. I would try to be open and engaging, but June was having none of it. The visits continued, but our relationship never seemed to improve. I wasn't about to give up, but it was really beginning to bother me. I confided my dismay to Michael.

"Oh, that's just June." Michael reassured me. "She doesn't like anyone. She doesn't like me, either."

June's bout with cancer had left her feeling bitter and angry. Up until then, she had been a big wheel in her small town, known and respected by all. June was one of the biggest fish in the small pond that was Maysville. She had a certain celebrity there, and she reveled in it; after all, she had worked hard to earn it.

But when the cancer came, she felt, as so many women do, that it had robbed her of her femininity. As a result, she no longer liked to be around people. This, in turn, robbed her of her stature. She deeply resented that; but she could hardly take it out on the cancer. Instead, she took it out on the few people that she did have contact with.

I could hardly blame her for her feelings, so I kept up the good fight. I would not let her get me down, and if I could, I would bring her around. Eventually, I did wear her down. June did not want to give up her resentment either, at least, not easily. She held onto it tightly, as if it were a prize possession. As the weeks progressed, she began to loosen her grip on it and she warmed up, little by little. Soon enough, we had an actual for-real friendship going—to her surprise as much as to mine. There was no single moment of change. It was a gradual evolution; and when it was done our relationship was completely unrecognizable from what it had been.

June became my "Maysville mother", always fussing over me. "I don't like you living on that farm out there—that's a hunter's haven. It's no place for a girl on her own." She was always worrying. "Are you eating? Have you been eating? You don't look like you're eating. Come out to the house for dinner tonight." Her tone of voice left little room for argument.

Living on that old farm, with its single light switch in the kitchen, I did not exactly have extensive laundry facilities. The old hand pump and washboard just wouldn't cut it. So every week I would haul my laundry to the laundromat. It didn't take June long to figure it out either. She would instruct me, "I want you to come to dinner tonight. And bring your laundry."

We would get the washing machine going and have dinner while it did it's work. Dinner was always warm and wonderful; and afterward, we would sit contentedly, with full bellies, talking and relaxing while the dryer hummed in the background.

On some nights we would read Bible verses and talk about what they meant to us, while sitting on the floor of her posh purple bedroom. Leaning back against pillows, we would gaze up at the ceiling and ponder the mysteries of heaven and earth. Until the drier buzzed. Then I would reluctantly climb to my feet to fold my laundry.

"You stay right there," June ordered me, time and again. "I'll take care of it. You relax." If she had had her way, I would never have folded a sock or washed a dish.

"If you're not going to let me help," I would chide her each time, "then I won't be able to come back." At which point, she would reluctantly accept my help.

June was forever offering her spare room, so that I might stay the night. "You shouldn't be sleeping alone in that old hideout." The offer was always tempting, and I took her up on it a time or two. It was still a long drive from June's house to the farm, and it was always cold, dark, and a little scary when I got home. The only lights, for miles around, were my headlights. Or the stars.

I spent many a wonderful evening with June, and she became a friend that I would treasure forever. To think, we might

When life gives you lemons. . .

Create memories!

People get strength from knowing they're part of something bigger, and that they've weathered rough storms before. "History" can help us put our own life in context. We can see patterns, correct misconceptions, and recognize how much of ourselves we owe to the people who came before us.

have missed out on all of that, if not for that chance meeting with Dr. Cross. If he hadn't pointed out Michael's clinic to me, June and I might never have met. I thank God every day for little "chances" like that.

What's more, if not for that little meeting, I might never have run into Michael again. Of course, when June found out that we were casually seeing each other, she had plenty to say about that. "I was saving him for later!" she informed me, indignantly. "I'm just not ready for him yet!" I began to worry that she was actually serious. But at my look of alarm, she slipped me a little wink and let me off the hook.

"We're only just friends . . ." I replied, lamely.

Every year, there was one big night out that I never missed. The American Cancer Society Gala was quite the formal ball. In years past, when I was president of the society, I would always attend the big event. They were so beautiful and elegant that I couldn't bear to sit at home, knowing it was going on. If I had to go alone, I would—even if it meant playing a wallflower. I just had to watch. Sometimes, I did go by myself; other times I attended with one of my favorite clients. Either way, I was going.

When Michael asked me to attend the gala with him, to my surprise and his, I was hesitant. I should have been jumping for joy. This was a *real* dress-up date—a glamorous night out on the town—and I was the official "date-ee". But the medical community was as much about politics and gossip as any other. He was recently divorced. So was I, but my divorce was a matter of record—old news. However, *his* divorce made him a prime target for the husband-hunters that permeated the field. A successful doctor recently released from captivity was serious big game. No doubt there were dozens of nurses planning his recapture at that very moment. I didn't want to get caught in the feeding frenzy. I thought it over very carefully. I didn't want to feed the rumor mill. The last thing Image Insights needed was bad PR. I had to maintain a good, solid image in the medical community.

Besides, I wasn't looking for a trophy husband. If that's all that other women wanted him for, then "they" could have him. If I married again, it would be for life. My previous experiences with marriage had been devastating. To my deep regret, I had chosen poorly. Not that I had even been thinking about marriage, to Michael or anyone else. But if I was given another shot at it, I would move slowly and carefully. There had been too much turmoil and heartache for me to treat the matter lightly. In thinking about it so much, I realized that I was getting ahead of myself. I was worrying about gossip and evaluating his marriage potential like a school girl with her first steady. It was just a simple date. *Why don't we take this one day at a time?* I told myself. The plain and simple truth was, I really enjoyed being around Michael. So I agreed to go with him, but we would go as friends. *Who could have a problem with that? No one,* I told myself. *That's who.*

We had a wonderful time at the Gala. Michael was a perfect gentleman. Handsome and charming, he made sure that the whole evening went perfectly. *This is a far cry from the blowfish date!* I thought to myself happily. Between the dinner, the dancing, and the conversation, I was having the time of my life. It had been so long since I'd had a night like that. In fact, until that night, I don't think I'd *ever* had an evening quite like it. At one point, Michael left to refill our drinks and a friend turned to me and said, "That man absolutely adores you. Have you been dating long?"

I laughed and replied, "This is our first 'real date.'" I smiled, and hoped she couldn't see me blush. "We're only friends."

"Oh, no!" she said. "He adores you. I can tell by the way he looks at you." My smile fell away. *Me?* I wondered girlishly. *He really likes me?* "You guys are great together," my friend said with a wink, as she wandered off. Michael returned to the table, his usual cheerful, gracious self, and I plastered on a happy smile. Inside, my mind was racing. *Adores me, huh?* I looked at him in a whole new light. For the rest of the evening, I found myself thinking about what my friend had said.

After that night, Michael and I began trading regular phone calls. Every few days or so, we would have a long talk. We talked *a lot* about our children. He had four teenagers, John, Phillip, Luke and Claire, and things had been challenging for him since the divorce. They were all good kids, but there had been a lot of hurt feelings to soothe, and a lot of issues to sort out. Michael was working hard to make sure that his children stayed on course. He didn't want any of the mistakes their parents had made to sour them on the idea of marriage and family. Having been through divorce and the trials of the teen years myself, I could relate to much of what he had to say. We would talk at length about the challenges of raising teenagers. While I was certainly no expert, I was willing to share my opinions. I was also pleased that he listened so well and really seemed to consider what I had to say. More than anything, I was grateful that my boys were becoming young adults by then.

One afternoon, about six months after the ACS gala, I was at June's house again. Her illness had taken a turn for the worst, and she was feeling very poorly that day. I was there to see if there was anything I could do for her—but mostly I was there just to keep her company and cheer her up.

We had been chatting for a while, when my cell phone rang. It was Michael. "Do you mind?" I asked June.

"No, go ahead. See what the big fool wants." She still pretended to carry a torch for him. While June may have been feeling down and out, at least her spirits were picking back up.

I took the call, and kept it brief. When I finished, June arched an eyebrow at me, as if to say, "Well . . .?"

"He just wants to know if we're still on for dinner," I said by way of explanation. "Getting near feeding time."

June snorted, "Ha! He's lucky you got to him first. Probably couldn't handle a woman like me . . . Too much for him!" Her spirits were definitely picking up.

I chuckled at her bravado, and we returned to our discussion. While I wasn't watching the clock, it couldn't have been more than fifteen minutes before the phone rang again. I pulled out the phone for a look. "Michael," I shrugged helplessly.

June nodded for me to take it. "Must be getting hungry," she quipped.

I took the call, again. It was the same question, again. "I'm over at June's," I told Michael, "I'll leave in a few minutes and call you when I'm on the road. I'll meet you at your house." I hung up and looked at June, wide-eyed. "Sheesh! What a nag." I grinned and shook my head.

"You know how it is with men and their stomachs," June shook her head sympathetically.

We had gone back to chatting, and it couldn't have been but another fifteen minutes when the phone rang again. Michael. "What? Is he counting the minutes?" I asked. "What's the rush?"

"Maybe he wants to pop the question," June smirked.

"Yeah, right." I took the call.

When we finished, June said to me, "You better get going, before I get hungry and decide to take your place!"

I hadn't been on the road more than five minutes, when he called again! "Are you on your way yet?" Michael asked. "We need to talk." Now I was no longer curious; I was downright anxious. *I wonder what's got his underwear in such a twist?* June's house was an hour away from Michael's, so he would just have to wait.

I had just pulled up to Michael's house and opened my door when Michael offered his hand. He practically pulled me from the car. "Come on," he said urgently, "This can't wait." We walked a short distance down the street. He was quiet, and walked briskly all the way. There was a small wooded area at the end of the road, and he found a nice shade tree. Coming to a stop, he motioned me toward it. "Sit down. Please."

Michael paced around for a moment, his hands going in and out of his pockets as he searched for the right words. Not finding them there, he sat down beside me. Taking my hand in his, he looked at me and said, "Gayle . . . ." Then he popped back up and started pacing around again. He was alternately pocketing his hands or waving them about as he explained, "with all I've been through," and "after such a difficult divorce . . ." It wasn't making much sense.

Then he stopped and looked at me. "I never thought I'd be serious about someone again." Michael seemed to calm down then, and he sat beside me and took up my hand again. "I don't want to live the rest of my life without you," he finished.

At least, I think he was finished. He'd stopped talking anyway; but I wasn't sure where that left me. I really wasn't sure how serious this was. It had seemed pretty serious when he dragged me down here, but now I wasn't sure. Was he just expressing his feelings, or was there more to it than that? "Are you asking me to marry you?" I asked, eyebrows raised.

"Yes." Michael nodded. "Yes, I am."

If I had been a little confused before, now my head really began to spin. *This is serious! He wants to marry me!* I was stunned. *Me!* This was a man I had always looked on with admiration. *He's so kind and caring,* I mused, *so loving and thoughtful.* I was amazed that he actually wanted to marry *me!* So while part of me wanted to shout "Yes!", another part of me actually hesitated. *How do I know I'm making the right choice?* Believe it or not, I was still lugging around a lot of emotional baggage. Old habits really do die hard.

I could almost see the little cartoon angel and devil hovering over my shoulders! "What are you? Crazy?" The little angel shouts, jumping up and down in a panic. "Say YES! Say YES!" Then the little devil leans in and whispers slyly, "Not so fast, Gayle. What if he's a phony? What if he's hiding something. You know how badly you chose before . . ."

Long before my days at The Lemonade Stand, long before I opened Image Insights, I was a single mom. After a pair of divorces, I really felt like a failure. As a young Catholic woman, I'd *tried* to take the teachings of the church seriously—tried but failed. *Look at me,* I thought. *A single woman with two young boys and no husband. A divorceé. No, a double divorceé!*

What a mess I've made, I thought reproachfully. *Good job, Gayle.* The first marriage was doomed almost from the beginning. I was young and foolish. I tried to make it work; but there are some things no one should have to take. I knew that it was time to go, and I would just have to deal with the consequences as they came along. As to the second, short marriage, I was a little less young but no less foolish. A shiny, happy lifestyle had tempted me into a relationship with a man who cared not a whit for my sons. That one was dead before it started; I'd just been too slow to catch on.

"What God has ordained, let no man put asunder." That first marriage was supposed to be a good Catholic marriage, but I'd sundered it all right. It didn't matter that it had needed sundering. That, if I hadn't, I might not have been around long enough to make any choices at all, foolish or not. None of that mattered. In my mind, I had screwed up. I made the poor choice, so the results were my own fault.

Church was still important enough to me that I wanted to continue to go; but when I walked in, I felt distinctly out of place. Part of me was always afraid that someone would turn and point at me, crying "Sinner! You don't belong here!" Silly, I know; but I was young, and foolish. I hadn't really put two and two together. After all, if church is not a place for sinners to be welcomed, then what is? What better place to be warm, open, and inviting to a sinner than in church? Church is about forgiveness, is it not? It is about encouraging you to do better. Church should lift you up, help you to see the light, and teach you how to reach your full potential. Most of all, if you should stumble on your way, church should be there to give you a hand up again.

It took me some time to understand it. We've all made mistakes; we've all failed. It's not so much how one fails that is important, as it is how one recovers. *So you failed. Are you sorry?* Yes, I am. *That's good; are you doing a better job this time?* Yes, I am. *That's even better.* If only I had understood such things a little sooner, I might have saved myself some grief—and years of regret.

At my tender, young age, I had missed the point of church completely. In condemning sin, I thought they were condemning me. I felt unworthy. It was my misunderstanding; but that's what led me to feel like a second-class citizen. Since I felt like I didn't belong, I sat in the back of the church and hid from the priests, trying to get a little peek at God from way in back.

I didn't want my mistakes to mess up things for my boys, so I took them in anyway. Besides staying busy with after-school sports and helping out at the shop, Adam and Nicholas became altar boys. They were good and faithful ones, and the priests came to know them as solid, hard-working, and dependable. I guess some of their good reputation must have rubbed off on me. Even while my sons were altar boys, I continued to hide out in back, hoping that no one would notice. But, of course, they did.

One Sunday, a priest at St. Thomas church asked me to stay after Mass; he wanted to sit and talk with me. "Why are you always hiding in the back row?" he asked. I told him my sad little story, reliving my "disgraceful" past. Inside, I actually expected him to tell me to leave. That shows just how badly I'd misjudged him, and the church. I had thought that, because I was a divorceé, I didn't belong. I didn't think that they would have me. It hadn't occurred to me that they weren't in business to help perfect people. Youth, and a lack of solid information, had led to some foolish conclusions. When I was finished with my tale, the priest asked me, "Gayle, are you sorry for your sins? Are you sorry for their repercussions?"

I looked at him, and I thought, *I wish it had gone better—but we were wrong for each other.* I was never going to be the woman he wanted me to be, and no amount of his hitting or yelling was going to change that. Was I sorry I got the divorce? Yes and no. The divorce *had* to happen. I was sorry I'd made a poor selection; but I was not sorry that it had given me my sons. However, I was sorry for the damage it might do to them. So was I sorry? What finally came out was "Yes. I am sorry."

"Do you repent of your sins," he asked me.

"Yes, I do," I answered.

"Then you are forgiven," he said. Simple as that. "See you next Sunday, *up front!*"

My eyes went wide. "Really?" I asked hopefully.

"Oh, yes!" The priest nodded emphatically. "Come to communion, move forward, and live your life. It's time you stopped living in the past."

I was so relieved! That part of my life had weighed so heavily on me. That I could put it behind me was almost unbelievable. For so long I had lived with the misguided notion that I didn't belong, that I was unworthy. That day, the priest had quoted a Bible verse to me that helped me understand my mistake. "Trust in the Lord with all your heart and lean not on your own understanding; in all your ways acknowledge Him, and He will make your paths straight" (*Proverbs 3:5-6*).

To top it all off, my priest encouraged me to petition for annulment. "You're kidding!" I said, in disbelief. "An annulment. For me?" I was sure he was mistaken. "How do I rate *that*?" I'd never thought I was worthy of such a thing, and *never* would have asked on my own. The priest explained that, while the church considered marriage sacred, they were well aware that some unions were serious mistakes. Naturally, they would prefer that their parishioners work hard on their marriages, to grow them and sustain them. In their eyes, divorces were too common, and all too easy to get. They had become an easy out for many who were unwilling to face the hard work of marriage. But that didn't mean that the church couldn't see the truth. We're only human; sometimes people choose poorly—very poorly. Sometimes there were marriages made that should never have been ordained. Which is why there were annulments.

But this would be no easy out. It took almost two years to complete the process, the investigations, and the reviews. When the annulment of my first marriage was finally granted, I felt like the weight of the world had been lifted from my shoulders. The second marriage had been made outside of the church, so it was not entirely valid in their eyes. The second divorce was enough to clear up that mistake. While that may have been a convenient loophole for me, I regretted my foolishness in that case just as much. I had worked hard not to repeat the mistake. So hard in fact, that all these years later, I was having trouble recognizing a good man when he was right in front of me!

Long after the church granted my annulment, I went in to have another serious talk with a priest again. This was several years after I'd opened Image Insights, and I had just turned 40. I told the priest that, if it were God's will, I would like to be married again one day. I was seeing couples like Sue and John every day. They inspired me, and I wanted so much to be part of a relationship like theirs. However, I didn't have a lot of experience in picking good men. "How do I know if a man that I'm interested in is the one that God chose?" I asked the priest. "How do I know it's not my poor judgment again?"

"For a woman in your situation," the priest began, "there are criteria that a man should meet before you even consider him." *Criteria?* I thought, *I probably should have looked into this a long time ago.* Then he proceeded to outline them for me.

"First," the priest said, as he held up a finger, "you should look for a man who has never been married," *At 40? That sounds promising,* I thought sourly. *What's wrong with him?*

"Second," he said, as another finger came up, "you could look for a widower." *Oh great, and be called by the wrong name for the next 20 years!* I sighed.

Another finger came up. "Third, you can always try a divorced man." The priest paused, and pursed his lips as he stared at the three fingers. He put his hand back down, and looked right at me. "But if *you* are serious about the church, then *that* would suggest that *he* is not." I shook my head. *No thanks. Been there, done that.*

The priest folded his hands together. "If *he* was serious about church, then he would already have an annulment." The priest finished, "That is your fourth choice." *And what are the odds of that?!* I thought forlornly.

I thanked the priest for his time. *I guess single life isn't so bad.*

ow several years later, I was sitting on the grass with a truly wonderful man. That wonderful man had just asked me to marry him. I could see myself being happy with him for the rest of my life.

"You're really asking me to marry you?" I said to Michael.

"Yes," he smiled, "I am."

"But, you don't meet the criteria!" I blurted out.

Michael blinked at me in astonishment. "The criteria?" he laughed. "Says who?"

"Well, you can't ever have been married . . .," I said, as I counted off one finger. Michael's eyebrows went up.

"Or you have to be a widower." He frowned, as I counted off two.

"Or, you can be divorced," I continued, while I held up three fingers. "But that means you're not serious." His forehead wrinkled and one corner of his mouth turned up in a half smile.

"Or else, you have to have an annulment," I finished, and held up all four fingers. Michael's forehead smoothed out and the other corner of his mouth came up into a full smile. *He's not mad!* My mind worked furiously, *He doesn't think I'm crazy. And he hasn't stormed away.* "Do you have an annulment?" I asked hopefully.

He took my hand. "Yes," he said, "I do."

"Then, yes." I replied, "I will."

Not exactly a moment fit for the silver screen, but it was everything I had ever hoped for. Michael had taken the time, years before, to do things right. That sealed the deal for me. However, his careful preparations weren't entirely complete. In his haste to ask me, he had overlooked one minor detail. We were short one ring.

"Be nice to have something to remember the moment by . . .," I suggested. Then I squeezed one of his fingers, gently but firmly.

"Oh, yeah!" Michael blinked, "the ring." He smoothly pulled off his favorite ring and slipped in onto my finger.

Nice recovery, I thought, as he kissed me. Then he called me his "pearl of great price" and I thought, *Oh, that IS good.*

I'm going to be an old married woman! I thought, with a grin. I was so excited I could barely contain myself—really! At long last, I was finally going to have a loving husband, and a big family full of people to love and care for. I could hardly believe it was happening. For nearly a decade, I'd been working so hard to keep Rita's dream alive. Now, within weeks of my 10-year anniversary, God had set the perfect man in my path. I had kept my promise, and now all of the hard work was finally paying off. Not with a financial jackpot, instead, my reward was to have my fondest dreams come true.

Naturally, Adam and Nicholas were the first to hear about the proposal. They were a lot less surprised than I had been; I guess they'd seen it coming. I was lucky; the boys thought as highly of Michael as I did and they were very happy for us. After my boys, Michael told his kids. Then I told each of my family members and all of my closest friends; I was so thrilled. When I was done, I called my old friend Bill Huston to tell him all about Michael.

It occurred to me later that I probably should have called him *first.* Bill's opinion was important to me. It was so important, in fact, that if he'd said "bad idea," I would have thought seriously about saying "no". And then, I would have had to call everybody back and tell each and every one "nevermind!" Over the years, I'd kept in touch with Bill, and he had become my Rock of Gibraltar. At 77, he was my sage, my wise old man. Even more, he was my center—especially in times of trouble. Bill was always able to show me how my life and the world of the Bible should fit together. Everything made sense around him. So it was important to me that Bill give us his blessing.

On the phone, Bill surprised me by saying, "Honey, before I do, I'd like to meet Michael first." *Oh,* I thought, *I guess he's not*

going to hand that blessing out without checking up on me first.
"Yeah," he drawled, "I'd like to meet him alright." Another pause,
then Bill finished seriously, "Alone." In my mind, I could almost
hear a shotgun chamber a round. I knew Bill was a gentle soul,
and he probably hadn't touched a shotgun in decades—but that's
how I felt. I swallowed nervously, and agreed. If Bill didn't
approve, then Michael was going home single. Besides, you never
really know just who has a shotgun.

Half nervous and half excited, I told Michael all about Bill,
and how he had been so very important to me. At first, Michael
thought that the request was a little unorthodox, and he was
reluctant to go. When he realized how important it was to me—
no Bill, no Gayle—Michael agreed to meet with him.

The next afternoon, I dropped Michael off at Bill's house.
Then I drove away. I so hoped that he would make a good
impression. *How could he not?* I thought. But I was nervous just
the same. I wanted so badly for Bill to approve. I told Michael to
call me when he was ready for a pick up. I was about as anxious
as I'd ever been. I went looking for a way to kill some time.
Maybe a coffee shop, I thought. I needed something to do with
my hands. I was very fidgety. But by the time I'd found a little
shop, I was so nervous that the very idea of coffee was repellent.
I would probably explode in a blast of nervous energy. They
would be cleaning the place up for weeks. Instead, I just drove
around and around. And around some more. *If this goes on much
longer,* it occurred to me, *I'll have to gas up again.*

After a while, I even drove all the way to Image Insights. I
went back into that old broom closet and prayed for some
strength. I felt a lot better after that. So I drove back to Bill's side
of town and went looking for ways to kill time. I even circled
back by Bill's house once or twice, just to make sure that Michael
hadn't been tossed out into the gutter.

It was several hours before Michael finally called me. Of
course, I shouldn't have worried. When I returned to Bill's

house, he and Michael were talking and laughing just like long lost friends. I don't know why I'd let my imagination get the best of me. After all this time, I guess I wanted our marriage to happen so badly that I was afraid of anything that might stop it. Seeing the looks on their faces, as I walked up Bill's steps, made me terribly jealous. I wished I had been there to enjoy the visit with them, instead of driving in circles all afternoon. Together, they had been laughing up a storm, while I was almost all out of fingernails. But the wedding was on!

The man who would be marrying us was a priest by the name of Father Jim. He was one of the those people that just radiated positive energy. His faith and confidence was infectious, and when he spoke, he truly did lift the congregation up. Typically, to ensure compatibility and a safe, solid marriage, the church asked for six months of counseling. "You guys are grownups," Father Jim said to us, "I think we can do it in three."

There would be marriage classes involved, too. The classes would be followed by a marriage test. Our score would be determined by how well our answers agreed. We were all ready to sign up for the classes, but Father Jim said to us, "I think you guys are a little too old for that. Why don't you just take the test?" That sounded like a good idea, but when it came time for the test I grew anxious again. It was like the nightmare where you get to class only to find that there is a test that day and you've missed the entire semester. Only now, I was living that dream. *At least I'm not in my underwear,* I thought. It had taken me so long to get there. The idea of our marriage had passed muster with Bill, Father Jim, our parents, and our kids. What if the test actually said we were incompatible? What would that mean?

As it turns out, I was worried over nothing. "Your test scores are so high," Father Jim told us, "that you guys ought to be marriage counselors." *Isn't that ironic,* I thought to myself. All of those phone calls, dinners, and chats out on the porch really seem to have paid off.

Michael's brother Dave, Luke, John, my husband Michael and myself, Phillip, Claire, Nicholas, and Adam. After ten years of working hard and waiting for the right man, God blessed me in a big way. My cup runneth over, indeed!

Michael and I were married just over a year after our first real date. It was a beautiful ceremony, as most weddings are, but there was one part I especially liked. Okay, three parts. After "I now pronounce you husband and wife," and the kiss, I loved the part when Father Jim talked about lemons. He spoke of how we had each found Christ, and said, "Now you are making lemonade together, from two lives that had seemed like lemons." I hope it was our story that inspired the phrase. Although I suppose it could have been the explosion of lemons that was our wedding.

There were lemon slices in the bouquets, lemon slices in the boutonnieres, and lemon slices in the corsages. The beautiful arrangements were courtesy of my friend Jim Case, who was an amazingly talented florist. He was so dedicated that he attended our wedding just to be sure everything was perfect. There were lemon centerpieces on the tables and, of course, lemon slices on the cake. To top it all off, each guest had a wedding edition bottle of Nantucket Lemonade to wet their whistle. What can I say? Sometimes I get a little carried away.

After the whole "kiss the bride" moment, when I was expecting to walk down the aisle together as husband and wife, Michael turned and dashed up the aisle alone! *Isn't it a little late to leave me at the altar?* I thought. My look of surprise must have been telling, because I saw it reflected in the faces of many of our guests. We all listened in confusion at a deep and rapid *thump, thump, thump, thump, thump.* It was the kind of sound a big man would make if he were leaping up a flight of stairs, two at a time.

Michael emerged on the choral balcony a moment later, looking slightly out of breath. He took a few seconds to gather his wits, then he waved a signal to the choir behind him. The music rose and the singers came to life, while Michael snatched a few more hurried breaths. Then, he serenaded me with "Love Never Fails," with full choral accompaniment.

Fortunately, for everyone involved, Michael has a beautiful singing voice.

After the song, and to enthusiastic applause, Michael rejoined me at the altar. Then we walked down the aisle as husband and wife. It was an awesome day.

CHAPTER

16

Cha-Cha-Cha Changes

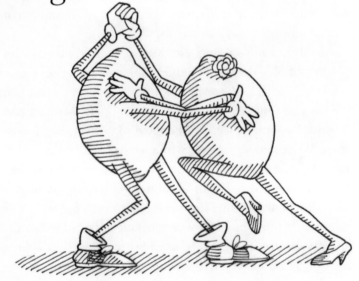

Michael began helping out at Image Insights almost as soon as we began dating. *In for a penny, in for a pound,* I thought to myself happily. We were remodeling our Covington location again, expanding and upgrading the store. It seemed as if I were forever remodeling. No sooner did one project stop than another one began. There were always building improvements to be done; but, sadly, I was no Bob Villa. My stumbling efforts were more along the lines of Tim "The Tool Man" Taylor. But that's okay; I never claimed to be an expert. My skills lay elsewhere. Fortunately, I had a lot of talented help that I could count on. God had blessed me with many skilled and knowledgeable volunteers,

Me and my husband, Dr. Michael Zinda. A kinder, more compassionate man I have never known.

and my latest recruit was pretty handy himself. Most people don't think of doctors as do-it-yourself-ers, but Michael knew his way around a hammer and paintbrush as well as anyone.

To liven things up a little, Michael would bring in his CD player and play the most wonderful music. His tastes were a tad eclectic; classical, Motown, blues, jazz, gospel . . . you name it, we listened to it. We even tried a bit of opera. Michael had that beautiful singing voice, and he liked to put it to work now and then. We would sing along while we painted and moved furniture. From our first days as a couple, we pulled together as a team. He helped me with absolutely everything, which was a new experience for me. I was used to going it alone; but I had a "for real" partner now. It was a constant source of wonder to me. *If our marriage is going to be anything like this,* I thought, *then I have definitely found the right man.*

Image Insights was doing well, humming along smoothly, and my staff and I were helping people like never before. With the help of the foundation, the stores were even supporting themselves. All those years of chaos and struggle were beginning to seem like a distant memory. To my great relief, life had become stable. I'd been taking home regular paychecks for awhile now, and for the first time, my personal finances were actually in pretty good shape.

That being the case, there was one thing that I wanted to change. For more than ten years, I'd been driving all over Kentucky, Indiana, and Ohio in one beat up old car or another. I had probably driven to the moon and back; but I'd never had a nice, solid, reliable new car. It seemed as if everything in my life was 40 minutes away. The Ohio store was 40 minutes away from the Kentucky store, and the Indiana store was 40 minutes away from either of them. My cabin on the farm was more than 40 minutes from all three! Sometimes if felt like I spent as much time on the road as I did caring for my clients.

Wouldn't it be nice to have a car that always started? I would think longingly. *I would love to have a heater that always worked. And upholstery that wasn't cracked. And a stereo that came on. And a car that didn't rattle. And paint that wasn't dinged or dented.* It was high time that I started looking for something a little more professional.

I began by looking at new cars; but nothing felt very exciting to me. There wasn't a single car I saw that had me thrilled about parting with all of that hard earned cash. They were either too boring, too expensive, or both. In moments of wishful thinking, I fantasized about my dream car . . . a Mercedes. *It could be used,* I thought. *Er, . . . I mean, preowned.*

It would be practical, I rationalized to myself. *What could be more practical, for driving across three states, than a car that never breaks down?* And it would be so comfortable. I was spending more and more time in the car. The drives were getting so long, and I was on the road all alone. I thought it would be nice to have a car that was utterly and completely dependable. I knew it seemed far-fetched, but if I was going to dream, I would dream big. *Why not?* I said to myself, *it couldn't hurt to take a little look.*

Oh yes, it could. I looked. It hurt. *Maybe I can milk the Chevy for a few more years,* I thought. *At least it will save me a car payment.*

While this was going on, Michael had bought himself an SUV. I was over at his house, visiting, so that he might have the chance to show it off. But as I was still stuck in my old clunker, part of me was a little envious. "What on earth do you need with a big old truck?" I teased him.

"Well, you never know . . . I might have to haul around a bunch of stuff," he explained, "or a bunch of people." Apparently, Michael was thinking farther ahead than I was.

"Then why is that old boat still here?" I asked, nodding at the station wagon still squatting in his driveway.

"I haven't figured out how to sell it. I'm not very good at such things," Michael explained lamely.

"Oh, that's easy," I frowned at him. "I'll do it for you." I called the paper and placed an ad for him. I had them bold-face the first line, "little old lady drove to church on Sundays." I thought that the old chiché would get a laugh, and maybe some attention. Then I plainly listed the particulars.

The ad got some attention all right—from a well-to-do woman in a swanky neighborhood. We drove the wagon out for her to see, and she bought it from Michael right away. We were walking away, our transaction complete, when she opened the garage door to put the wagon away, I couldn't believe my eyes. In the second space was a blue 1986 Mercedes E300 sedan. Propped up inside the back window was a For Sale sign.

I was too stunned to speak. It was my dream car. I had loved Mercedes all my life. I'd read everything there was to read about them, knew everything there was to know. The way that some people are with airplanes or muscle cars—or sports—that's the way I was with Mercedes. I knew the history, the stats, the performance. I just admired them through and through. I had even cruised the dealerships over the years, just to keep up. *Someday,* I'd always told myself.

I grabbed Michael's arm and squeezed. "Did you see that?!" I hissed, excitedly.

"Yeah," Michael nodded. "Nice," he said softly. He was playing it cool. "If you'd like it, I could buy it for you," he told me quietly. So much for playing it cool. I shook my head "no." He frowned at me then, with a look of *why not?*

"We're not even married yet," I said to him. His eyebrows went up as his chin came down. *So what?* his expression read. "No," I told him, "If I do this, I have to do it on my own."

That car was a symbol to me, a four-wheeled seal of approval. It was confirmation that I had worked long and hard enough to earn a nice reward. To me, that car meant that I'd made it, that I had made a success of myself and my business. If Michael bought it for me now, it would look like I had cashed in. Marry a doctor, get a Mercedes. I had earned this on my own. I wanted to do it myself.

I thought about that car all night long. I even prayed on it. The next day I drove back to see that lady, and to find out how much she wanted for the car. The price was a good one, but even so, I didn't have that kind of money just lying around. I went into the bank, to see about a loan. To my complete and utter astonishment, they said "yes". After all these years of denying me a business loan, they decided that a used Mercedes was a good risk. I couldn't believe it. In their eyes, a used car had more intrinsic value than a functioning business! Not that I was complaining.

That nine-year-old "pre-owned" Mercedes was my graduation present to myself. My first "new" car; it was a badge of honor to me, a sign that I'd made it. The old days were gone; no more struggling as a single-parent and overextended business woman. I was still a working mom, but soon I would be a *married* working mom. And while I might be marrying a doctor, I was proud that I had managed to swing that Mercedes on my own. That made it especially sweet.

I was right about the reliability, too. It never gave me an ounce of trouble. And man, was that ride smooth . . . and the heater worked . . . along with the stereo. Perfection truly is in the details.

Now that I was an old married woman—pleased and proud of it—things really began to change. For the first time, I had a wonderful husband who met or exceeded every one of my dreams and expectations. After so long as just the three of us, for Adam, Nicholas, and me, it was an amazing feeling to be part of a large family. Sometimes, when we were all together, I would just sit back to watch everyone. I was amazed that this was my life now, and it affected me in ways I'd never imagined. Michael and his children, my boys and I, were all stirred together into one big stew. While I understood that it would take a while for the flavors to blend, I knew we were creating something good.

It wasn't all smooth sailing. Like any family, we had our share of choppy seas and a few storms. As compatible as Michael and I were, we had widely different backgrounds and histories. Naturally, that affected the way we raised our kids. Michael and I had to learn to work together—and we both had things to learn from each other. Of course, none of the kids were very interested in our parental re-training. They preferred to leave things just the way they were. In the end, we all had to learn to adapt to one another.

I wanted Michael's kids to know that I wasn't trying to replace their mom. Just as, in theory, Michael was not trying to replace my boys' dad. Although, truth be told, my boys were probably pretty happy to have this new father figure. I hoped and prayed that I would have just as good a relationship with Michael's kids as I had with my own. John, Luke, Philip, and Claire were becoming hugely important in my life, and I wanted so much to play a similar role in theirs. What I really hoped for was that, one day, they would come to see me as their bonus mom. Our relationship should be a plus in their lives—not a negative—in other words, a bonus. It would take time, and work, I knew that. But no matter what it took, it was better than the alternative. Now, we were creating one big, new family where two broken ones had existed before.

We came at this from different perspectives, so it would be a challenge to integrate them all. My boys had grown up in a single-parent household. My divorce happened when they were very young. After that, their father was never around. He'd never been able to recover from his addictions so we'd stayed away from each other. My boys didn't need that kind of trouble in their lives. Eventually he and I made our peace with each other, but there was no role model for them there. When we lost him to cancer in 1995, that hope was removed forever.

Now, into their lives walks Michael—as fine an example of a man as there ever was. Even though my boys were grown young men by then, they welcomed the addition. Michael was open, honest, and loving with them, and they responded to it. At last, they had someone they could take their cues from as the years progressed. More than anything, they were glad to see that their mother would no longer be alone.

Michael's kids saw things a little differently. To them, the divorce was more recent, and they still had a good relationship with their mother. In their eyes, the change was a little less exciting. It was a perfectly understandable point of view.

I tried my best to do the right thing, but mistakes were made. I know I made my share. I worried and wondered, *Am I doing a good job? Are we coming together?* My biggest fear was that we might make too many mistakes, and that we would be forever fragmented. I was constantly asking myself, *Am I doing this right?*

Several years later, I got an answer, of sorts. We had moved into a new house, one with a second story. At the top of the stairs, a long hallway branched left and right. With the upstairs doors all on the stairway side of the hall, the opposite wall was one long, unbroken expanse. Since we had to travel that hall several times a day, it made the perfect place to hang our collection of family photos.

Michael and I each had dozens and dozens of framed photos of every shape and size. One by one, they went up, over the course of several days. Painstakingly, Michael arranged and re-

When life gives you lemons. . .

Learn to use the internet!

It's the information highway for researchers in every field. You can find out who's doing what, their results, discoveries, and future plans. Beyond that, there's a Disneyland of interactive entertainment. It's so good, millions of people call it addicting. It's easier than you think and you'll never, ever get bored.

arranged, until every last one was hung. It was a photo montage of each of our lives, right up to that point. When it was finished, the arrangement was a sight to behold. Climbing to the top of our stairs, visitors would emerge into a hallway to find themselves facing a good 50 feet of photos, almost floor to ceiling. That long hallway was our little family history museum. Michaels' photos stretched away to the right, and mine off to the left.

Michael's kids were off to college, so we would only see them one or two at a time. As each of them came by, we pointed out Michael's handiwork. It had been a big job, and I was quite proud of his efforts. Each of the kids climbed to the top of the stairs and took it all in; but none of them said very much. They would walk up and down the hall, looking things over, from one end to the other. There was an occasional brief smile at a recognized picture; but there was none of the happy responses that I had hoped for. *Oh no,* I fretted to myself, *they hate it.*

"Well," Michael would ask each one, "what do you think?" The kids would kind of shuffle their feet, or stuff their hands in their pockets, and think for a moment. "Oh. Umm. It's nice," was the usual polite response.

By the time Claire came to visit, I had almost given up. I hoped that Michael wouldn't bother to ask. But as Claire looked things over, he did.

Claire stopped and folded her arms. "Why are the pictures all divided up?" she asked. Michael and I looked at each other, puzzled.

"Why aren't we all mixed together? If we're a family now, why are we still all 'his' and 'hers'?"

For a moment, I was completely speechless. I finally said to Michael, "Yeah. Why aren't the pictures all mixed up?" I looked at him meaningfully, as I thought, *Well, this is a good sign.*

Almost as if he'd read my mind, Michael nodded. "I guess we'll just have to do it all again," he replied with a smile. If we hadn't arrived at our destination yet, at least it looked like we were on the right track.

J ust as things were finally coming together for me, they were also going quite well for Michael. Over the years, he'd received frequent offers, each one representing a jump in responsibility and reward. His latest position had him at the University of Kentucky, so we found a nice little house in Lexington. Life was good. The only drawback I faced was my commute. By now it was an hour and a half drive to my main store in Covington. It was a lot easier to take in the Mercedes than it would have been in my old Chevy; but even so, it was a long drive and a lot of wasted time.

It wasn't long before Michael was offered an even better position and we were relocating once again. It seemed like I'd been moving almost once a year for a very long time. It was usually a little disorienting. While the improvements were always nice, I began to find myself longing for some real stability. *It would be nice to put down some roots one day,* I thought wistfully. Michael's new position had us moving in the opposite direction, all the way to Chilicothe, Ohio. My commute to the Kentucky store now stretched out to two hours. It was an exhausting drive.

We discussed finding a house closer to the store, but it wasn't really practical. How can you be a doctor and live an hour or two away from your patients? To me, that didn't make any sense. If I were a cancer patient, I think I'd rather have my "wig lady" looking a little sleepy, than have my doctor nodding off at work! Resolved to tough it out, I continued to make that long, long drive. I wasn't about to give up the ship; my clients needed me. At the same time, I didn't want the store to become an anchor for Michael, holding him fast, or worse, dragging him down. So for the time being, I decided that I would take it one day at a time. We'd wait and see just what the future brought. In other words, with no good choices to make, I did nothing. *Who knows? We might decide to move the store,* I told myself. *Or maybe Michael's next position will move him closer in.* Hope springs eternal.

I kept up my daily grind, but it was really starting to take its toll on me. It was simply too much time in a car for this human being, no matter how nice that car was. By the time I got home at night, I was exhausted, and so sore that Michael would have to come outside to pull me out of the car. He was such a devoted husband, with dinner always ready and waiting for me. But it was all I could do to swallow a pain pill, have a quick bite to eat, and collapse into bed. Then, I would get up the next morning and do it all over again.

My lower back was really beginning to bother me, and I should have known better than to push it like that. There is a little expression that doctors are always using, "Pain is a signal that something is wrong." One might think a nurse would pick up on that—I had heard the phrase often enough. But I was so determined to be all things to all people, that I ignored what my body was trying to tell me. I could not let my clients down. Neither would I hold Michael back. Instead, I would mess myself up and try to pretend that I wasn't.

The worst part was, I'd been through all of this before. I *really* should have known better.

B ack in the days before I met Rita, I used to work several jobs at once. Besides my nurse administrator position, I did the insurance physicals, I did home health care, I did anything I could fit in. I had my two boys to support, and there was a nice financial mess to clean up, courtesy of the divorce lawyers. So I spent every waking hour trying to make a buck. For a while, I even worked part-time at a weight loss center.

I was working Christmas one year, and it was *really slow.* Imagine that. A weight loss center slow at Christmas. *Can you think of a better place to do your last minute shopping?* I thought, as I knocked about the empty store. *Why are they even open?* I supposed they felt like *we*—meaning me—had to "be there" for their clients. If they saved even one person from gorging themselves on turkey and mashed potatoes, or eggnog and pecan pie, then it was worth it. *Yeah, right,* I thought. *Mmmm, pecan pie.*

Still, I wasn't complaining, not out loud anyway. They were paying extra by the hour and I was glad to have it. *Since I'm here anyway,* I thought, *I might as well make myself useful.* The place was in need of a little tidying up, so I got down to work. I swept, mopped, scrubbed, or wiped almost every surface in the store. A few hours later, the place looked as good as new. I still had time to kill, so I decided to clean the break room. There was a small refrigerator in there that needed cleaning, too. *A dirty job, but someone's gotta do it,* I smiled to myself. So I did. After I was all finished, I surveyed my handiwork with some satisfaction.

Any *normal* person would have stopped there. In truth, any normal person would have stopped hours ago. Not me. Oh no. I thought to myself, *I'll bet no one's cleaned behind that thing in years.* I tugged it out, wiped up the dust, and pushed the beast back into place. As I did, something in my back went *boing!* Just a little sprain, or, so I thought. A few days later, when my right leg went numb, I realized that there was more to it than that. X-rays confirmed it, and it took emergency surgery to repair a ruptured disk.

More than a decade later, I was feeling that same pain all over again, and foolishly trying my best to ignore it. I had complained about doctors and their God complexes time and time again. And their stubbornness—oh, how stubborn "they" could be. Apparently, nurses are not above such foolishness, either.

"You've already had one surgery," Michael warned me. "Are you looking for another?" We were discussing what kind of changes could be made, but I couldn't see any way to do things differently. A doctor simply cannot be "on call" and be two hours away. I was not about to let my troubles interfere with Michael and his patients.

After many years of hard work as a radiation oncologist, Michael was finally getting where he wanted to be in his career. Besides treating patients, he administered entire cancer centers. Not long after we had married, Michael spent a couple of years in an Executive Master's of Science program for Health Administration. He'd spent more than enough time commuting himself, running back and forth to the University of Alabama in Birmingham.

Michael was finally in a position where he could put to use both his clinical skills and his administrative talents. I thought it was important that that not be interrupted. While our work was related, there was one important difference—*his* work actually *saved* lives. Then, my work put them back together again. Sure, there were a few things that I thought doctors ought to do differently. I tried to teach them to see their patients as people, to see that the work was not finished when the patient left the doctor's office. But my efforts were totally in support of theirs. If Michael and his colleagues weren't doing their jobs well, then I wouldn't have a job to do at all.

I simply was not going to interfere with that. So I continued to make that long drive to care for my clients. And sure enough, I drove myself right back into another date with the surgeon.

During my recovery, the doctor warned me about doing too much driving. Apparently, it was just about the worst thing I could do in my situation. The problem was, once I recovered, I still faced that long, lonely drive. I'm embarrassed to admit that, as soon as I was well enough, I went right back to my old habits. Looking back, it reminded me of the doctors I used to see standing around outside the hospital—on their cigarette breaks. *You guys should know better than that!* I would fume silently to myself. I suppose I wasn't any smarter than they were. In fact, I *knew* I wasn't. Once upon a time, I'd been one of them, too—standing outside with a cigarette in hand. I was finally beginning to see a pattern.

This stubborn refusal to deal with reality went on for the best part of a year. Something had to give. There was plenty of soul-searching and real-estate searching. I made dozens of visits to my broom closet to ask God for a little guidance with my predicament. I prayed, and looked for a new location for the main store. I searched for new talent—someone to come in and take some of the load off my shoulders. I even wished for a transfer, or new opportunity, for Michael—something a little closer to Image Insights. But there were only so many cancer centers within driving distance. In the end, I knew that was a hopeless prospect.

Eventually, I realized that I'd been praying for specific solutions while the answer had been staring me in the face all along. It reminded me of the old joke about the two rowboats and the helicopter.

I n case you haven't heard it: A man is flooded out of his house. He climbs up onto the roof and prays for salvation. The waters are rising through the first floor, when a man in a rowboat paddles by. "Come on, jump in!" the boatman shouts.

"No thanks," the man yells back. "God will save me. I'll be fine."

The waters rise through the second floor and another boat happens by. "Hop in! Let's go!" the second boatman cries.

"That's all right," the man calls back, as he shakes his head. "I'll be fine. God will save me."

The waters are rising up the roof and lapping at the man's toes, when a helicopter comes to a hover over head. The pilot drops a rope ladder and shouts, "Climb up, and we'll get outta here!"

"I'll be okay," the man yells back, as he waves the pilot off. "God will save me!"

A short while later he drowns.

When he gets to heaven, the man complains to God, "I don't understand what happened. I thought you were going to save me!"

"Oy," God says. "What do you want from me? I sent two boats and a helicopter!"

A s much sense as that story makes, it's not like I got it all at once. At first, I tried streamlining the business a little bit. The Indiana office had never grown beyond a part-time satellite location. Now that I had my clients' measurements and preferences, there was little need for them to drive all the way in. We were handling most of the work by phone and mail order anyway. When a client needed something, they called. We placed an order, customized as necessary, and shipped it right to their front door.

The store had become almost superfluous—and I was no longer up to the extra drive. While it pained me to do it, I closed the Indiana office.

The closing did lighten my burden, and the impact on the business overall was almost negligible. While it had supported itself well enough, the Indiana office just hadn't grown the way the main Kentucky shop had. The loss in income was more than offset by the reduction in stress, both mental and physical. Since we were still able to care for those clients, and the drive would only continue to beat me up, the closing made sense.

What I hadn't reckoned on was the logical extension to that way of thinking. For another eight months, I continued to shuttle between the Covington and Glendale stores. All the while, I was reawakening old injuries. In time, I realized that what was true of the Indiana office also held true for the Glendale store. While that location had done better, the solution was the same and any losses would be more than offset by the growth of the main store. The Glendale store closed too, and we soldiered on.

While the business didn't seem to suffer, and we still managed to care for all of our clients, I began to feel like all of my hard work was coming undone. That wasn't really true. The main store was giving people help and doing business like never before. But it felt that way to me.

That's when I remembered the story.

I had spent so much time looking for a way to stay, that I hadn't realized it might be time to go. Could it be that it was time to look for a successor, someone else to carry on in my place? I had promised Rita ten years, and Image Insights was fast approaching its twelfth anniversary.

The business had taken a lot of time away from me and the boys. It had also provided us with many rewards, personal and spiritual. I'd made friendships that would last a lifetime, and there were others I would never forget. But I had a new, larger family at home now, one that needed my attention. Perhaps, this was my first rowboat, the first sign that it was time for a change.

In its day, The Lemonade Stand had operated in a vacuum. Before Rita, there was next to nothing in the kind of care that we supplied to our patients. In our part of the country, Rita had blazed a new trail. She and The Lemonade Stand cared for patients, and educated doctors, at a time when most people were very tight-lipped about cancer. Following in her footsteps, Image Insights had set the bar for that kind of care. We were unmatched in professionalism, compassion, and charity. But now, stores like ours dotted the country. People were getting care; and they were talking openly about cancer, its treatment, and its effects. Image Insights was no longer the only game in town. Was this my second rowboat?

As I continued making my long commute, those old pains began to flare up again. The third sign. The spirit was willing, but the body was wearing out. Those pains were a warning that change was overdue. I'd ignored them before, to my own peril. This time I listened more closely. Did I want another surgery? If not, then it was time to grab hold of the rope ladder and ride the helicopter out of harm's way.

17

A Glass Half Full

For a dozen years, I'd done everything I could to make my company grow; but I had to admit, the business had reached its limits under my guidance. In fact, over the past year, I'd even begun to pull back. That was not what I wanted for Image Insights. I wanted it to grow. To help others. To expand. But even now, with only my main location, I couldn't keep up. Image

Insights was doing great. As for me, not so much. I felt like now I was holding the company back.

To grow to the next level, Image Insights needed a leader with a stronger business sense than than mine. For me, compassion and charity were our touchstones—the foundation upon which Image Insights was built. It was imperative that those ideals remained it's guiding lights; they were the heart and soul of the company, indeed, the very reason for its existence. But if Image Insights was ever going to be more than a "one-woman show", it had to have a leader who could see the bigger picture. I had a feeling that my vision was probably too focused and narrow, too small time.

My apologies to my staff and volunteers for the "one-woman" exaggeration; but the phrase refers more to my weaknesses than my strengths. The one-woman character of the business kept it chained to its smaller stature. I had tried to learn and grow—and to a great extent, I had. By now, I was managing things I'd never dreamed of when Rita welcomed me into The Lemonade Stand. Even so, I had never been a "business" woman at heart. I was a caregiver. If the company were to grow, and reach more people, it would need a leader who better understood business. Image Insights needed someone who could choose store managers, delegate authority, secure financing, and oversee expansion.

Even after so many years, I was still trying to do too much on my own. To make matters worse, I was wasting energy on things I wasn't any good at. I couldn't even keep my books balanced without all kinds of help. Nor did I have any interest in it. I loved caring for my clients. I loved teaching and reaching out to people. Everything else was secondary, a chore to be slogged through, or avoided. For so long, I tried to do it all alone. *Money is not the point here,* I said to myself. *The clients are. I can do this.* But I had failed to ask myself one question: What would happen when I could no longer do it all?

Trying to manage every aspect of the business, I was wearing too many hats for my own good. In truth, I micromanaged some parts of Image Insights, while I failed to manage others at all. The worst part was, I was wearing myself out trying to do it. Now my body was trying to tell me that I had to stop. The signs were unmistakable. I couldn't go on this way forever. But if I didn't do it, who would? Image Insights would die without me—unless I got some help.

After much discussion and soul-searching, Michael and I came to a decision. It was time to find a successor and train that person to eventually take over the business. Unfortunately, I had no idea how to go about that, so I talked to my banker. He was eager to help and knew of a business broker who would screen candidates for us. "I will handle it all," the broker promised us. "Everything goes through me first, so it's perfectly safe and you are fully protected." It was just what I needed to hear. No sooner had we made the decision than things began to happen.

Our search had hardly started, when the broker set us up with what seemed like the perfect candidate. Barbara was a kind, good-natured lady from Texas; a true Southern belle with a sweet accent that literally hooked you and reeled you in. A smart, professional woman, she knew her business; and she knew how to put a person at ease while she did it. Barbara had sold her medical services business in Texas and was looking to re-establish herself up north. Divorced and childless, she had the time to devote to business. She also had all of the assets, instincts, and lawyers that she would ever need. This was a woman who knew how to get things done. Barbara had it all— she had all of the skills and talents that I never had.

This looks like the right woman for the job, I said to myself. But I'd been burned before; this time we would do things carefully, and use lawyers to dot every i and cross every t. Barbara couldn't have agreed more. We would do it all by the numbers. Her lawyers contacted mine and they set to work. While I wished we could have done it all with a handshake, sadly it seemed to me that those days were gone.

Unfortunately, our broker dropped out of the picture at that point. He had some serious family troubles to attend to and he dropped completely out of sight. But before he did, he said, "Just tell her everything she wants to know and you'll be fine."

We took it slow at first, but as we got to know her, it wasn't hard to see that Barbara was perfect for the job. For all her success, she was very down-to-earth, with the gift of gab as well as a head for numbers. It was a good combination. Barbara's experience really showed, too. Observing our techniques and talking with the employees, she really seemed like a good fit with the crew. She also had a voracious appetite for information, reading reports, reviewing figures, and wading through paperwork. As Barbara learned the business, it seemed like she took to it almost without effort. Over the next six months, she got to know Image Insights like the back of her hand.

At the same time, we had meetings with accountants, meetings with bankers, and meetings with lawyers. There was a lot of red tape to wade through, but everything had to be done officially and by the book. I had thought the transition would involve chaos, stress, and lots of sleepless nights, but I was pleasantly surprised. While things were moving slowly and carefully, they were also going very smoothly. *It's nice to work with professionals,* I thought. Those lawyers, bankers, and business people really knew their stuff.

One day, I took advantage of a quiet afternoon to visit Michael at work. The office assistant told me that he was busy with a staff meeting, but she brightly suggested that I wait in his office—to surprise him. She promised she wouldn't tell.

Sitting in Michael's big armchair, I poked idly through the jumble of papers on his desk. One of them caught my eye. It was a color brochure from a cancer center in Madison, Wisconsin. Michael's family was in Milwaukee, and I knew it was beautiful there. Clipped to the brochure was a letter—one that made an offer of the director's chair to Michael. *Interesting,* I thought. *He didn't say anything to me.* I read the rest of the letter and examined the brochure. I liked what I saw. The position was a good one, and Michael would be able to spend time with his mom and dad, and his brother, Dave. After all, he'd been away from home for almost 25 years.

Michael wouldn't be back for a few minutes, so I gathered everything up and slipped outside. Once I was settled in the quiet of my car, I flipped open my phone. I dialed the number at the bottom of the letterhead, and asked for the name beneath the letter's unreadable signature. *What is it about doctors and their handwriting?* I wondered. A man came on the line and, after introductions, I said to him, "I understand you guys are interested in Dr. Zinda. Well, this is not the doctor, it's the wife. If you want the doctor, you'll have to make the wife happy. What are you offering?" With a chuckle, the man politely answered my question.

He made the wife happy. It was a good offer.

Michael returned to his office a bit later, and I said not a word. We had a nice relaxing lunch together. We talked about this, and we talked about that, but about Wisconsin, he said not a word. I waited and waited, but he never brought it up. *I thought we were partners,* I grumbled silently to myself. *Why didn't he mention it?*

All afternoon, I waited for a call—nothing. By the time we sat down to dinner that night I was fairly bursting with curiosity. That cancer center seemed like the perfect place for Michael. I couldn't believe he wasn't bringing it up! But if he could play it cool, then I could play it cool, too. Michael began cutting his first bite and I took a sip of water. I was cool as ice. By the time he'd pierced the bite with his fork and raised it all the long way up to his mouth, I could stand it no longer. "Why didn't you tell me about the offer?" I blurted out.

The fork stopped in midair with his mouth half open. "What offer?" Michael asked as he lowered the fork back to his plate.

"The one in Wisconsin!" I replied snappishly. "I thought we were partners!" I was working up a head of steam, all on my own.

"We *are* partners," Michael grinned as he took his first bite. "I hadn't thought it was an option." He took another bite.

"You mean you don't want it?" I asked, almost indignant.

"Well sure, it would be nice," he explained around mouthfuls. "But I didn't think you'd want to go so far from home. From the boys. Or from the shop."

I'd thought about all of that, I'd even prayed on it. The kids were off taking care of themselves. A few more hours of travel time weren't going to make a difference. Things were going well for Image Insights and the transition was moving forward about as smoothly as I could have hoped. And Wisconsin was his home; I knew he'd be happy there. I told Michael what I thought and he put down his fork, frowned and cocked his head at me. With a half smile, he replied tentatively, "Really?"

I nodded. "I say we go for it."

"Okay, partner," he replied with a grin. Then he picked up his fork and dug in.

Chaos did enter my life at that point; but it was a good chaos. There was a house to pack and sell, and another one to buy. The distance made things tough, I'd never moved so far; but it was an exciting time. Everything just seemed to come together all at once.

I had promised Rita that I would continue her good work for another decade, and the years had run to an even dozen. But times were changing, and my body was delivering unmistakable signs that it was ready for a change, too. About seven months after we'd first met, Barbara was ready to take over with Image Insights. The lawyers and bankers had lined up all of the ducks, and they were waiting for me to sign on the dotted line.

By December, I was ready for the change. The kids were doing well and Michael had a terrific new position waiting for him in Wisconsin. There was nothing to hold us back. We were moving to a new home in a beautiful part of the country, and I was ready to begin the next stage of my adventure. It was time to do something new with my life, though I did not yet know what that was.

For years, I'd spent every waking moment doing what I *had* to do. Suddenly I was faced with the prospect of doing what I *wanted* to do. It would require some serious thought. I actually had a choice as to how I would spend my time. Besides seeming like an almost decadent prospect, it was a daunting one. I was being given a golden opportunity. This was a chance that some of my patients, like Sarah, could only have dreamed of. For their sakes, it was important that I not waste it.

Of course, that December I wasn't thinking quite so clearly and logically. That kind of clarity would only come later. I'm as human as the next person; at the time, I was simply excited to be going someplace new. I was looking forward to setting up our new home. And, to be honest, I was thrilled that I no longer had to scrape and scrounge just to get by. Oh, it's not like we were royalty or anything. Michael would be working harder than ever to provide us with this opportunity. But the impending sale of Image Insights would leave me with enough seed money to make a good start at whatever came next.

I was fairly certain that, no matter what it was, it would still involve helping people. And, of course, it would still involve Rita. The work, and her message, were just too powerful to walk away from. Over the years, I'd learned to enjoy making my presentations to doctors and other groups of people. Speaking before a crowd had actually become something I looked forward to. Maybe I could find a way to continue telling Rita's story, to inspire people with her courage. If she could make such wonderful lemonade with the lemons that life had given her, then anyone could.

There must be a way, I thought, *some way to teach others how to make lemonade with their lives.* I might try my hand at counseling. Who knows? Maybe I would try speaking, advocating for patients. I might even go back to the book I'd meant to write. *Wouldn't that be something?* I thought to myself.

The day after the Christmas holiday, we were all packed up and ready to go. On our way out of town, we made one last stop in Kentucky. We had a final meeting, together with the employees, and they understood what was going on. The papers were signed and in the mail, so the transfer was complete. While ownership was changing hands, their work would continue just as before. Everyone, patients included, would be well-taken care of. I would be back in January to sign off on one last thing, and I would take Barbara around to meet a few people who would be important to her business. But other than that, my part was over. If that meeting was not a bittersweet moment, then I don't know what was. The only thing worse was saying goodbye.

Michael had gone ahead, so Adam and Nicholas were there to help me make the trip. For a little while, it was just the three of us again, and it felt like we were driving away from our old lives. Leaving the store behind, was one of the hardest things I ever had to do. I felt like I was leaving a huge part of my life behind. But I also knew that it was time to move on. Besides, the store was no longer mine. As we crossed Ohio and put Kentucky behind us, I began to relax and look ahead. It was time to take the leap into the great unknown, time to begin the next stage of my adventure. As I thought about the future, my spirits picked up and I started planning what came next. With wild fantasies of books or speaking engagements in my head, we rolled down the highway. It was a long drive to Wisconsin. I had plenty of time to dream. I loved every minute of it.

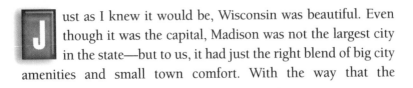 ust as I knew it would be, Wisconsin was beautiful. Even though it was the capital, Madison was not the largest city in the state—but to us, it had just the right blend of big city amenities and small town comfort. With the way that the

University of Wisconsin snaked through the downtown high-rises, it was hard to tell where the university left off and the city began. It gave the place a youthful energy that contrasted well with the stately old buildings. I liked it there. Michael was glad to be back in familiar surroundings, and I felt like I would fit right in. The future looked promising indeed. *This is going to be a good New Year,* I smiled to myself.

Michael and I had been unpacking and organizing for a couple of days, and our new house was beginning to look like home. For so many years, I had bounced around from houses to apartments, to a cabin, and back to more houses. It felt so good to finally settle down.

I was working on my last stack of boxes, when Michael disappeared into his newly set up office to check his email. He emerged a few minutes later, looking pale and more than a little ill. "What's the matter?" I asked, when I saw his ashen face.

"She changed her mind," Michael replied in dazed disbelief.

"Who did?" I prodded.

"Barbara." Michael replied in disbelief. "She's not buying."

"You're kidding." I said, not really understanding what I was hearing. "What did she say?"

"Her email said simply, 'Sorry. No longer interested.'" Michael rubbed his eyes wearily and sighed a huge sigh of frustration.

Now it was my turn to stand there in shock. "Well, what do we do now?"

That night was a long, sleepless one, and I tossed and turned as I tried to figure out what had happened. We'd tried all day to contact Barbara, and we would try again. But is seemed like she had dropped off the face of the earth. Phone, fax, cell phone, email—nothing worked.

Why did she do this? I agonized. We had worked for seven months to make it all possible. There had been miles of red tape and weeks of meetings and negotiations. When it was all said and done, we had turned over a fully-functioning, self-support-ing company. Now, several days later and four states away, she says she's not interested. "How can she *not be interested*!?" I asked myself aloud, startling Michael awake.

Sleep came only in fits and starts as I did a little crash course in the seven stages of grief. I skipped a few of the stages, prefer-ring to concentrate on my favorites: shock, anger, and despair. Especially anger and despair. *How could she do this to me?* I fumed. *Why didn't she say something while we were still in Kentucky?*

In the morning, when we failed to reach Barbara again, I knew what I had to do. I had to go back. I had to see what was left—and I would probably have to close it all down.

"You can't keep it open, Gayle," my lawyer had said to me, after he'd calmed me down. "You don't have a professional man-ager in place. Barbara was it. Now she's gone. There is no one else."

"Maybe, I . . ., Maybe, I can . . . ." Fumbling for words, I was trying desperately to find a way out.

"Maybe, what?" he replied. "Maybe you can run it from *Wisconsin*?" He took a deep breath and sighed sympathetically. "Gayle, you can't do that. If the employees knew you were that far away, the temptation would be too great."

"The temptation for *what*?" I asked, confused.

"For *theft*," he returned, emphatically. "You think you can trust them—and you probably can. But someday, with you eight hours away, someone is going to crack."

The whole thing was devastating. I had worked so long and hard to breathe life into Image Insights. Then, we'd groomed it and handed it off to someone we thought would help it to grow and mature. Now, my lawyer was telling me I had to go back and put an end to it myself. Even worse, he was telling be I had to do so because I couldn't trust my people. It was all too much to hear. It was all too much to believe.

I thanked him, hung up, and hit the road. Maybe I could find a way out.

Saundra would drive in to meet me at the shop. Together, we'd see what we could come up with. I still couldn't believe it was happening. Insurances had been canceled, leases were transferred, and bank accounts closed. Ownership had, for all practical purposes, completely changed hands. The only problem was, my trusted and worthy successor had walked away from the deal only days after we were gone. So much for trust.

When I arrived back at the shop, I found everything to be still in order. My old employees were all at work, the doors were open, and business was going on as usual. Nobody seemed to know that Barbara had bailed out. I made a few phone calls and got my employees together for a meeting. Saundra had also arrived, so she sat in on it quietly.

"Barbara has changed her mind," I told them. "She skipped out on signing the papers and left us high and dry." My old employees looked suitably puzzled. "But as you know," I continued, "Michael and I live in Wisconsin now; and we don't have a replacement manager to keep things running here. Unless I can come up with something fast, it looks like we'll have to close up the shop." I felt absolutely horrible, and the staff looked as bad as I felt. "This is the last thing in the world that I had hoped for," I told them. "I am so sorry."

I told the staff that we would have two more weeks in the shop as we wrapped up our outstanding orders. Those weeks would be light ones though, as we'd have to stop taking in new appointments. I would also pay them another two weeks' severance after that; which gave them the best part of a month to find new positions.

Hopefully it won't come to that, I told myself. But I knew it was best to prepare for the worst. Everything had been so *final* a few weeks before. I wasn't sure what could be done—or undone. And my lawyer was pressing me to shut it all down. It's funny how you can always find experts to tell you what you *can't* do.

It's a lot harder to find any who will tell you what you *can*. "We'll think of something, Gayle," Saundra said to me as the meeting broke up. "We'll find a way out of this mess."

A few days later, Saundra proved to be as good as her word. She came into the shop with her brother, Steve, in tow. While I had been worrying about how to take it all down, she had found someone we could trust to keep it all going.

"I'll buy the business," Steve said as he took a seat. "I'll take over the business for you."

I couldn't believe my ears. "Are you serious?" I asked in amazement. So many years ago, Steve and his brother had offered to come to my financial rescue by becoming partners in the business. I had turned them down because I was afraid of the kinds of decisions a "business man" might make. All these years later, it was my search for just that kind of person that had put me in the fix that I was in now. And now Steve was back, offering to rescue me once again.

"I know just how important this place has been to Saundra," Steve replied passionately. "If I can help to keep it going, then I'm darn sure going to try."

Naturally, I wanted to jump at his offer; but part of me still held back. This time it was for his sake, more than for mine. "You don't have to do this," I said to him. "When we talked about this before, it was when I would still be involved. Now, I'm too far away."

"I've been thinking about that," Steve replied confidently. "After all, it's not like you won't take my calls. While I won't have you here to do the hands-on work, I'll still have you around for advice. All I have to do is pick up a phone."

Nodding thoughtfully, I said, "This could work."

"The way I see it," he continued, "all I need—at bare minimum—is a good stylist for the wigs and makeup, and an employee who is good at fitting the prostheses."

When life gives you lemons. . .

Spend money!

Most people spend their whole life saving for a rainy day. Looks like the rain is here.

"Or one who can do both!" I said, thinking fast. "I have some of each."

"Perfect," Steve came back. "The bookkeeping and business management, I can handle. The problem is that I don't have any experience in patient care. If we can cover that, then I can add people back in as the clients begin to return."

"Great!" I said, my enthusiasm returning in a rush. "Let's see who we have that will stay!"

I had several employees who expressed a guarded willingness to stay. That's okay, I couldn't blame them for being careful. With Barbara bailing out and my having to close the store, they'd had the rug pulled out from under them twice already. However, one of the hairdressers, Patty, was down-right thrilled about the prospect. She was both a talented stylist and skilled at fitting prostheses. She was perfect for the job. After a moment of awkward hesitation that I didn't quite understand, she jumped in with both feet and agreed to be Steve's "point man". She was excited, Steve was excited, and I couldn't believe how well it was all working out! "Well, good," Steve said, clapping his hands together. "Let's get this done!"

I called my banker, Gene, to let him know I'd found a way out of the bind we were in. There was no answer at his desk, so I left a voice mail message, "We've found a new buyer! He's ready to go. Call me as quick as you can!"

Over the next few days I was busy tying up loose ends—or, more precisely, untying knots I thought had been all tied up. I still hadn't reached my banker, but I knew Gene would come through for me. We'd known each other since we were kids. Over the years, we had developed a good business relationship, too, as I proved that Image Insights was sound. A few years before, we had even cared for Gene's wife while she fought her own battle with cancer. I knew I'd hear from him soon, and together we would get the financial details all worked out.

In the meantime, there was a lot of running around to be done, as I rushed through the process of handing my business over to a successor—again. But with the way things were going, I was much happier this time. Now that Steve was taking over, it would almost be like I was keeping it in the family. After the way Barbara had dropped out of sight, I was so happy to be dealing with someone I knew and trusted. Steve would do the right thing. As a talented businessman, I knew he could grow the company in the right direction. But as a friend—and Saundra's brother—I knew he understood what the business was meant to be.

Saundra and I were in the car together, shuttling between appointments as we tried to bring it all together. We had to move fast. I was a full day away from home and I had been weeks away from Michael. The business was folding up, and soon the patients and employees would all have drifted away. There wasn't time to waste on the ponderous processes of lawyers, bankers, and their staffs. So we were rushing around, trying to do in days what had taken all of those people weeks to accomplish the last time around. While I couldn't do the tricky legal or financial stuff, I could run errands and keep everything else moving along.

As I drove, I called the bank again and asked for Gene. I'd been trying to reach him all week, but I still hadn't heard from him. It was beginning to feel like Gene was avoiding me. I got his voice mail again, so I left another message. "Why aren't you returning my calls?" I asked him. "Have I done something to offend you? I have another buyer and I'm running out of time!"

I don't know if I guilted him into responding, or what; but to my surprise, Gene finally returned my call. At first, he was awfully chatty, going on and on with small talk. *This is not like him at all,* I thought. *Why is he being so weird?* It was like he was dancing around the subject, trying to avoid talking business. I finally dragged him around to the subject at hand and quickly retold my story about Steve's willingness to buy.

After that, Gene warmed up and began to get excited again. I could almost feel the relief rolling off him. At that point, a question occurred to me. "What do we do with all of the checks that are still coming in?" I asked him. "You know, the insurance reimbursements, the private pays . . . . Do I have to sign something to transfer them over to Steve?"

"Oh, no, no," he said. "Just have them forwarded to the bank and we'll apply them to your loan. Then, when Steve buys the business, he'll pay off the rest." I promised to do just as Gene said. "That's great about Steve," he said, wrapping up the phone call. "I'm very excited. Now we can keep your store *and* Barbara's open."

"Yeah! I'm excited, too!" I said, about to hang up. "We'll just . . . Wait a minute," I paused, suddenly confused. "What did you just say?"

The silence on the line was deafening.

"Barbara has a store!?" I asked him.

No response.

"We haven't been able to reach her and I . . . "

"Uh, oh. I think I've said too much." He hung up.

"What was *that* all about?" I said to Saundra. She shrugged.

I called back. No answer. I called the bank. The woman on the phone said smoothly, "I'm sorry. He stepped out of the office."

A s we drove back to the shop, I began to put two and two together. It was adding up to a dreadful sinking feeling in the pit of my stomach. *I asked about Barbara and a loan,* I thought. *He panicked and hung up.* I knew what that meant. *Barbara has a loan.* I kept thinking. It got worse and worse. *Barbara knows how to open a business . . . Barbara studied my business.*

This is bad, I thought. *Do I have "sucker" written all over my forehead?* My eyes involuntarily flicked to the rearview mirror to check. *How could I not have seen this coming?*

We'd barely walked through the door when Patty dropped what she was doing and rushed over to me. I knew I couldn't have looked too happy, but she was clearly pale and distressed. Clearly, something was bothering her—something serious. "Gayle. There's something I should have told you the other day." She paused, wringing her hands, "Barbara offered us jobs in her new store." *Oh, the hits just keep on coming,* I thought. "It opens in a few weeks. I wanted to tell you, but . . . I was hoping it would all work out with Steve."

That's okay, honey," I said dully. "I understand." *What else was I going to say?* I left her and walked numbly back to my office. Saundra followed me in and closed the door.

"Can you believe this!?" I sputtered angrily, stalking across the room to my old desk. "It's happening again!" Saundra shook her head sadly and waited for me to blow off some more steam. I punched the padded headrest of my chair. It didn't help much. I flopped into it and slid down lifelessly, sighing a huge, disconsolate sigh.

I was angry at the betrayal, and hurt. I had been sure that Image Insights was in good hands. Just as Helen had trusted me with her store in Glendale, I had trusted Barbara with mine. I thought she cared as much about the people, and the business, as I did. Caring for clients and their families, dealing with doctors and suppliers—I'd taught her everything that she would need to know.

Patient lists, vendors and suppliers, doctor and hospital contacts—she had it all. In fact, that had been the idea from the start. In order to carry on the business, she *had* to know everything. Besides, the lawyers had required full disclosure agreements; so I did just as the broker instructed—I gave her everything. But once she had all that she needed, Barbara decided that the only thing she didn't need was Image Insights itself. That hurt.

"We'll have to tell Steve," Saundra said softly. I nodded and picked up the phone.

After that, it went just about the way I'd thought it would when I'd first returned to the store. We wrapped up the orders that remained unfinished, and after the two weeks was up, we closed the doors.

I'd told Steve everything we had learned; and even then, he wasn't quite willing to throw in the towel. "Let me think about this," he'd said. But in the end it was clear. He would have been taking over a business in which he'd had no real experience. For that challenge, he was prepared. With a little help, he could have done it. But now he was faced with a *local* competitor— one who was skilled and experienced—and one who was equipped with every bit of information that Image Insights had ever acquired. Right down to the clients themselves. It was truly a lost cause.

Over the next couple of weeks, we boxed the shop up and hauled it away. It took several trips, back and forth, one load at a time, with Michael, the boys, or Saundra to help and keep me company. It was a painful time. The first time leaving had been bad enough; but at least then I'd only had to say goodbye. Now I was back to dismantle my business by hand—piece by piece.

As I looked around my lifeless shop, I thought about all of the living that had gone on within its walls. Tears started welling up as I thought about my clients. My volunteers. My staff. So much good had been done here. But now, even that was over.

I lost the whole thing, I thought, as I stuffed the boxes with the now useless products. *It's all gone.* Inside, I felt like I'd really let Rita down. At that point, the whole thing looked like a big failure. *How is this a happy ending?* I wondered sadly. I had a few choice words for God about then; but apparently the Complaint Department was closed. He didn't seem to be listening. I registered my complaints anyway. *How is this justice?* I fumed to Him. *How is this the answer to my prayers?* He left me to stew in my own juices—and I did. *A little divine retribution might be nice,* I sniffed to myself. I knew one person who could use a good plague of locusts.

On the outside, I tried to pretend that it didn't bother me too badly; but everyone knew better. So we would spend our days packing boxes and stacking them in the truck, while whoever was with me tried in vain to cheer me up.

I don't know when the change came over me, but after a while I noticed that things didn't bother me quite as much anymore. Maybe it was just the distraction of the job at hand. The initial shock was over and we had work to do. Besides, it's hard to stay down when you're busy. If idle hands are the devil's workshop, then what does that say about busy hands? Maybe my complaints had been heard after all, because at some point, the storm clouds in my head blew away, and I began to think clearly.

Would Rita want to see me grumbling and griping like this? I asked myself, *Would she want to see me feeling sorry for myself?* Of course not. She'd had more reason to feel down than I had ever known. But not once did I see Rita complain about her lot in life. Not a single time.

In fact, it finally occurred to me, I had a lot to be thankful for. *What do you have to whine about?* I asked myself. *Ohhh, so someone took your store. Too bad. You were done with it anyway.* Yes, the financial loss would hurt, but it's not like it would put me back in the poorhouse. I'd find a way to move on, even without my seed money, just as I had done before. More than anything, it was my pride that was hurt. Besides, my body had been telling me that I was done with Image Insights for longer than I cared to remember. Yes, it was a disaster, a financial meltdown, and a humiliating end to a dozen years of good hard work. It was also *not* the end of the world.

I hadn't been tossed out into the cold, or left homeless in the street. I had a husband, indeed an entire family, to attend to. There was a wonderful new home in Wisconsin, just waiting for me. I had plenty to be grateful for. Besides, wasn't I supposed to be moving on to the next stage of my adventure? As I began to put it all behind me, the work became a little easier to bear and the day began to look a little brighter.

I realized that, eventually, I would have to forgive and forget. And in time, I knew that I could. It's not like I just flipped a switch and got over it. Not at all. Things took a good deal longer than that. But once the decision was made, my outlook began to improve immediately. I finally made it to that seventh stage of grief—acceptance. Oh sure, in the months ahead, I would occasionally indulge myself in a little taste of bitterness, a big bite of anger, even a whole slice of despair. But it was emotional cheesecake to me now. That kind of thing might sound good at first, but once I'd had a few bites I would realize that I was satisfied—and for a good long time. To overindulge would be self-destructive, so I would mentally push the plate of negativity back, get up from the table, and go and do something positive with my life.

Brooding was not positive; I knew that. On the other hand, looking on the bright side while loading the truck was. *So the store is closed,* I reflected. *Does that make it a failure?* The answer, plainly, was "no". We had done good work here. *Would Rita consider it a failure?* I asked myself. The answer there was most emphatically, *No!* Over the past dozen years, Image Insights had helped more than ten thousand patients. We had also educated, consoled, or counseled tens of thousands more—from doctors and nurses to family members and friends. We'd made a difference here, all of us—my staff, my volunteers, and myself.

I'd heard it thousands of times, "Gayle, you don't know how much better that made me feel." From one patient after another, "You don't know what that meant to me." In a hundred different ways, "You guys are wonderful." And best of all, "You made me feel like *me* again."

Yes, we'd made a difference, I realized, as I closed and latched the truck. *Really, who can ask for more than that?* As Nicholas pulled tight the last of the tie-downs on the tarp, I locked the front door of the now empty shop. Sure, it was a sad moment; but I didn't feel nearly as bad as I had a week before. I was beginning to look ahead again, rather than behind.

As we pulled away from the curb, I took one last look at my old shop through the rear window. *Goodbye,* I thought. *Things don't always work out the way we plan.* But they do work out in the end. Life goes on and we move ahead. Onward and upward.

Some time later, I found out that Barbara's store hadn't made it too far past the one year mark. *Wow,* I thought, *even with all she had going for her.* I wish I could say that I felt sorry for her. I tried to. I was really more worried about my former clients. But times had changed for the better, and shops like mine had sprouted up everywhere. There was no shortage of care for them anymore.

One thing that little piece of news did do—it made me hugely proud of the twelve years that we'd managed at Image Insights. I guess it helps to have your heart in the right place.

We were flying down the interstate in Northern Kentucky when we hit a few bumps in the road—literally. A rough patch on the highway momentarily rattled my teeth. "Wow!" I said, "Your tax dollars at work."

"Or, not." Nicholas replied, as he glanced in his rearview mirror. "Uh, oh. Someone is flashing their lights at us . . ."

I turned to look behind us, but I couldn't see anything over the covered boxes.

"Oh, no . . ." Nicholas groaned, and he immediately began pulling off the highway onto the shoulder.

"What? What is it?" I cried, over the roar of the tires in loose gravel. "Do we have a flat?"

"No," Nicholas shook his head, as he put the truck in park, "but it's trouble." He jumped out, slamming his door behind him. The truck shuddered under a blast of air, as it was buffeted by the slipstream of a passing semi. In my mirror, it looked like an unending river of eighteen-wheeler's.

What on earth is going on? I wondered as I climbed out of the passenger door. "Nicholas! Be careful out there!" I yelled over the roar of the passing traffic. I couldn't see over the bulk of our cargo, so I made my way around the back of the truck. *The tarp looks okay,* I thought, as I tugged on a line to make sure it was secure. But as I came around the back end, I saw that the tailgate was down and a couple of boxes had overturned.

"Nick?" I called out. "What's wrong?" I came around his side of the truck, expecting to find him retying the ropes or examining the tires; but there was no one there! I looked back up the highway behind us. Nicholas was about a hundred yards up the road, jogging on the shoulder *away* from the truck. "*Where* is he going?" I asked aloud. Holding a hand up to shade my eyes, I watched him jog into the distance, wondering what he was after.

Just then, I noticed something puzzling. *What is that all over the road?* I wondered. There were small pale polka dots scattered across the interstate. Another semi blasted past and the tarp at the back of the truck snapped in the breeze like a sail come loose from its lines. *What are those things?* I wondered, as I squinted at the polka dots. I started walking down the shoulder toward Nicholas.

Just then, he dashed out onto the highway.

"Is he crazy?" I asked aloud, and started running toward him. He was darting around the road, from point to point, picking up the polka dots. With one eye on the traffic, he would scramble back out of the way, to avoid an oncoming car or truck. A second later, he would dash out onto the highway again! "Nicholas, stop!" I shouted; but my words were swallowed by the roar of speeding big-rigs.

Again and again, he would dart out into the traffic, using the spaces between the vehicles to scurry around and pick up those polka dots. "Nicholas! No-o-o-o!" I yelled as I ran. *Why was he being so stupid?* I was panicked. He was going to get himself killed.

As I ran down the shoulder towards Nicholas, I could see some of the oncoming semis, in the distance, braking and swerving. They were trying to avoid the pale pink polka dots that were scattered even farther up the road far behind us. Horns blared at me as vehicles continued to fly by. Nicholas went on scooping up the polka dots, oblivious to my cries.

They're breast forms! I realized in disbelief, *the polka dots are breast forms!* "Stop, Nicholas!" I shouted, growing hoarse. "Please, stop!" Looking like pale pink land mines, at least a hundred breast prostheses of various sizes were sprinkled along the interstate. Tumbled from an overturned box in the back of the truck, they were scattered everywhere. And now my son was running around, risking his life, for a bunch of fake boobs!

I was close enough by then that Nicholas could hear me. He was wearing down anyway, so he stopped and turned in my direction. With an armload of breast forms, Nicholas walked toward me as he tried to catch his breath. His head was hanging low. I was grinning with relief, laughing and crying at the same time. As we got close enough to talk to each other, Nicholas lifted his head up and said, "I'm sorry, Mom. I couldn't get them all."

I wrapped him in my arms and held him tight; useless, gravel-speckled breast forms, and all. "It doesn't matter," I practically sobbed. I took a deep breath and squeezed him harder. "I'm just glad you're okay." I held him for a moment more, and said a silent prayer of thanks.

We started back towards his truck, still chuckling at the surreal nature of the whole episode. *Weird,* I thought, *It was like a bad Driver's Ed film, "Busts on the Highway."*

A few of those polka dots had found themselves on the wrong side of sixty thousand pounds of tractor-trailer. Apparently, breast forms and big rigs are not a good mix. "They look so pathetic," I said, pointing to one of the prosthetic victims. It looked like a dead jellyfish, washed up on the beach.

We repacked the truck and tied it down securely, again. Then Nicholas put the truck into gear and we pulled back onto the highway. "Well. That was the perfect end to a perfect day," I mumbled to myself. Nicholas smiled wryly. Then I laughed out loud. Everyone was okay. It really *had* been the perfect end.

CHAPTER

18

When Life Gives You Lemons . . .

O nce we were settled back in Wisconsin again, with our new home comfortable and complete, I began to look for something to do with my time. It was a strange position to find myself in, unsettling. I was not accustomed to having time that was unaccounted for. Besides that, closing down Image Insights had left me feeling a little beat up and burned out.

Positive outlook or not, my mental state was still not what it was supposed to be. What I needed was a change.

I wanted to do something that would be a little easier on the emotions. Dealing with matters of life and death had left me exhausted. *Let someone else ride that roller coaster,* I thought. *Somebody else can worry about keeping the doors open, too.* I taught classes at a fitness center for a while; then I tried my hand at selling Mercedes. The jobs were interesting and, in their own ways, fun; but neither of them was satisfying. The best part of each was spending my days around lots of people. But it didn't take long to realize that something was missing.

While I wasn't looking to open a new business, I knew that punching a clock for someone else wasn't enough. I missed knowing that I was really helping people, and I missed spreading Rita's lemonade message. I thought I could just walk away after closing the doors at Image Insights, but I couldn't. Being away for a year had really opened my eyes. Suddenly I knew why I couldn't leave it all behind. For twelve years I had been sharing Rita's message, telling her story, and living up to her fine example. What I hadn't realized was that, somewhere along the way, her message had also become mine.

While I'd never had to make lemonade in the same way that Rita had; over the past dozen or more years, my life had been all about taking lemons and making lemonade. And if I wasn't doing it myself, I was trying to teach others how to do it. I missed it. I missed the meaning that it gave my work. I liked teaching people that when life gives you lemons, you don't have to just sit there and suck lemons.

So I began to pursue some of the things I'd always dreamed about. I took classes on speaking, I went to seminars, I joined associations and I went to workshops. And I practiced, too. I used everything that I had learned from giving seminars and doing our TV show. It wasn't long before I was really pretty good at speaking before a crowd—any crowd. I got to the point where

I couldn't wait to get up and tell The Lemonade Stand story to a roomful of people.

Rita inspires me every day. To get up and communicate that feeling to others, to actually *inspire them*, is very rewarding. It feels good to light another person up, just by telling a story. The very idea is both thrilling and satisfying. Of course, it helps to have a good story to tell.

That is precisely why I decided to finally write it all down. To tell the story well, I had to get it out of my head and down on paper. It is a difficult thing to do. Distilling a lifetime of experiences and emotions down to nouns, verbs, and adjectives is, well, almost impossible. I'd met so many wonderful people; how could I do them justice in a few pages, or paragraphs? The answer is— I couldn't. I could barely scratch the surface. But telling the tale, even with my small ability, is still better than not telling it at all.

When I tell the story out loud, I let it all hang out. Nobody wants to just *listen* to a story; they want to *feel* it. Stories inspire emotions; not only in the audience, but in the speaker as well. So when a part of the story makes me mad, I let it make me mad. When the story is sad, I remember how I felt—and I get teary-eyed all over again. And if the story is happy, I end up grinning like a fool. I never hold back. I can get tongue-tied, mixed up, or use the wrong words entirely, but the audience is always forgiving. That's because they know that they're seeing a real person.

Writing is so trying because there is none of that give and take. *How do I present myself?* I wondered when I began to write it all down. *I have to sound intelligent, don't I?* This is a *book*, after all. Besides, the people in the story were so important to me. I had to treat them with dignity. *I have to write like a grown-up*, I thought. I couldn't make a fool of myself, or, by extension, anyone else. So I tried writing intelligently, with dignity.

Big mistake. It didn't take much of that to realize that I was swimming upstream. *No one wants to read this*, I chided myself. *They want to feel it.* Just like an audience, a reader wants to connect with a real human being—flaws and all. So I tried again. This time, I let it all hang out. But when it came to the end of my tale, I was worried, *What do I do now?* The story didn't end with a great epiphany. If anything, I ended up looking a little foolish as my hard-won business closed down. What's more, I hadn't come up with all the answers—or even very many. I hadn't solved the mysteries of the universe or found the meaning of life. For so many years, I tried to help others as they walked the line between life and death. I looked for the meaning behind it all, I tried to make sense of everything. Now, all these pages later, the best I had come up with was "make lemonade." *Is that it?* I wondered. Was my glass-half-full, sunny-side-of-the-street outlook really all that I had to offer?

So, everything falls apart and I say, "Well, things could be worse!" And yet, it was true.

Write it the way you felt it, I said to myself. And I did. It was a long, arduous process. We were finally nearing the end, putting on the finishing touches, and getting the book ready for the printer, when I got an interesting bit of news.

"We found a mass," the doctor said. "We found a mass in your chest."

Yeah. Things could be worse all right.

A few weeks before, I'd gone into the hospital for a hip replacement. Yes, I was a little young for that; but it had needed doing. Just another body part that I'd worn out from years of abuse, and miles of wear and tear. A little bone on bone friction is more painful than you might imagine. On top of that, I was fresh off the table from a hysterectomy only a few months before. Suddenly it seemed like I was in and out of the hospital all the time. *I might as well move in,* I began to think. *Maybe they can turn my room into a condo.* Happily, the hip surgery went smoothly, and my recovery was ahead of schedule. I was up on my feet again within a day— although *carefully,* I must say.

Things were going well enough that, not much more than a week later, I was even preparing for a public speaking engagement. *No sense waiting around,* I thought. I was moving around again, and if I wasn't a hundred percent yet, then I was in the nineties. I was ready for it.

Getting a good night's sleep before putting the final touches on my speech, I woke up in the middle of the night. As I stood up to find my slippers, I noticed the room was beginning to tilt and sway on me. I felt like I was falling, standing up! I got back into bed, but the dizziness only increased. I was holding still, but the planet wasn't! *What on earth is going on?* I wondered.

"What's the matter?" Michael asked, "What's wrong?" I told him about my extreme dizzyness. He got up and began to get dressed. "Dizziness is okay," he said. "Vertigo is not. We're going to the emergency room."

"No. I'm okay," I protested. "It's probably just the pain medication. Or maybe I got up too fast." I didn't want to go and I tried to pretend that he was overreacting.

Michael wasn't buying it. "We need to run some tests," he insisted. "We have to make sure there aren't any blood clots loose. You don't want to have a stroke, do you?"

"It's not that serious," I stalled. "It's just the pain meds. Maybe I need some food."

Michael shook his head. "Gayle, what have you got to lose?" he asked. "If you're right, we waste some time. If I'm right . . . and I hope I'm not . . ."

We went in. Michael explained his suspicions to the ER doctor and he agreed. A short while later, I was sliding headfirst into a CAT scan machine. They ran the test, and it all looked good. As far as clots go, there were none. No surprises were waiting to happen. I breathed a big sigh of relief. *Maybe now I can get back to bed,* I thought hopefully.

Just to be safe, they ran a set of chest X-rays on me, too. As the image came up on the screen, the doctor pointed. "We see a little shadow," he said. "So we'd like to take another look." He did. It wasn't a shadow.

Events moved quickly after that. In that respect, I was blessed. After the doctors found the shadow, they did a biopsy a week later. As quick as it was, it was still a *long* week. Of course, the biopsy came back positive. I had a small spot of lung cancer; but even a little bit is too much. I had dabbled in smoking and it looked like the foolishness of my younger days had come back to bite me. Either that, or my DNA had picked up a few faulty genes. Maybe it was both. Either way, it sucked—to coin a phrase.

How's that for lemons? I thought, stunned. *After all that hard work, this is the thanks I get.* Believe me, God heard about it—loud and clear. I was angry, I was bitter, and I was scared. I prayed and complained. I prayed and pleaded. I prayed and mourned.

It's a good thing that events were moving along so quickly, because I was definitely in a downward spiral. Right down the drain. Intellectually, I understood what was happening to me, and I tried to fight it; but it seemed like I was losing my mental battle. Some days were better than others; some *hours* were better than others.

What if my time with Michael is over? I worried. *What if I don't get to see the kids anymore? Or my grandson, Colin?* After all those years of caring for cancer patients, now I was under the gun. And I was panicked about it. When I wasn't panicked, I was grief-stricken. *I haven't had enough time with them,* I prayed to God. *I need more time with my family.*

If I thought I'd known about the stages of grief before, then I was getting a graduate education in them now. Although, I never was one to do things in stages. I usually dived right in and tackled everything at once, in as haphazard a way as I could manage. One moment I was miserable; the next, angry; a little later, I was silently pleading or bitter again. Then hopeless. And then I'd start all over again, in random order. *Where are all your easy answers now, Gayle?* I asked myself angrily. Didn't I have some Bible verse to spout? Or some old country wisdom to fall back on? *What's the matter?* I demanded of myself. *No words of comfort?*

I had to admit, *I've got nothing.* My downward spiral was deepening, and it seemed unbreakable. *How is this the answer to my prayers?* I said to God, bitterly. *I don't remember asking for this!* Some reward. God didn't answer—at least not immediately—preferring instead to remain silent on the subject.

Physician, heal thyself. After a few hours—or maybe it was days—of emotional oscillations, something finally occurred to me. Rita hadn't asked for it either. But did I ever hear a word of complaint? *No.* Did she make the best of her situation? *Oh yeah.* And did it affect her faith in God? *Not. One. Bit.* If anything, her faith only grew.

On the face of it, her response seems like a contradiction. After all, if you dump enough tragedy on a person, you are bound to break them. After the ninth time she lost her hair—or the ninetieth time she went in for an exhausting, debilitating treatment that seemed to do less and less good—you would think she'd have lost her taste for God. That she'd be angry with Him. That she might curse Him. But she didn't.

Instead, Rita prayed to God to ask for strength and guidance. Then she looked to Jesus for inspiration. She would need it all, simply to handle what life had dished out for her. She got all three, in spades. In God, Rita found the strength to deal with her illness. In Jesus, she found the inspiration to help others, even as she struggled. And she was given the guidance to do it all. Rita found ways to do things that she'd never done before. That guidance had even led her to me. Looking back, I suppose it appointed me to follow in her footsteps. Rita's favorite verse came to mind again, "I can do all things in Christ, who strengthens me." Wasn't it time I walked in her footsteps again?

Every single day, Rita made a choice to look up, not down; to move forward, not back. Rather than wither away in a stuffy, stale den of self-pity, Rita chose the fresh air of life. She made lemonade, and drank in great gulps of it. Rita would never drag others down with her tales of woe; instead, she would lift them up. She brightened her own life by lightening the burden of others. Every day, she put on her best face and set out to do good, always encouraging and inspiring others. In return, their happy responses buoyed her spirits as well.

I decided to give it a little try.

Big surprise. It worked—almost right away. Oh, I wasn't nearly as good at it as Rita had been; I still needed some practice. There would be moments when I would backslide into depression or despair. But over the next few days, I got better at catching it, and reversing it. I adopted a positive attitude, and I got a big positive response from the people around me. This fed my spirit and made it even easier to maintain my positive outlook. It was a kind of circular, snowball effect—a self-fulfilling prophecy.

Instead of spiraling down, I started spiraling up—and it was all a matter of choice. I decided to take my latest lemons and make a new batch of lemonade, as best I could. Rather than sink in a sea of sadness and self-pity, I decided to strike out for shore. The best way to do that was to continue to meet life head on. I had a book to finish, and there were speaking engagements scheduled. One speech was lined up for little more than a week after my upcoming surgery. I left it on the calendar. One way or another, I was going to make that speech. Rita had given seminars in worse shape.

Being busy also helped. There were moments of worry and fear; but a few quiet words with God would help to settle my nerves. I was blessed to have all kinds of support from my family and friends. And I was very fortunate that things were moving along quickly.

Counting my blessings, I thought back to the patients we'd cared for at Image Insights. Many of my clients weren't so lucky as I. For some, the treatments had dragged on endlessly. Others

Live in the present!

Too many people spend their whole life trying to "get it" or "get there." Until we make our way to heaven, there is no "there" there. It's the quality of the journey that sets us free.

had little or no support from family or friends. Image Insights was all the family they had. It made me proud, once again, of the job we had done. Now that the shoe was on the other foot, I understood the difference we'd made like never before. Back then, I was always an outsider. I could feel for the patients. I could empathize. I could even imagine how badly they felt. But I could never *know*. Not for sure. Not until now.

Now that I was a cancer patient, too, I saw firsthand how much the little things really mattered. When our clients had complimented us at Image Insights, they weren't just being polite. They were speaking from the bottom of their heart in ways that I'd never fully understood. Every kind word, every gentle touch, every moment of human contact was important to them. It all made a difference; just as it did to me now. Every prayer spoken with them mattered. Every prayer said *for* them counted. So many things, that seem so little to us on the outside, make a huge difference to those of us on the inside.

The idea of "making lemonade" could be what mattered most of all. A positive attitude allowed all of those other little things to do their part in lifting the spirits, whether they were mine or my clients. "When life gives you lemons . . ." Sounds like a cliché, doesn't it? A bit of cheesy, old-time country wisdom. But they don't call it wisdom for nothing. There is more truth in those old sayings than most of us realize.

See a glass half full.

Look for the silver lining.

Accen . . . tuate the positive. Elim . . . inate the negative.

Just direct your feet, to the sunny side of the street.

And of course, there is always my favorite: "When life gives you lemons, make lemonade." Those are words to live by—all of them. In truth, what other choice is there? See a glass half empty? Walk on the gloomy side of the street? We *have to* make lemonade. Life is *always* handing out lemons. And we don't get to choose our lemons, either. Our only choice is in what we do with the ones we are given. What do we make with the lemons in our lives?

So I decided, again, to make some lemonade with my latest bushel of lemons. Adam had moved up to Wisconsin to help me start my new business, so together we got back to work. In fact, he had moved up only a week before I was diagnosed. His timing just could not have been any better. Michael and I would both come to rely on him to help us get through this difficult time. Nicholas took over Adam's business for him—after all, he had a family to take care of and a child in school—and Adam moved in with us. The poor kid thought he was there to work with me. He had no idea how tough the work would be.

My surgery was almost a week away, so I tried to stay busy. There were speaking dates to schedule or confirm. There were technical details to iron out on the book, and press dates to arrange. And now there was a new final chapter to write. Yes, it would throw the whole process into disarray, but it would also allow me a chance to sort out some feelings. There was a lot to be done, and I wanted to do it all quickly.

There was a certain sense of renewal to the work. I was re-energized by it. Not that it was easy; I struggled through my ups and downs. But having a purpose made it much easier to get back on top again. More than ever, I felt driven to tell the story. I had watched so many people make lemonade. I had to tell their tales.

On top of all that, my son was getting married, and the wedding was only a month away. Nick was ready to tie the knot. But his beautiful bride-to-be, Lisa, had lost her mother to cancer when she was just a teenager. They were both hopeful that I could continue to help. I was determined not to let them down. And in the back of my mind, I realized that things had been no different for my clients. Even as they had struggled and stressed, they still had to deal with day-to-day life. The world didn't stop because they were sick. It went right on without them. Their choice, and mine, was to stop and get run over, or to get up and go along for the ride.

There was so much to be done, and I felt like the clock was ticking. *How am I going to fit it all in?* I stressed, *There just isn't enough time!* There were days when I pushed myself to exhaustion. I had to keep things moving! I was almost panicked about getting the lemonade message out; but even as I worked to assemble that message, the message itself was evolving.

Nothing is going according to plan, I anguished. *For all I know, I'm running out of time!* But then, in a moment of lemonade clarity, I realized something and the panic fell away. *When has my life ever gone according to plan?* I smiled at the thought; the very idea was ludicrous. Lots of things had happened that I hadn't planned on. I'd dealt with them all. Having cancer was just another one. *You're gonna have to deal with it,* I told myself. Making lemonade is about adapting and improvising, every day. It is a process, not a one-time event. *If life doesn't go according to plan,* I laughed to myself, *then change plans.* It was time to adapt, to improvise.

The whole thing reminded me of the old John Lennon line: Life is what happens while you're making other plans.

So as my next date with the doctor approached, I made my plans—knowing full well that they might be tossed out the window again. If circumstances changed, then I'd change with them. But at least I would be ready. We continued to revise the book. We lined up more speaking engagements; allowing a little time for recovery first. We worked on a website, created business cards and postcards, and finalized the cover. And we planned a beautiful wedding for Nicholas and Lisa. There were a million things to get done, so we took care of them one at a time.

The only other important thing I had to plan for was my hospital stay. I packed clothing, and makeup, and nice pajamas; no cheesy hospital gowns for this patient. If I were going to be stuck in bed, I was going to look like I was happy there. There's nothing more demoralizing than an ugly old cotton gown hanging open at your backside. At least, when you're in your own pajamas, you still feel like *you*.

Which is exactly why I was packing street clothes, and makeup, too. I was not about to lie around in bed all day, looking battered and helpless. How would that improve my morale? As soon as humanly possible, I was determined to make myself presentable. When I looked into a mirror, I wanted to see *me*. And as soon as the staff would allow it, I planned to be up on my feet and moving around again. I would not wither away in bed; I was determined to roam those halls and get back in shape. The sooner the staff saw me up and moving, the sooner they would let me go home. And I would not do it in jammies, either. I planned to be up, dressed, and moving, as much as I could get away with.

I know that's just not possible for *every* patient. I wasn't even sure that it would be possible for me; but that was my plan. If circumstances changed, then I would adapt; but always with an eye towards moving ahead. Once again, onward and upward.

The big day arrived and, as the doctors and nurses prepared for surgery, I was as scared as anyone. As a former surgery scrub nurse, I may have been more scared than most. There was no blissful ignorance for me. I understood the ramifications of nearly everything that was said and done. My doctors and nurses were professionals, and I knew that I was in good hands. Even so, I'd spent a dozen years working with cancer patients. For some, things had gone pretty well; for others, not so much. Better than most, I knew just what was at stake.

I tried hard to put on a happy face, as I had for the past week or more. Sometimes it was really difficult; but making lemonade can be hard work. Occasionally, my mask slipped, or a chink in the armor showed. My confidence would start to slide, and my spirit would stumble. If that happened, a few quiet words with God would usually put me mentally back on my feet. With so much support from Michael and Adam, and the rest of our family and friends, it was easier to maintain that positive attitude. I was truly blessed to have so many people pulling for me.

As the anesthesiologist gently put me under, he said, "We'll see you in a little while, Gayle." I remember smiling briefly, and then I remembered nothing else.

It was a long day for the surgical team. They were going all the way in to remove a small portion of the lung that was showing the early stages of cancer. I'm happy to say that I missed out on the excitement.

The next day, I felt battered and bruised, worn out and run down. In some ways, it would have been nice to lie there and feel sorry for myself. I hurt, and I was tired. Once again, I learned first hand how Rita, and my clients, had felt. Like they did, I chose to make lemonade instead. Michael brought in everything that I had packed, so we set about putting me back together again. Once we'd finished, I *did* feel a little better. Over the next few days, we even did a little bit of editing on the book.

I'm grateful to Pastor Bill and his wife, Rose. They had visited daily to pray for a successful result and a rapid recovery. They also provided me with some much needed company. Having family and friends around to pull for you really makes a big difference. I found out that there were more people pulling for me than I knew. Pastor Bill began a prayer chain for me and had his entire congregation involved. And it spread from there. At the same time, Saundra was doing likewise at her church. All of those prayers meant a lot to me.

According to the doctors, the surgery had gone well. They got what they were after, and everything else looked good. During the following week, the test results came in. It was official. Thanks to the hard work of my surgical team, I was cancer free.

There would be more tests to come, and we'd still have to keep an eye on things, but it looked as if I'd been far more fortunate than many of my clients had been. As I thought about it all, I felt bad for being angry with God. Upon discovery of the cancer, I had asked Him angrily, "How is *this* the answer to my prayers?" Now, I had a different perspective. If it was going to happen, wasn't it better that I found out sooner, rather than later? If it hadn't been for that night of vertigo, and the subsequent tests, we might never have caught it in time. Things could have gone much, much worse. Looking back, I thanked God for that dizzy spell. And I thanked Him for Michael's stubborness too, his insistence that we go to the emergency room.

The big know-it-all.

CHAPTER

19

. . . *Make Lemonade*

What a relief it was to have the scary stuff behind me. Once again, it was another demonstration of how my patients must have felt—the more fortunate ones anyway. The sense of relief, of optimism about the future, *of freedom* was so strong I could taste it. *What a blessing,* I thought. *What a gift I've been given.* There would still be follow-up examinations, to make sure I remained clear of the cancer—and there was still a lot of recovery time ahead of me—but the feeling of redemption was overwhelming. I could well imagine how it must have felt to a client who had endured so much more than I had.

After several surgeries in a very short period of time, my body needed some time to heal. I gave it some. I had to; the doctors left me with no other choice. But a week later, I was raring to go, just itching to get out of that hospital.

"You're getting ahead of yourself, Gayle." The doctors told me, "Your mind is leaping ahead of your body. You need to take it slow."

"Who has time for that?" I protested. "I have a wedding coming up. I have talks to give, and a book to finish. I gotta get going!"

The doctors kept me still as long as they could; but when I showed enough progress, they gave in and let me go home. They may have been a touch reluctant; but as I showed them, there was no reason to keep me there.

That's not to say that I was all better again. There were frequent follow-ups, and I was on a cabinet full of pain medication. According to my doctors, I was to stay at home. Take it easy and slow. I tried—for as long as I could. Gradually, we ramped up our efforts to finish the book. Requests for speaking engagements were still coming in. I was finding it hard to remain still.

As to the speech I had left on my calendar, the one I had scheduled for a week after surgery—I almost made it. I tried so hard to be there; I was all dressed up and ready to go. But one look at me swaying on my feet was enough to put a stop to that. Michael put me back in bed, and this time I listened. Together he and Adam left to pinch hit in my place.

I wanted so badly to go. My friend Francine's daughter had set up the event. Melissa was a high school student and she had to set up a community service event as a senior project. Her interest was in fashion, and she had heard about the show we had done years ago. Mel decided her show would benefit the

Wisconsin branch of the American Cancer Society; and she hoped I would be their special guest.

After the fashion show, I was supposed to give my first ever talk about the upcoming book. I had planned to tell The Lemonade Stand story, as I'd done before. Only now, the story had a new finish—and so did the book. But this time, for a change, the Pink Lemonade story would be told by two big, strapping men.

My friend Francine and her daughter, Melissa. For a senior project, Mel put on a fashion show that raised over $4,000 for the ACS.

Adam and Michael donned a pair of pink shirts and took to the stage in my place. As guest hosts, they were fabulous. Their speech was a big success and the audience response was overwhelmingly positive. When they came home to tell me about it, I couldn't have been more proud. I'd been terribly disappointed not to go myself; but now I found myself wishing even more that I had been there to see their take on the Pink Lemonade story. Getting up on stage is never easy, unless you've had *a lot* of practice. It brought tears to my eyes to know that they would stick their necks out like that for me.

"I am so proud of you guys," I said to them both. "To think, just last month, I'd said I was done with it all." It was true. A few weeks before, as the book was nearing completion, it had looked to me like that part of my life was over. After all, The Lemonade Stand and Image Insights were long gone. They were history. Michael and I had been discussing what I planned to do next. I was thinking about joining up with a charity, but which one? I'd even done a good deal of praying on the question.

I was trying to decide where to direct my efforts in the days ahead, when Francine and Mel had presented their idea. *Well, why not?* I thought, *one last cancer speech, and then I'll move on.* But in

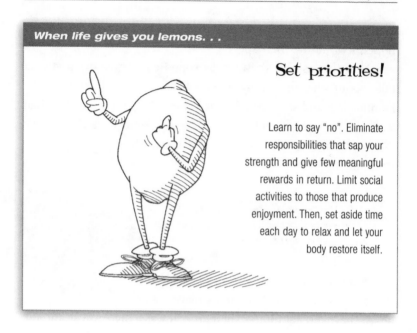

When life gives you lemons. . .

Set priorities!

Learn to say "no". Eliminate responsibilities that sap your strength and give few meaningful rewards in return. Limit social activities to those that produce enjoyment. Then, set aside time each day to relax and let your body restore itself.

the few short weeks between scheduling that speech and its delivery, I had crossed over to the other side. I'd gone from being a cancer care provider to a cancer survivor. I couldn't give up now.

It looked like I was in this game for life.

Mel's first charity event raised over $4,000 for the Wisconsin ACS. She'd hit a home run on her first time at bat. Mel handled everything with a little help from her mom. I wish I'd been there to help. I was so proud of that young lady.

While I missed my first post-surgery date, I did make the second, with Saundra at my side for support. Just one week after Michael and Adam had tried walking in my shoes, I stepped back onto the stage again. Our church had put together a big event for women, and there were hundreds of people present. As I approached the microphone, I remembered how scary it had once been. I thanked God for the second chance—the opportunity to reach out to people once more. It felt good to be back on track again.

The return to my old habits brought about a return to my old mindset. I hadn't been off the operating table for all that long and I was already thinking, *go, go, go!* So much for taking it slow and easy. Nick and Lisa had a wedding coming up fast, so I had all the reason I needed to push myself. I had to get myself back in shape.

Lisa had fond memories of vacations in Florida, with her mom, so the wedding would take place there. But having lost her mother so many years ago, Lisa was short-handed when it came to making the arrangements. "I can do weddings!" I quipped. "Yes—weddings, I know how to do!" I was thrilled to be able to help, and we made a trip to Florida a few months before my surgery.

Nick may have been a little nervous about his mother spending so much time with his bride, but he needn't have worried. We got along so well together. I was determined not to be the stereotypical mother-in-law; I would give Lisa all the help she asked for, and all the room she needed. As it turns out, she didn't need that much of either. While I know my help was appreciated, she would have been fine without me. And as for room, I was prepared to give her plenty, but she seemed to need none at all. We spent a lot of time together and I loved every minute of it.

With so much time in each other's company, we had plenty to talk about. I knew I could never be but a shadow of Lisa's mother, and wouldn't dream of trying to replace her; but I did hope that Lisa might recover a little bit of the relationship that she had lost, with me. I knew it was possible that I was setting myself up for disappointment. Let's be honest, does any bride *really* want to pal around with her mother-in-law? But as they say, hope springs eternal. It was my second-favorite saying.

Lisa and I talked about everything, as we ironed out all of the wedding arrangements. Working together, we quickly and efficiently planned and arranged the entire event in four days. While we did it, we shared our thoughts about family, about God, and

My son Nick, my grandson Colin, and my new daughter-in-law Lisa on the wedding day.

the future. It seemed like there was nothing we couldn't discuss. She is a terrific girl and I was so happy for Nick.

Lisa was the perfect bride for Nick and I know she will make him happy. I'm just as certain that he'll do the same for her. He'll make a good husband—kind, gentle, and supportive. I know this to be so because I've already seen the kind of father he is. Nick is a patient and loving father, and Colin has grown into a beautiful, intelligent little boy. It took me almost twenty years to complete my family. I'm so happy that the three of them have found each other so soon.

The wedding was upon us before we knew it and I was as ready as I could be. After so much surgery in so little time, I was still a little shaky—but I was not about to miss this event. Our preparations paid off and the wedding was as beautiful as we hoped it would be. After working so hard to keep us all together, I was so proud to see our family growing again on its own. For me, one of the best of the many terrific memories we made in Florida was something that Lisa said during our time together. "You're not just the mother of the groom," she said earnestly to me. "You're also the mother of the bride, mom." Like the wedding itself, that was one teary-eyed moment.

After their wedding, I spent a week in Kentucky with my grandson, Colin, while Nick and Lisa went on their honeymoon. During my stay, I spent a lot of time with my parents, and my brothers and sister. I was also able to share some time with Saundra, too. She had suffered a death in the family, and it was my turn to offer some of the same care and support that she had shown so often to me. After the bright and beautiful high of the wedding, and the happy time with my family, a family tragedy like Saundra's made for a heartbreaking low. Over the years, it had always helped to have each other to rely on. I hope I was as big a help to her as she has always been to me.

After the roller coaster of emotion that had been the last few months, it was a welcome relief to return home. It felt good to focus on my work again; but as I tried to pick up where I had left off, I found I was having some difficulty maintaining that focus.

For the past month or more, I had been running on adrenaline. Now that the pressure was off, I found I was losing my motivation. At first, I attributed it to simple exhaustion. But after a few days, my lethargy still hadn't gone away. *This isn't like me,* I thought. I was even getting crabby and moody—which is not like me at all!

Looking back, the cause of the problem seems obvious; but at the time, I hadn't put it all together. It wasn't just sheer force of will that had kept me going in those hectic weeks after my surgery. I'd had a little bit of assistance. While force of will may have kept me energized, it was the prescription painkillers that made it all possible.

After realizing that I wasn't getting back to my old habits, I went to my doctor to find out why. Besides my sluggishness, and new cranky attitude, I began to feel an annoying tingling in my fingers and toes. I was not myself, and I couldn't figure out why.

"It's the narcotics, Gayle," My doctor said to me. "You have to get off of those things." She paused and folded her arms, "The thing is, after so much surgery, I'm not sure what to recommend. I'd like to talk to a specialist."

Now that I knew what the problem was, I didn't want to wait around. I made some calls of my own. After finding a narcotics specialist, I explained my dilemma to him. "I'd suggest going cold turkey," was his considered response. "Just take off the patches and get rid of the pills." He made it sound so easy.

"Cold turkey! You're darn right," I replied. I was furious that those little pills had taken my normal life away from me. When I got home, I dumped those pills into the garbage, and then I hauled the trash can out to the curb. *That's enough of that nonsense!* I thought, triumphantly.

When Michael came home that night, I told him of my discovery, my bold decision, and my decisive actions.

"Umm. I don't think you want to do that, Gayle," Michael warned. "We need to titrate you off those things gradually."

"No," I returned confidently, "I'm in control." I refused to be weak. "I can handle this on my own," I said boldly, "but don't let me slide." They were my famous last words.

As the narcotics began to wear off and the post-op pain returned, I came to regret my earlier rash behavior. Even so, I was determined not to let those little pills run my life. I began gulping down the milder, non-addictive painkillers that the doctor had prescribed—right up to the maximum limit.

It wasn't helping. After the worst night of my life, I was considering how I might sneak out to the trash can on the curb, without anyone noticing. Digging around for those little pills sounded awfully good about then. Unfortunately, it was trash day.

Listening to that big truck pull away, I realized that temptation had just been removed. At that moment, I wasn't sure whether I should thank God or not. In the end, I did thank Him, and decided to tough it out.

What followed were the worst few days of my life. I spiralled down like never before, with severe depression, massive panic attacks, and almost nonstop uncontrollable crying. There were times when I was certain that I was dying. Worse than that, there were moments when I thought I already had, and my mind just hadn't caught on to the fact yet. My body was fighting the detoxification, and words like "miserable" and "horrific" don't even begin to describe that nightmarish experience. I'm almost certain I would have stayed in bed, withered away, and died if not for Michael and Adam. My motivation, even my will to live, was gone. They were constantly dragging me out of bed, getting me up and moving around, taking me outside, and convincing me to eat. And they endured my crying and yelling while they did it. The whole thing was so bad that I was ready to give up, to curl up and die.

Michael understood what I was going through and asked, over and over, if I would like to get some help. Each time, I refused. "I can't," I wailed, "I have to do this myself!" If I didn't, it meant I was weak—or so I thought. *How could my clients have endured so much?* I wondered in painful astonishment, *How could Rita? When I can't even beat those stupid pills!* I'd begun to think that, if I couldn't overcome them, then I wasn't worthy of association with the people that I had known.

After a few days, my morals and standards went right out the window. "Please give me a patch!" I wailed hysterically, "Pleeease!" I had cracked. All I wanted were the drugs so that the pain would go away.

Michael couldn't stand to watch me suffer through withdrawals. He was also baffled as to why I'd followed the advice of another doctor over his—especially when it meant so much needless pain and suffering. "Are you ready to try this gradually?" he asked.

I said nothing. All I wanted was that narcotics patch.

"Why are you fighting this battle?" Michael finally asked me. "There are more important things for you to do."

So after two days of misery, the light finally came on in my head. I blinked at him in surprise. He was right. "Why didn't you put it that way before?" I asked.

Funny thing. As a radiation oncologist, Michael actually knew something about treating cancer patients. Imagine that. He put me back on the patch, but only after I promised to follow his instructions. The pain went away. Physically, I was overwhelmed with relief. Mentally, I was disappointed that I had succumbed. But then, in a moment of clear thinking—something that had been all too rare in recent weeks—an idea occurred to me. *Could it be that your judgment is not as sound as it should be?* I asked myself. *Yeah . . . could be.*

Trusting in Michael's judgment, again, I went on a gentle detox program. He gradually titrated me off of the narcotics, until I was back to normal again. We went from the patch, down to pills. Then we slowly reduced the number of pills until there were no more. The process took more than two months. It also gave me new insight into the struggles of addiction—insight I *almost* wish I'd never had. That specialist I'd talked to . . . he specialized in addicts—not post-surgical patients. I'd called the wrong man. Apparently cold-turkey is good for addicts. After major surgery, it's not such a hot idea.

The whole thing just reconfirmed the soundness of my husband's judgment. Okay, I'll say it. "Michael was right." There will be no living with him now!

Now That I Think About It . . .

We don't get to choose our lemons—only what we do with them. I learned that lesson every day. Making lemonade is a way of life. Through little steps, moment by moment, we choose to make the best of what we are given. At The Lemonade Stand and Image Insights, I watched my clients do it every day. And I watched Rita do it. And Sue. And Sarah. My best friend Saundra makes lemonade every single day. With role models like those, how could I do otherwise? So I thank God every day for granting me time with such wonderful people. And I thank Him for giving me a mentor like Rita. It looks like I will continue to follow in her footsteps.

What a journey it has been—and the road ahead looks just as amazing. When I started out, I wasn't sure what was guiding the events in my life. How much of it was God? And how much was luck? Chance? Coincidence? I wasn't sure. I had spent plenty of time in church, but it hadn't *really* sunk in, not completely. I had never taken it to heart.

Not until Rita said the seven strange little words, "Honey, I've been waiting for your call." She opened my eyes to a new way of looking at things. And a few years later, after Rita was gone, Bill Huston said those same seven words. Over time, he helped me to see even more clearly. And I began to recognize it for myself in that old broom closet.

Now, I know for sure. There was no coincidence. God has been working in my life all along—just as He does in all of our lives. He uses the people around us to build our characters; just as He is using us to build theirs. In a way, we are all working on each other, with most of us never knowing it. The goal is that we all become more Christ-like. We are to learn to do as He did, to treat others in the same way.

The trouble is we overanalyze. We try to pick and choose—to decipher which moments are "God-inspired" and which are not. And once we figure out which ones are, we try to determine what they mean.

My graduation meant *this*. My beautiful marriage means *that*. The birth of my precious child means *something else*. We try to pick the big moments and decide what they mean. But what about that cashier at the grocery store who was so nice today? Or that short-tempered waiter who was obviously having such a bad day? Each of those were opportunities. Each was a chance to grow and become more Christ-like. Not only the good moments, but the bad ones, too—and even the tragic ones—they are all moments for us to choose.

With every moment in our life a chance to grow, how can we determine what they are all supposed to mean? The answer is: we can't. The questions and relationships are far too complex to puzzle out. It would take a lifetime. A thousand lifetimes.

But there is something we can do. We can continue to learn and grow, following always the example set by Jesus himself. I have learned not to be swayed by the negative attitudes of others. Their character-building moments are different than mine, and different than yours. Besides, a negative attitude itself may be a test of our own character.

So I have learned to stay steadfast in what God is teaching, no matter what goes on around me. It is all too easy to become angry, bitter, or hateful when things go wrong. Being bad is simple. Being good is hard. Doing the right thing can be difficult; but walking with God has taught me character, perseverance, and forgiveness. I try to share that idea with others.

If you've learned a little something about how to treat others, then share that information, put it to use. If you've learned a little something about God, then share that, too. It doesn't matter if you're not perfect yet. It is okay to teach others even as you are learning.

Think about an overweight man who has just learned the joy of working out at the gym. Does he have to wait until he is fit and trim before he can share what he is learning? Or consider a clumsy man who is learning how to dance. Does he have to wait until he is Fred Astaire before he can teach the thrill of a new step? How about a young pilot, just learning to fly. Does he have to solo before he can teach you to . . . ummm, okay, bad example.

You don't have to be an expert to share what you have learned. You don't have to be a saint to talk about God. Believe me, I know. After all, I'm a work in progress, too.

Well that's one woman's opinion, anyway. Remember, I'm still learning and growing right along with you.

When you've been handed a pile of lemons in life, it can be hard to see the lemonade inside. In this story, the lemons were cancer—just about as sour and bitter a lemon as anyone can get. But if the people I've known could make lemonade with lemons like those, then surely we can make lemonade with the lemons in our lives—no matter what they are. I know I'm going to try. Every day, I will make the choice to do the best I can with whatever I have. Sure, there will be bad days. But if life knocks me down, then, like the song says, "I pick myself up and get back in the race. That's life."

I don't know how true this is, because I don't really remember. In the moments right after they wheeled me out of my cancer surgery, I was in and out of consciousness, not really all there. When I started to come around again, in the recovery room, I said three little words out loud. As soon as he heard them, Michael told me, he knew that I would be all right. Before we had the results of the surgery, the tests, or anything, I had apparently already decided to "make lemonade." According to Michael, I mumbled three fuzzy words that pointed the way to the road ahead.

"Where'th my lipthtick?"

Stir your faith!

If you are interested in having Gayle Zinda speak to your organization, please call us at (866) 841-1021.

Were you inspired by this book? Would you like to know more? Explore Gayle's list of informative and entertaining presentations.

The "Lemonade" Story

Gayle's shares her amazing story of a chance encounter with a women who reshaped her "purpose," changing her life forever. This is Gayle's most sought-after talk.

This is a highly motivational and inspirational presentation. (30 to 90 minutes)

Raising Kids with Morals Not Money

Gayle's testimony of raising two boys with no child support and little money. Gayle shares five great ideas on how to raise boys with morals and wisdom in today's world, like "Surround yourself with those you want to be like, and run from the one's you don't." Gayle also brings you up to date with what her boys are doing now, as young adults.

This is an informative and motivational presentation. (30 to 60 minutes)

Patient Advocacy—Don't Drop the Ball

Gayle talks about the importance of Medical Professionals and the recovery process before, during, and after an illness. Gayle recounts her frustrations after having two major back surgeries, a hip replacement, and a left lower lobectomy.

This very informative talk is usually presented to Medical Professionals and their staff. (30 to 90 minutes)

Burnout and the Healthcare Provider

"Thank God for the peace and tranquility of my broom closet." Gayle recounts her use of a broom closet in her office as a private chapel, to pray, reflect, and remember her purpose.

This funny and motivational presentation is directed toward healthcare providers. (30 minutes—Great for a luncheon)

Facing the Difficult Patient

Gayle shares her personal experiences of how prayer and hard work helped her win over some of her most difficult clients.

This very inspirational presentation is directed to healthcare providers. (30 minutes—Great for a luncheon)

Patient Advocacy in the Healthcare Jungle

It takes a good health care team, a supportive family, and an army of friends to conquer a serious illness—and to keep your sanity. Gayle shares four important key points to help patients and their families through the difficult times before, during, and after a major surgery or serious illness.

This very informative and positive message is directed towards patients and their family's. (30 to 60 minutes)

Lemons to Lemonade

"We have choices when we face difficult situations!" Gayle shares some of her toughest challenges in life so far, and how a positive attitude plays a vital role.

This is an inspirational and emotional presentation. (30 to 60 minutes)

Looking Great to Feel Awesome!

Gayle shares her experiences with her own recent lung cancer diagnosis, and why she believes that her positive mindset—like wearing her own pajamas in the hospital and applying lipstick just hours after a left lower lobectomy—aided in her recovery.

This is a highly motivational and inspirational presentation. (30 to 45 minutes)

Success is Not Always "Show Me the Money"

Gayle shares how providing care and inspiration to more than 10,000 clients truly defines her success—and how money acted as a temptation to divert her from her purpose.

This inspiring presentation is sure to raise some questions on money, morals and business ethics. (30 to 60 minutes)

A Leap Of Faith

"Don't wait for your deathbed to make your faith real!" Let's face it; if we were told we were going to die tomorrow, we would all pray to someone. Gayle shares the challenge that her mentor, Rita gave her. She covers the road that followed, as she gave up a great job with security to venture out on a journey of hope.

This highly motivational and inspirational presentation will challenge you and your position with your faith. (30 to 60 minutes)

TO ORDER ADDITIONAL COPIES OF

Pink Lemonade

FRESHLY SQUEEZED INSIGHTS TO STIR YOUR FAITH

Call Toll Free: **866-841-1021**

Fax Orders: **608-873-9345**

On the Web: ***www.lemonmotivators.com***

Mail Order: Pink Lemonade Presentations
PO Box #526
Stoughton, WI 53589

Name: _____

Address: _____

City, State, ZIP: _____

Telephone: _____

Email: _____

Sales Tax: Please add $5^{1}/_{2}$% for products shipped to Wisconsin addresses.

Shipping by Air: U.S.: $5.00 for first book and $3.00 for each additional book.

International: $11.00 for the first book, $7.00 for each additional copy (estimated)

Please call for quotes on orders of over 6 copies.

☐ Visa/MasterCard   ☐ Check

Card number: _____

Name on card: _____   Expires: _____

Questions or comments: 866-841-1021

_____

_____

_____